+3

THE RELIGIOUS STUDY OF JUDAISM

Description, Analysis, Interpretation

The Centrality of Context

Volume 2

Studies in Judaism

THE RELIGIOUS STUDY
OF JUDAISM

Description, Analysis, Interpretation
The Centrality of Context
Volume 2

Jacob Neusner

UNIVERSITY
PRESS OF
AMERICA

LANHAM • NEW YORK • LONDON

Copyright © 1986 by

University Press of America,® Inc.

4720 Boston Way
Lanham, MD 20706

3 Henrietta Street
London WC2E 8LU England

Library of Congress Cataloging-in-Publication Data

Neusner, Jacob, 1932-
  The religious study of Judaism.

  (Studies in Judaism)
  Includes index.
  Contents: v. 1. Description, analysis, and
interpretation—v. 2. The centrality of context.
  1. Judaism—History—To 70 A.D.—Historiography.
2. Messiah—Comparative studies. 3. Midrash—History
and criticism. 4. Bible. O.T.—Criticism, interpreta-
tion, etc., Jewish. 5. Death—Religious aspects—
Comparative studies. 6. Judaism—Relations—
Christianity. 7. Christianity and other religions—
Judaism. I. Title. II. Series.
BM170.N46 1986   296.3   85-30411
ISBN 0-8191-5450-4 (v. 2 : alk. paper)
ISBN 0-8191-5451-2 (pbk. : v. 2 : alk. paper)

All University Press of America books are produced on acid-free
paper which exceeds the minimum standards set by the National
Historical Publications and Records Commission.

For my gracious hosts, teachers, and friends

at the

UNIVERSITY OF TORONTO

A token of thanks for a constructive and cordial
hearing of my ideas
and for exemplary hospitality

and
with special thanks to (among many)

William Callahan
Harry Fox
Warren Jevons
Hans Küng
Jane McAuliffe
Willard Oxtoby and Julia Ching
John Simpson
Peter Slater
Wilfred Cantwell Smith
Brian Stock
Ronald Sweet
Donald Wiebe
Irving Zeitlin

A memento of December 10, 1985

CONTENTS

Preface

Taking things out of context distorts them. Interpreting in context provides the sole correct perspective on meaning. But while thoughtful people concur on these verities, the identification and definition of context justifiably provoke disagreement. For the thing interpreted may define the limits of its context, whether a poem or an idea or a book (as I shall show in Chapter Four). So the inner structure and proportion of a system viewed entirely distinct from the larger framework in which the system -- a religion, a philosophy, a political construction -- endures constitute a viable definition of context. That is, working outward from inner detail, one may propose to see the whole, as if, from the inner structure of the crystal, we perceive the entire snow-flake. That view finds its counterpart in the position that the definitive framework of interpretation -- hence, by definition, the context -- of an idea, a poem, or a religious system finds definition in the social setting in which that idea, poem, or system discovers its audience and its meaning (as I argue in Chapters Five, and Seven). Short of braving the entire blizzard, this other view reasonably maintains, we do not really know anything about the snowflake either. In framing the two extremes, the one insisting that questions on social and historical setting effect reductionism, the other maintaining that asking only about the thing itself yields formalism and academicism, I of course exaggerate, if not by much. For in the camp of literary criticism today, on the one side, and in the circle of marxist and materialist interpretation of culture, on the other, worthy exemplars of each viewpoint find an honored place.

My modest contribution to the theoretical issue at hand is to explore some of the subtleties involved in taking account of context. Specifically, I experiment with the role of context -- defining the larger setting, following the dictates of logic of that larger setting -- in the concrete work at hand, which is the religious study of Judaism. My interests flow in three parallel streams, one, describing the whole, two, analyzing important components, that is, the parts, and, three, interpreting the result of the first two. In the exercise of asking about the definition and role of context in description, analysis, and interpretation, I believe I contribute examples of a number of distinct meanings to be imputed to the word context. Specifically, I deal with two, first, context as a statement of the social and historical setting in which a work is brought into being and finds its audience, second, context as a statement of the inner logic, the interior structure, of the thing subject to interpretation. In the former category -- the role of social and historical context -- are the essays of Chapters Three, Five, and

Seven. In the latter -- the role of the inner traits of proportion, structure, and interior logic -- are the essays of Chapters Two and Four. A broader theoretical statement of the first of the two approaches to the definition of context -- the historical, the social -- occupies Chapters One and Seven. Chapters Two and Three then illustrate the definitive power of seeing things in two distinct contexts, interior (Chapter Two) and social and historical (Chapter Three). I define Judaism twice, once in the one context, once in the other. The equivalent theoretical statement on the search for the context to be inferred from inner straits of structure, the generative logic of an idea seen in its own terms, the movement from inside to outside, is in the beginning and end of Chapter Four. Chapter Six stands pretty much by itself; here by context I simply mean regnant opinion, which I accepted to my sorrow. So in this book, over all, I wish to experiment with two distinct approaches to the appeal to context in the description, analysis, and interpretation of the givens, the data, of the religion, Judaism.

These essays are free-standing. I do not assume that they will be read in sequence and in a single sitting. They do not flow from one to the next, but all of them do serve to illustrate the larger issue of the definition and role of context in the study of a religion, its texts and its ideas. I wrote each paper for its own purpose. Now they come together because, on their own as a group, they permit a broader audience to derive some knowledge of the concrete work of describing documents and systems, analyzing documents and their structures, and interpreting systems and components of systems (as in the figure of Moses), which, in the course of my studies, I have accomplished. My pattern in study is fixed.

I first address a specific, important text in the canon of Judaism in its formative age. This I translate and describe, pretty much in its own terms. I make the effort to introduce this text to the world that does not know it at all (that is, nearly the whole of the academic community) or that does not know it whole but only in bits and pieces (that is, nearly the whole of the Judaic scholarly community). An example of that work, in the results I can communicate to a broader audience, is in Chapter Four and Chapter Five. In Chapter Five I speak mainly to historians of religion, with special interest in issues of the fourth century. Each of my translations and introductions to canonical documents of Judaism, the Mishnah, Pirqé Avot, Tosefta, Talmud of the Land of Israel, Talmud of Babylonia, Genesis Rabbah, Leviticus Rabbah, Sifra, Sifré to Numbers, has led me through precisely the same program. One example, on the narrowly literary side, is *The Talmud of the Land of Israel. 35. Introduction. Taxonomy.* The most recent, by way of example, is represented here: *Sifré to Numbers: A New American Translation* (Atlanta, 1986: Scholars Press) I-II, and *Genesis Rabbah: The Judaic Commentary on Genesis. A New American Translation* (Atlanta, 1985: Scholars Press) I-III.

My second exercise, in sequence, is to focus upon the text that I have translated and described a broader issue: that is, the text in context. By context I mean yet another dimension, specifically, the intellectual one: the setting in humanistic learning in which I can situate the text at hand. My specific task? I try to find the question that the text at hand answers. When I work my way through a canonical text and grasp the principal points of stress and tension, I find myself filled with answers to someone's questions. But what are those questions, and are they my questions? And am I able to generalize -- for the study of religion is a generalizing science -- from the answers and the questions to matters of broader concern, importance to scholars of other religious traditions and of religion? That I take to be my task in the work of moving from text to context. Examples of this exercise comprise *Judaism in Society: The Evidence of the Yerushalmi. Toward the Natural History of a Religion,* (Chicago, 1983: University of Chicago Press), *Judaism and Scripture: The Evidence of Leviticus Rabbah* (Chicago, 1986: University of Chicago Press), and *Judaism: The Classic Statement. The Evidence of the Bavli* (Chicago, 1986: University of Chicago Press).

My third vocation derives from the history of religion. Specifically, I wish to offer a general theory of the history of Judaism to make possible the inclusion of Judaisms and their histories into the larger history of religion. I have in mind, also, to contribute to the history of religion the example of a general theory of the history of a religion, for I cannot point to any at this time. Judaism in this way will help to shape the history of religion by exemplifying how a general theory of a religion may exemplify the general theory of religion. I cannot point to anyone to whom that example may prove meaningful, but perhaps the product will create its market.

This vocation requires a separate work from that beginning in the study of specific documents and their traits. The other exercise brings me to examine the unfolding of ideas in the canonical literature, carried out, for example, in *The Foundations of Judaism. Method, Teleology, Doctrine* (Philadelphia, 1982-1984: Fortress Press). *I. Midrash in Context. Exegesis in Formative Judaism. II. Messiah in Context. Israel's History and Destiny in Formative Judaism. III. Torah: From Scroll to Symbol in Formative Judaism* . In those works I traced the history of the three principal constituents of the Judaic system that comes to full expression, in late antiquity, in the Talmud of Babylonia. Building on the results, which pointed to the fourth century documents as the point of initial statement of the definitive outlines of the Judaism that would emerge in the Talmud of Babylonia as classical and normative, I completed another trilogy. The three books are these: *Judaism in the Matrix of Christianity* (Philadelphia, 1986: Fortress Press), *Judaism and Christianity in the Age of Constantine* (Chicago, 1987: University of Chicago Press), and *The Death and Birth of Judaism: From Self-Evidence to Self-Consciousness in Modern Times* (New

York, 1987: Basic Books). In these two trilogies I have begun to outline a general theory of the history of Judaism.

So the present essays derive from three distinct and large-scale enterprises. I present them, as I said, as free-standing statements, because I believe they stand on their own and will reach their distinctive audience. That audience is composed of readers who bring to the study of Judaism only a casual interest, on the one side, but a well-developed program of inquiries of their own, on the other. They rightly want to learn something from Judaism for their own studies. To that audience, of which, in all subjects but my own, I am part, I contribute what I hope are examples of discourse on an issue of quite broad intelligibility, on matters subject to valuable debate. Just as I learn from others, when they take the trouble to teach me, as an outsider, things I should know for my own inquiries, so I wish to contribute to the discussions of others examples of general intelligibility drawn from Judaism.

The essays originate as follows:

Chapter One: The Coser Lecture at Hunter College, delivered on March 13, 1986. Not previously published. But the paper reworks ideas in the Preface and Chapter Two of my *Ancient Judaism and Modern Category Formation* (Lanham, 1986: University Press of America).

Chapter Two: Not previously published. This paper in substantially revised form will some day serve as the chapter on Judaism in a textbook on religion edited by Joseph Bettis, to be published by MacMillan. The project goes forward draft by draft, and this draft seems to me to stand on its own as an example of how, if we intend to describe a *religion as a system*, the work may be done.

Chapter Three: Not previously published. This paper, in substantially revised and abbreviated form, will some day serve as an article for *Biblical Review*. The issue of this paper is how to describe a religion within the category of history, that is, description worked out as a sequence of incremental developments through time. So this is an example of seeing how to describe a *religion as a historical phenomenon*: where it came from, where it was going, and why. This paper draws on materials in my *First Century Judaism in Crisis: Yohanan ben Zakkai and the Renaissance of torah* (New York, 1981: Ktav Publishing House), as well as on *Judaism and Christianity in the Age of Constantine*.

Chapter Four is a revision of the preface to my *Sifré to Numbers*.

Chapter Five is a revision of my introduction to *Genesis Rabbah. A New American Translation*.

Chapter Six is the Bokser Memorial Lecture at Queens College, delivered on March 12, 1986. It has not been published previously.

Chapter Seven is a lecture delivered at Bucknell University. It has not been published previously.

Jacob Neusner

February 28, 1986
The eve of the celebration of Margalit's
becoming a *bat mitzvah.*

Program in Judaic Studies
Brown University
Providence, Rhode Island 02912-1826
U.S.A.

Part One

CONTEXT AND DESCRIPTION

Chapter One

Description and Category-Formation

Categories dictate the intellectual processes of learning and so determine understanding: what we choose to learn, how we proceed to explain and make sense of it. Our category tells us what we want to know, and, once we have selected our data, we find out also what we wish to know about them. The category *Judaism* defines what we study when we wish all together and all at once to describe what the Jews believe, or the Jewish religion, or similar matters covering religious ideas viewed as a system and as a whole. It therefore constitutes a philosopical category, an *-ism*, instructing us to seek the system and order and structure of ideas: the doctrine of this, the doctrine of that, in Judaism. We invoke the category, Judaism, when we wish to speak of the whole of Judaic religious existence. There are, as I shall argue, other categories, other words, to tell us how to select and organize and order data to instruct us on that same thing: all together, all at once to speak of the whole. But the category we select will guide us to data appropriate to that category, and, consequently, that "whole" of which we speak all together and all at once will not be the same "whole" that finds definition in a category in the classification of an *-ism*. Accordingly, the category in the classification of an *-ism*, in our case, Judaism, tells us what we collect and what we do not collect, how we arrange what we have assembled and so how we are to construe the relationships among data deemed relevant, that is to say, Judaic. Another category, in a different classification, will teach us another way of speaking of the whole all at once and all together. For example, a category in the classification of a central symbol, something that, in itself, encompasses the whole on its own authority and in its own framework, will produce a different picture: different data, assembled along distinct lines, producing a quite distinctive view of the whole. My argument favors a symbolic, and, in this context of a textual community, therefore canonical, as against a philosophical, definition. Why so? It is on the grounds that the symbolic definition of the definitive category derives from an inductive reading of data, while the philosophical one depends upon an extrinsic and deductive reading of the same data. So at issue in this argument is the appropriate principle of category-formation.

I

Self-Evidence and Category-Formation

Where to begin? It is with the fault of the category, "Judaism," because that category appears to many to constitute a given in the study of Juda -*ism*. Some claim in behalf of the category, "Judaism," the authority of self-evidence, the universal acknowledgement accorded by common sense. How else -- they ask -- select and organize data than by the category, *Judaism*. They maintain that that forms a self-evident category, based on the only rational formative process, which is, common sense. But, as I shall show, common sense supplies uncertain guidance indeed in telling us not onlywhat are our categories but the principles that dictate their definition.

How shall I call into question the very self-evidence of the definitive, encompassing category, *Judaism*? And, second, how shall I identify a correct principle of category-formation, to yield on the basis of inductive inquiry an alternative category for the description of the whole, all at once and all together?

Let me violate all rules of rational discourse to show the that the category, Judaism, does not enjoy the status of self-evidence. Specifically, I shall argue from an anecdote. Why adduce a mere anecdote in evidence in a serious argument? Because people think the present categories, beginning with Judaism, self-evident. There are no others. But as I shall now suggest, there is nothing self-evident about them. If I can point to one instance, plausible on the face of it, in which the present category-formation does *not* prove self-evident, then choices open up. Nothing any longer may then demand the status of mere common sense. Why not? Because of the very character of a claim of self-evidence. For something to prove self-evident it must commonly make sense. A plausible exception, therefore, forms an insuperable obstacle, just as much as does a single exception to the claim of uniqueness. That is, if I claim something is unique, e.g., as to its species, or even as to its genus, then nothing else can form part of its species, or even its genus. Once we can find a plausible counterpart or parallel or equivalent, then what is alleged to be unique no longer is unique. To cite anecdotal evidence then constitutes a valid mode of argument against claims of self-evidence and common sense, just as a single exceptional case invalidates the claim of uniqueness.

As to plausible categories other than the received ones, therefore, I invoke the exception that comes to me from my grandmother.[1] My grandmother, who spoke Yiddish and came from somewhere near Koretz, in the province of Volhynia, in the northwestern part of the Ukraine, provides the unanswerable argument. She too sought language to speak of the whole all at once and all

---

[1] I choose my grandmother because, in discourse among scholars on the definition and character of Judaism, a fair number of colleagues, specializing in subjects other than in the study of Judaism, or in aspects of Jewish data other than the study of religion, invoke arguments from what their parents or grandparents or rabbis happened to tell them. So what my bubbee told me forms a valid counter-argument in the court of I-think-you-think.

together, that is, to define the things she lived for. She did not use the word we use when speaking of the things of which we speak when we wish to speak of when we say, *Juda - ism*. She used a different word, which in fact referred to different things. Her category of definition, serving for her speech as does the category, *Judaism*, serve ours, namely, to refer to the whole, all in all, taken all together, therefore instructed her to speak of different things. Her categories and ours, which are supposed to refer to the same data in the same social world, in fact encompass different data from those taken in by ours in our speaking, categorically, of *Judaism*. So do different categories imposed on the same corpus of facts turn out to organize different worlds in different ways.

The difference? When my grandmother wished to invoke a category that included everything all together and in correct proportion, she used the word-category, *Torah*. And so did many centuries of Jews before her. Our category falls into the classification of a philosophical or ideological or theological one, a logos: a word. Her category fell into the classification of a symbol, that is, a symbol that in itself encompassed the whole of the system that the category at hand was meant to describe. The species *-ism* falls into the classification of the genus, logos, while the species, Torah, while using words, transcends words. It falls into a different classification, a species of the genus *symbol*. How so? It is an object, a classification, an action -- an everything in one thing, and that is the power and effect, therefore the definition, of a symbol.

Our *-ism*-category, by contrast, does not invoke an encompassing symbol but a system of thought, as I shall explain presently. So today for a sentence meant to define everything all at once, we resort to the word-category, *Judaism*. By contrast, my grandmother resorted to a symbol-category, *Torah*. Why does this matter? It is because in fact the two categories do not correspond, though they are meant to function in the same way, and do run parallel to one another. So *Torah* as a category serves as a symbol, everywhere present in detail and holding all the details together.[2] *Judaism* as a category serves as a statement of the main points: the intellectual substrate of it all. If we uncover no such uniform substrate, we have problems -- unless we use our ingenuity to find what is not there. How may we test this proposition? It is by appeal to common language-usage, that is, to self-evidence. How in fact do people use language?

The conception of Judaism as an organized body of doctrine, as in the sentence, *Judaism teaches*, or *Judaism says*, derives from an age in which people further had determined that Judaism belonged to the category of *religion*, and, of still more definitive importance, a religion was something that *teaches* or *says*. That is to say, Judaism is a religion, and a religion is (whatever else it is) a composition of beliefs. In Protestant theological terms, one is saved by faith. But the very components of that sentence, *one* -- individual, not the people or

---

[2]That is why I called my prime textbook, *The Way of Torah*, and its companion-reader, *The Life of Torah*. But I see other ways to compose an introduction to Judaism and am now experimenting with one of them. My tentative title says it all:*From Testament to Torah*.

holy nation, *saved* -- personally, not in history, and saved, not sanctified, *faith* -- not *mitzvot* -- in fact prove incomprehensible in the categories constructed by Torah.[3] In fact in the Torah one cannot make such a statement in that way. We have rather to speak as our subject of *Israel*, not one, to address not only individual life but all of historical time, so saved by itself does not suffice, further to invoke the verb, the category of sanctification, not only salvation, and to speak of *mitzvot*, not of faith alone. So the sentence serves for Protestant Christianity but not for the Torah. If, according to the Protestant theological category, I want to study a religion, I study what people believe. So of course Judaism, for its part, will also teach things and lay down doctrines, even dogmas. But the category, faith, the work of constructing the system of thought of which the category is composed -- these do not serve for the study of the data we refer to, all in all, as Judaism.

Now, to revert to my grandmother, who in this setting serves as our native speaker: for my bubbee the counterpart of the statement, *Judaism teaches*, can only be, *the Torah requires*, and the predicate of such a sentence would be not, *...that God is one*, but, *...that you say a blessing before eating bread*. The category, *Judaism*, encompasses, classifies and organizes, *doctrines*: the faith, which, by the way, an individual adopts and professes. The category, *Torah*, teaches what "we," God's holy people, are and what "we" must do. The counterpart to the statement of Judaism, "God is one," then is, "...who has sanctified us by his commandments and commanded us to...." The one teaches, that is, speaks of intellectual matters and beliefs, the latter demands -- social actions and deeds of us, matters of public consequence -- including, by the way, affirming such doctrines as God's unity, the resurrection of the dead, the coming of the Messiah, the revelation of the Torah at Sinai, and on and on: "we" can rival the Protestants in heroic deeds of faith. So it is true, the faith demands deeds, and deeds presuppose faith. But, categorically, the emphasis is what it is: *Torah* on God's revelation, the *canon*, to Israel and its social way of life, *Judaism* on a system of *belief*. That is a significant difference between the two categories, which, as I said, serve a single purpose, namely, to state the thing as a whole.

Equally true, one would (speaking systemically) also *study Torah*. But what one studied was not an intellectual system of theology or philosophy, rather a document of revealed Scripture and law. That is not to suggest that my grandmother did not believe that God is one, or that the philosophers who taught that Judaism teaches ethical monotheism did not concur that, on that account, one has to say a blessing before eating bread. But the categories are different, and, in consequence, so too the composites of knowledge. A book *on* Judaism explains the doctrines, the theology or philosophy, of Judaism. A book *of* the

---

[3]My more sustained critique of the Protestant definition of religion and its affects upon the academic study of religion is in my "Theological Enemies of Religious Studies," *Religion*, in press for 1986.

holy Torah expounds God's will as revealed in "the one whole Torah of Moses, our rabbi," as sages teach and embody God's will. I cannot imagine two more different books, and the reason is that they represent totally different categories of intelligible discourse and of knowledge. Proof, of course, is that the latter books are literally unreadable. They form part of a genuinely oral exercise, to be cited sentence by sentence and expounded in the setting of other sentences, from other books, the whole made cogent by the speaker. That process of homogenization is how *Torah* works as a generative category. It obscures other lines of structure and order. True, the two distinct categories come to bear upon the same body of data, the same holy books. But the consequent compositions -- selections of facts, ordering of facts, analyses of facts, statements of conclusion and interpretation and above all, modes of public discourse, meaning who says what to whom -- bear no relationship to one another, none whatsoever. Indeed, the compositions more likely than not do not even adduce the same facts, or even refer to them.

How is it that the category I claim imposed, extrinsic, and deductive, namely, "Judaism," has attained the status of self-evidence? The reason, as I shall argue in a moment, is that the principles of category-formation rest on social foundations, and categories serve because they are self-evident to a large group of people. In the case at hand, therefore, Judaism serves because it enjoys self-evidence as part of a larger set of categories that are equally self-evident. In all of these categories, religion constitutes a statement of belief, so religions form a body of well-composed *-isms*. So whence the category, "Judaism"? The source of the categorical power of "Judaism" derives from the Protestant philosophical heritage that has defined scholarship, including category-formation, from the time of Kant onward. From the nineteenth century forward in universities a prevailing attitude of mind, particularly in the academic study of religion, has identified religion with belief, to the near-exclusion of behavior. In the hands of academic scholars religion has tended to identify itself with faith, so religion is understood as a personal state of mind or an individual's personal and private attitude. In the class room, after all, it is to attitudes of mind that we gain most ready access. Other matters lead us far beyond the walls of the lecture room. But the reason for the prevailing conviction is not merely adventitious: we study the data where they are convenient to us, hence, ideas in books. The reason for the categorical power of religion is theological, deriving from the Protestant character of universities, and the reason for the self-evidence of that category is social, deriving from haracter of the societies in which religion is studied. When we study religion, the present picture suggests, we ask about not society but self, not about culture and community, but about conscience and character.

So when we study religion, we tend, in the aggregate, to speak of individuals and not groups: faith and its substance, and, beyond faith, the things that faith represents: faith reified, hence, religion. Let me give as example of what I mean the observations by William Scott Green, as follows:

> The basic attitude of mind characteristic of the study of religion holds that religion is certainly in your soul, likely in your heart, perhaps in your mind, but never in your body. That attitude encourages us to construe religion cerebrally and individually, to think in terms of beliefs and the believer, rather than in terms of behavior and community. The lens provided by this prejudice draws our attention to the intense and obsessive belief called "faith," so religion is understood as a state of mind, the object of intellectual or emotional commitment, the result of decisions to believe or to have faith. According to this model, people have religion but they do not do their religion. Thus we tend to devalue behavior and performance, to make it epiphenomenal, and of course to emphasize thinking and reflecting, the practice of theology, as a primary activity of religious people....The famous slogan that "ritual recapitulates myth" follows this model by assigning priority to the story and to peoples' believing the story, and makes behavior simply an imitation, an aping, a mere acting out.[4]

Now as we reflect on Green's observations, we of course recognize what is at stake. It is the definition of religion, or, rather, what matters in or about religion, emerging from Protestant theology and Protestant religious experience. For when we lay heavy emphasis on faith to the exclusion of works, on the individual to rather than on society, conscience instead of culture, when we treat behavior and performance by groups as less important and thinking, reflecting, theology and belief as more important, we simply adopt as normative for academic scholarship convictions critical to the Protestant Reformation.

For my grandmother, and a hundred generations of Jews before her, the categories of the Protestant Reformation scarcely served in helping her to define the whole all at once and all together. She resorted to a different category from faith, meaning ideology, theology, or philosophy, a category deriving from the way of life and world view represented, symbolized, by the Torah: intrinsic, inductive, self-evident. And so did her Russian and Ukrainian Orthodox neighbors, and so did her Polish Roman Catholic neighbors not far away. To that entire universe of human civilization, the nation, the language, the religion, the way of life, clothing, food, occupation -- everything stood for one thing, and one thing stood for everything, whether the cross, whether the Torah, whether (I suppose) the hammer and the sickle. The Torah stood for the Jewish language, the Jewish food, the Jewish garments, the Jewish occupation, the Jewish way of treating other people, and on and on and on: the whole, all at once, all together. What has a mere -ism to do with all of that!

---

[4]Personal letter, January 17, 1985.

II

The Importance of the Correct Category and the
Right Generative Principle of Category Formation

Why, in the study of ancient Judaism, do I find it necessary to pursue the rather abstract question of category-formation? The reason is that the issue of category-formation dictates the character of learning. So the matter is urgent. Until we have explained the answer to the question of why we want to know what we investigate, that is, the principle of category-formation that tells us what we want to know and what we do not want to know, we labor without learning at all. We pursue unexamined careers of collecting and arranging, like the cavemen who went hunting and gathering. We compile information for a purpose we cannot specify, sort out data the cogency of which we cannot explain. What question, therefore, does the analysis of category-formation answer? It is what we want to know, how we propose to find out, and why, to begin with, we ask.

Nothing in learning derives from nature, that is, the nature of the data. All things come from nurture and therefore culture, that is, the social exercise of learning. Each of the categories we invoke to impart meaning and order to our minds comes from somewhere. Categories so deeply mark our minds that they appear to us to be self-evident. That, indeed, indicates the effect of a category. But, as I have shown, each category finds self-evidence solely in its larger social context, therefore forms a construct, not a given, of learning. Therefore categories, and the principle of category-formation that generates them, ultimately express an aspect of culture, serve political or economic expediency, or even introduce into the processes of intellect the effects of consciousness and conscience -- what our Gallic masters call *interiority* -- as I shall explain presently. I have now to make these allegations stick.

III

The Social Construction of Categories

Categories take form in the context not of the unconstrained mind but of the social intellect: the imagination formed, made plausible, by society, culture, politics -- that is to say, context and circumstance. What we want to know society tells us we should find out. How we shall find out what we want to know culture explains. And beyond the two lies the social compact that imparts sense and acceptance to the facts we think we know and to the categories that legislate the rules of comprehension and collective understanding. These are common sense and self-evidence. They in the end form the criteria for description. Description lends order and meaning to discrete pieces and bits of information, so forming the beginning of comprehension, of knowledge. So what we want to know, that is, the categories of knowledge, and how we find it out, namely, through selecting appropriate data and analyzing them, come to us as the gifts and the givens of our social world. Our context, provides the technology of finding things out, identifying sources we want to study and determining how to read them, also specifying sources we ignore and explaining why they contain only gibberish. All these, when brought to the surface and examined, testify to the formation of the categories of our minds, the structure and construction of all knowledge. So category-formation forms the critical component of consciousness and defines the structure of understanding.

To give a simple example of the centrality of social reality in the definition of how we shall undertake category-formation, I point to a case far away from the recognition of *Judaism* as a category. Rather, I refer to the recognition of *the* Maori as a social entity and -- more to the point -- as an organizing category of learning. In turning to far-off New Zealand, I want to know why that remote society falls into two parts, Maori and Pakeha (European), and, more especially, who first discovered that the Maori are *te Maori* -- that is, *the Maori*, a social entity, a group -- and why the discovery that various groups form *te Maori* mattered. To frame the question simply: Did Maori know they were *the Maori*,[5] and, if not, who told them? The parallel question: did my grandmother know that the Torah was Judaism, and if not, why did her grandson have to find out? What we shall see is that just as "Judaism" is the invention of philosophers, so the Maori as a category is the invention of people pressed to make sense of an unknown world. The answer to that question follows:

> ...in attempting to describe *the* Maori and his culture, we are creating a stereotype that did not exist; for there was no one typical Maori but many Maoris; no one Maori culture but regional and tribal varieties of culture. Moreover, most observers were expert in the culture of only one or two areas, though they often passed off that information as representative of the Maori people as a whole. Even the name, Maori, is an abstraction, created in the nineteenth century. Cook called them Indians, though the name New Zealanders was soon applied. Maori (ordinary) was first recorded about 1800 as an adjective in the phrase *tangata maori*, an ordinary person, as contrasted with *tangata tupua*, a supernatural being, as the Europeans were first thought to be. By the 1830s Maori was being used occasionally as a proper noun, but it did not come into general use as such until about the 1860s. Since then it has been used retrospectively to describe the early inhabitants....[6]

---

[5]The counterpart: did my grandmother know that she "practiced" or "believed in" Judaism? And if not, how and why did my father find out? And why did I take up the questions? We enter deeply into the history of the Jews in America when we study ancient Judaism. And when our Israeli counterparts do the same, they too would do well to ask some rigorous questions about their own intellectual roots.

[6]M. P. K. Sorrenson, *Maori Origins and Migrations* (Auckland, 1979: Auckland University Press and Oxford University Press), pp. 58-59. My dear colleague, Ernest S. Frerichs, and I stumbled on the book when visiting the Auckland Museum, and he found it first, so to him goes the credit for seeing it. But it is in the writing of Jonathan Z. Smith that both of us developed our interest in the Maori/Pakeha relationship as an example of the problem of the outsider.

In fact when the Europeans came, New Zealand consisted of two dozen different groups (social entities), at war among themselves, unaware that, as a whole, they formed a distinct society or nation or culture-group. They were no more a "the" -- "*the* Maori," (*te maori*) -- than "the Jews (believed in and) practiced Judaism" -- in that order. The category in neither case derived from the data or emerged out of inductive inquiry. The category in fact derived from the imagination of hard-pressed outsiders, seeking to make sense of an unknown world, to which known categories did not apply.

All the aboriginal inhabitants of New Zealand knew they had in common was that they lived on the same islands. When Europeans came, *te Maori* therefore were not *te Maori*. That is to say, the diverse social entities of the two islands shared the same planet, just as much as we share the same planet with Ethiopians or Peruvians, without regarding ourselves as part of a single entity (short of the human race, and that category bears slight consequence, beyond a rather trivial sentimentality). Were explorers from a distant galaxy to come and call us all "the weirdos," the sense -- the self-evident appropriateness of the name -- would strike us as no different from the self-evident appropriateness of the name Maori, when applied to the twenty-four perpetually warring groups ("nations"? "tribes"?) of the North and South Islands. Someone from the moon might as well have appeared on the Somme in 1916 and announced that the French and the Germans formed (under God) one indivisible nation. Such a statement, in that circumstance, would not likely have enjoyed universal self-evidence. Whatever the diverse Maori called themselves, they saw differences where outsiders saw sameness, and, in consequence, they fought unceasing wars, living out their lives in stockades. So, descriptively speaking, the generative category, Maori, derived from elsewhere. To them it was not only not self-evident, it made no sense at all.

But under other circumstances, at a different time, and for a fresh purpose, the categorical self-evidence of *Maori* struck the Maori quite forcefully. So even to the Maori *te Maori* became a self-evident category. But it was not because of the character of the data to which the category applied. In fact the category proved contingent on circumstance: politics and interest, things not of the mind at all. So much for context and self-evidence! As Sorrenson says, *maori* meant ordinary, that is, the normal, *us*, as against the extraordinary, *them*, the supernaturals. But that is not what the word means now. Then it was a mode of organizing unfamiliar experience by distinguishing natural from supernatural data. Now it serves as a political category, classifying for racial purposes a diverse and mixed population. So do categories form and reform, now supernatural, now political, now economic, in response to changing circumstance. When the New Zealand government today asks incoming travellers whether they are Maori, it does not mean to raise a theological question: are you ordinary or supernatural? And the question the government does address travellers remains one of classification. But the category has shifted, *and therefore also the facts.*

IV

The Circumstantial Character of Categories
and of their Formation

Knowing consists in more than merely following the intellectual equivalent of the rules of syntax for language. Knowing always rests on selection among the things that are there to be known, as everyone knows. We may choose to ignore, as the Australian aborigines did when the Europeans came, or we may choose to recognize and take charge, like the Maori in New Zealand, who carefully constructed a myth to account for their ownership of the land and much else:

> ...Maoris had their own purposes to serve in reciting and recording oral traditions, myths, and legends. Above all there was the vital question of establishing titles to land, since genealogies showing descent from Maui and the commander of the ancestral canoe from Hawaiki could be used to establish a charter to land....Far from dying out as the Europeans expected, Maori traditions, myths, and legends, including those elaborated in the nineteenth century, have continued as a vital part of what is still very much an oral culture.[7]

> The Maori created categories in response to circumstance, and the categories then dictated the kinds of information they would collect or invent, as circumstance required.[8]

Understanding the categories that dictate what we want to know and how we shall find it out defines our problem. Yet, as is clear, I find much to learn in a field so alien, so distant, to the one at hand. For where on the face of the earth can we go further from the Near East and Europe, and what age can we locate, beyond our own, more remote from that of the Jews of late antiquity, in the first through the seventh centuries, than nineteenth century New Zealand. And how astonishing then is it to know, as Sorrenson says:

> ...the ethnographers nearly always found in Maori culture what they expected to find; their expectations were kindled by the prevailing anthropological theories of their day. In this respect the ethnographic record on the Maori is a fairly faithful reproduction of changing fashions in anthropology...Descriptions which purported to be of the Maori as he

---

[7]Sorrenson, pp. 84-5.

[8]Indeed, I wonder whether the pre-historic, traditional tale, first told to be sure in the later nineteenth century, of the primeval or prehistoric migration by great canoe may in time turn out to be a restatement, with exquisite irony, of the (by-then-well-known) fact of the First Fleet, bringing the original settlers to Australia. But that is not our problem.

was at the time of Cook were often considerably influenced by the condition of contemporary Maoris.9

What conclusion do I draw from this observation? It is that theologically-motivated anachronism flourishes, not only in the study of the history of the Jews and Judaism in antiquity, but also in anthropology.

In fact *everything* we know, we know because, to begin with, we require knowledge of one sort, rather than some other. And our context, that is to say, our circumstance in society and among the cultural groups of our own country, in our country among the countries of our region, and on upward, tells us what we need to know and why. In the study of social groups, for example, before recording facts, we know that the facts concern the social group at hand, and not some other. So we start with a definition of traits that distinguish a social group. The consequence is simple. If you have those traits, you are in the group, and if you do not, you are not in the group. I know the traits before I know the group that is defined by them, so to speak. That is why, as Sorrenson says, observers see what they anticipate seeing, and their expectations come from what they have already seen: the categories established in their minds.

The history of knowledge monotonously reminds us that people see what they expect to see, rarely noticing merely everything there is to see. In Sydney, I was told, when the ships of Captain Cook's fleet appeared at Botany Bay, the aborigines, farming on the shore, simply did not see them at all: they just did not *see* them. Not expecting such a sight, their eyes -- so people report -- perceived nothing at all. Whether or not the story is true, I cannot say. But it does conform to the rule that we see what we expect to see. In broader terms, we perceive through analogies, think in metaphors, interpret and understand the unknown in terms of the known, -- all this because there is no alternative.

Let me conclude with a simple example of these facts of learning and life. Describing the formation of knowledge about the Maori peoples of New Zealand, Sorrenson[10] further states:

> For most European observers were not content to record what they heard and saw; they had to interpret their information and above all to answer intriguing questions about the ultimate origin of the Maori and their coming to New Zealand....Europeans' answers to these questions and interpretations of Maori culture were profoundly influenced by the prevailing philosophies of man and the latest scientific techniques....The idea that mankind had diffused from a single point, usually in the Middle East or India, offered a starting point for interpretation. Comparative techniques in physical anthropology, culture, philology, and myths and legends offered means of proving ancient racial connexions and of tracing the footsteps of primitive men, including the migrations of

---

9Sorrenson, p. 58.

10Sorrenson, p.82.

Polynesians. Darwinism offered a way of stretching the existing chronologies....These is no need to expand further on the absurdities of the Semitic or Aryan Maori theses -- both were attempts to apply the conventional wisdom of the day to the problem of the origin of the Polynesians....But it is worth pausing briefly to ask why the Maori was so favorably regarded: to be considered a Semite, when most other colored people were designated as Hamites; and, in the later nineteenth century, to be awarded the ultimate accolade of an Aryan ancestry like that of the Anglo-Saxon colonists? ....This was part of the wider ideal of an embryonic New Zealand nationalism. Nations are based on historical myths and New Zealand by the late nineteenth century was in the process of inventing hers.

So at the foundations of the category, *the Maori*, we uncover that demonic trinity, diffusionism, racism, and Social Darwinism! But as to the generative cause of the formation of that category, we uncover something considerably more within our range of understanding: the need of a new society, coming into existence out of the sherds and remnants of an older set of societies, to explain itself and its future.[11] And so too when it comes to "Judaism." What counterparts to such discredited ideas as diffusionism, Social Darwinism, or racism lie in the deep archaeology of these categories, of course, we cannot say. I see none. Nor do we know the human circumstances that made Jews look for a Judaism when they wanted to speak of the whole, all at once and all together, of their system.[12] But, to conclude, *Judaism* surely rests on a distinctive view of what we study when we study religion.

---

[11]The invention of the Maori formed into a single category all of the (to themselves diverse) populations extant on the islands at the beginning of European settlement. Today, I have the impression, the Maori assist the European-descended New Zealanders to accept their situation at the end of the earth and to let go of the long cord that binds them to "home," that is, "England."

[12]In his classic work, *The Uprooted*, Oscar Handlin argues that it was in America that the diverse immigrant groups discovered their shared nationality, e.g., as Italians. In Italy, if you asked, what are you and where do you come from, the answer would come as: from a village, such-and-so, in the province of X. In America, the *you* became Italian. So too the Jews of Eastern Europe described themselves by reference to village, near town, in province X. I never knew the name of my grandmother's village, all the more so that of the first Jacob Neusner, nor the name of their family, only, "near Koretz," in the "government of White Russia/Vohlynia. Jewish? Of course, so what? That did not count as a point of differentiation, therefore of category-formation. In America the immigrants gained that other identification, Jews as a group, Italians as a group. More to the point, the category made a difference. The self-consciousness that forces definition intellectually also expresses the power of homogenization working on internal points of distinction and differentiation within the social group. Wilfred C. Smith correctly has taught us that it is the outsider who names a religion, e.g., Hinduism. And, I would add, it is the experience of *being the outsider* that in the perception of the participant names the group.

V

How Categories Take Shape
An Inductive Approach

Now that we recognize the adventitious, indeed circumstantial character of categories, we need hardly dwell upon the distinction between inductive and deductive category-formation. That distinction seems to me self-evident. Such categories as *te Maori* and *Judaism* emerge when outsiders find it necessary to resort to available, therefore extrinsic rules of order and description in order to characterize the whole, all together and all at once. The alternative, an inductive principle of category-formation, will emerge from the data to be characterized. In the present case, the question that yields an inductive principle of category formation is simple: how do the data "describe themselves," so to speak.[13]

A study of the history of category formation in the study of ancient Judaism carries us not into the first six centuries of the Common Era (A.D.) and off to the Land of Israel ("Palestine"), but to nineteenth and twentieth century Europe and America. There we should expect to find out where and why people determined that *Judaism* constituted a principal category for identifying information, organizing it, and lending it proportion, sense, meaning and even significance. The category therefore dictates the rules of description, determines the issues for analysis, and governs the hermeneutical alternatives explored in the interpretation of data. None is teased out of the data it is meant to categorize. All come from without -- some from far away indeed. An account of modern and contemporary consciousness among Jews would certainly tell us much about the formation of these categories, as expressions of what proved self-evident in the unfolding consciousness of the social group at hand.

My purpose, however, is not to explore the modern and contemporary history of how Jews and outsiders formed the category *Judaism* and so identified data they determined would form *Judaism*. What I wish to pose is a different question. It is an inquiry intimate to, generated by, the data I study, which is to say, the documents produced in late antiquity and from then to now preserved by Jews as God's revelation to Israel. Specifically, I am trying to learn how to form appropriate categories for the description of *those* data, for the analysis of *those* data, and for the interpretation of *those* data. So my exercise in the study of category-formation begins not in abstract and philosophical reflection on nineteenth and twentieth century philosophy but in a particular body of the (to me) givens: the writings of the ancient sages, there alone. My study of category-formation therefore appeals to a particular authority: data already identified. It is inductive in a peculiar and curious way: I already know the limns

---

[13]Wilfred C. Smith's observation therefore is not the end, but only the beginning, of the matter. For knowledgeable people do come along and they are not outsiders to the data. And they too have their contribution to make.

and limits of my category,[14] and now I wish to find out what further categories have applied and whether they fit. My category is the canon of writings universally regarded by Jews from antiquity to the present day as Torah. My question is whether any other category than Torah applies. My answer is that none does. Specifically, such -*isms*, such categories as *Judaism* violate the limns and borders of the one category that forms from within the data and not outside of it, Those other categories, I shall try to show, therefore do not apply. That, sum and substance, is the argument at hand: that the only useful categories for the analysis of data derive from the data, in the case at hand, the analytical categories for the Torah inductively derive from the Torah.

VI

Canon, that is, Torah, as an Inductive Category

An inductive approach to category-formation requires that we take up the pieces of evidence one by one and propose by sorting out those data along lines they themselves dictate to find out what they mean. But an inductive approach presents us with its own circularity. Let me explain this circularity and how I propose to emerge from it, for this is the heart of the problem. How shall I know what data to select for organization in categories if to begin with I do not know what data I wish to organize and categorize? So knowing what I have to form into categories tells me the principles of category-formation. But if I already know what data demands categorization, then do I not already have my categories? That circularity confronts us first of all in our quest for a principle of category-formation intrinsic to the data and not extrinsic to them. My problem is to point to an initial and generative category external to the data yet (paradoxically) intrinsic to them. Lacking such a principle of selection and organization outside of the data I propose to describe, analyze, and interpret, I find myself at that same impasse at which I have located others. To restate matters as clearly as I can:

[1] we can know nothing without categories that permit classification, yielding the possibility of describing facts, analyzing them, and interpreting them.

[2] We wish to generate those categories out of the data themselves, rather than imposing categories external to the data, that is, we seek an inductive, rather than deductive, principle of category-formation.

[3] But how do we know what data we wish to categorize and classify, if not through some principle of category-formation that tells us one set of data belongs within the system, another set outside?

---

[14]Presently I confront the circularity of the present statement and show how to emerge from it.

So that is the circularity from which I have now to seek to emerge. Let us stipulate at the outset that all data -- all forms of evidence, in writing, in stones, in material culture, in reference in all writings -- pertaining to people regarded as Jews, and no data associated with people not regarded as Jews, to begin with require categorization for purposes of description, analysis, and interpretation. I believe philosophers will find that specification reasonable. But how, then, to begin the work of differentiation, if so external a category as just now specified tells me more merely that

[1] *everything in* is in

   and

[2] *everything out* is out?

Better the dreaded circularity with which we began. My responsibility, then, is to propose a category external to the data and yet appropriate to them.

I find that generative principle for category-formation in the matter of -- to state with heavy emphasis -- *the diverse institutional media by which the data are mediated from antiquity to the present.*

I refer to the differentiation among data imposed by the simple fact that some materials come to us in one medium, some in another. Some data reach us through the mediation of the diverse Christian churches. Some come to us through the continuous process of tradition of the Judaic religious institution, the synagogue, and its associated, and continuing institutions, e.g., the master-disciple circle, the school, and the like. Some data come to us by the happy accident of being preserved in the earth and dug up. These facts of transmission differentiate. How so? The third group of data -- that produced by archaeology -- bears no relationship to the first or the second, since, by definition, no one knew about them until they were dug up. They form a single group. The materials preserved by, respectively, church and synagogue scarcely overlap. The former constitute one distinct group, the latter, another. And, further, that latter group -- the writings preserved by the synagogue -- constitutes not a library but a canon. That is to say, the synagogue preserved the writings of late antiquity, where and when it did, because the group that kept the materials and copied them and handed them on and treasured them regarded them as holy, a statement of God's will to Israel: Torah. So that set of data stands quite distinct from the other two. Consequently, I claim an objective set of facts, external to the character and quality of the data, and yet enormously consequential in making differentiations among the data.

Accordingly, some data come to us [1] through the enduring institutions of the West, the synagogue and the church. Some data come to us [2] accidentally, through survival in caves. Some data come to [3] us in the form of writing, some data come to us [4] in the form of surviving buildings, artifacts, and other evidences of material culture. The one set differs from the other, and that in the merely adventitous sense just now specified: the medium of preservation and transmission. What is preserved and transmitted by people falls into [1] one gross category, what is preserved and transmitted by accident of nature falls into [2] another. And the people who did the preserving break up into [3, 4] distinct and scarcely intersecting groups as well.

Precisely what comes down to us from the Jews of late antiquity and how does it reach us? As is clear, the answer to the second question covers both: we have evidence in two media, material artifacts of archaeological provenience and writings of various kinds. The former then form one category, the latter another. As to the latter, the media for the preservation of documents -- deliberate or accidental -- once more supply us with our criterion for differentiation. What Judaism in its later history preserved as holy -- that is, the canon of Judaism from late antiquity to the present -- we must treat as distinct from what others than Jews preserved. The distinction -- the definition of the generative category -- therefore derives from circumstance and from without.

So we can indeed generate differentiating categories, variables that derive from the data themselves. Do these distinctions make a difference? For reasons already suggested, it makes a difference to know that (some) outsiders found materials worth saving. And, along these same lines and critical to the argument: it also makes a difference to know that (some) Jews found materials worth saving.[15] Some writings of Jews reach us through the medium of the copyists of the churches, others through the serendipity of preservation in dry caves. Some books come down to us only through the medium of the synagogue. And those for that -- adventitious -- reason form one distinct corpus of data -- for reasons of a nearly-physical, and essentially material character.

So, in my judgment, the simplest category at hand is how -- by what medium -- materials reached us. The items that come to us through institutions under Jewish auspices, therefore from the synagogue, fall together into one group, and that is *because of traits of all of these items and none of the others* . When we can point to traits characteristic of one set of data and not characteristic of another, we have found an appropriate category, and that category inductively derives from data.

I speak of course, of what later on became known as the Torah, that is, the canon of the Judaism that defined and preserved these books as a canon (not, for example, as a library).[16] The other data find their points of cogency elsewhere; they do not form our problem here. And, to proceed, once the books that for

---

[15]We do not know whether or not Jews thought so too, since we have these writings only from institutions under Christian auspices. If there were groups of Jews who cherished these books and also saved them, they did not succeed in handing on their holy books to the present generation.

[16]I work on the distinction between canon and library in *The Oral Torah. An Introduction* (San Francisco, 1985: Harper & Row), and on the distinction between a composition and a scrapbook or anthology in *The Integrity of Leviticus Rabbah* (Atlanta, 1985: Scholars Press for Brown Judaic Studies). These distinctions bear their own importance to me, but not here.

clear and distinct reasons fall together into a group define the broadest perimeters of our category, the mode of subdividing that encompassing category also is defined. From the canon, we divide by the same principle of category-formation as has led to the recognition of the canon as the principal category, namely, by the books that make up the canon. These categories then find definition in the books that the canon for its part preserved one by one (not as part of an undifferentiated mass) -- and so on down to the very sentences.

So I claim to move from the mass of evidence, delimited in a gross and completely external way, to the formation of categories that we recognize on inductive and external grounds. That is to say, on the basis of a descriptive and external approach to the diverse data that Jews of late antiquity produced, we locate a direct road to the categories formed by the canon and its components. These then define and constitute the categories, and so, I claim, the principle of category-formation derives from an inductive examination of the entire corpus of evidence, divided to begin with only among the media by which the evidence was preserved and transmitted to us, divided at the second level by the criteria themselves dictated by media internal to the first of the subdivisions of the data we chose to take up: the canon of that Judaism that preserved and handed on these books and not other books. And so the process proceeds.

VII

Describing a System Whole:
The Canonical Principle in Category-Formation
and How It Works

The limns of documents then generate, form, and define our initial system of categories. That is, the document to begin with is what demands description, then analysis by comparison and contrast to other documents, then interpretation as part of the whole canon of which it forms a part.[17] Now to the rules of description, which is to say, of category-formation along the lines of the canonical principle of category-generation.

Documents stand in three relationships to one another and to the system of which they form part, that is, to Judaism, as a whole. When we understand these relationships, we shall grasp the future of the study of Judaism in its formative centuries, therefore, also, of the study of the Christianity that took shape in the same context and circumstance.

Autonomy: Each document, it is clear, demands description, analysis, and interpretation, all by itself. Each must be viewed as autonomous of all others.

---

[17]I hasten to add, I do not take the canon to be a timeless category, as my analysis of the Mishnah and its associates indicates. Quite to the contrary, the canon itself takes shape in stages, and these form interesting categories for study. So things are considerably more complicated than I presently explain.

Connection: Each document also is to be examined for its relationships with other documents that fall into the same classification (whether that classification is simply "Jewish" or still more narrowly and hence usefully defined).

Continuity: Each document is to be allowed to take its place as part of the undifferentiated aggregation of documents that, all together, constitute the evidence of a Judaism, in the case of the rabbinic kind, the canon of the Torah.

How so?

Autonomy: If a document reaches us within its own framework as a complete book with a beginning, a middle, and an end, we do not commit an error in simple logic by reading that document as it has reached us, that is, as a book by itself.

Connection: If further a document contains materials shared verbatim or in substantial content with other documents of its classification, or if a document explicitly refers to some other writings and their contents, then we have to ask the question of connection. We have to seek the facts of connectedness and ask for the meaning of those connections.

Continuity: In the description of a Judaism, we have to take as our further task the description of the whole out of the undifferentiated testimony of all of its parts. For a Judaism does put together a set of once discrete documents and treat them as its canon. So in our setting we do want to know how a number of writings fit together into a single continuous and harmonious statement.

That is the point at which we do describe and analyze a Judaism. We therefore take up the task of interpreting that Judaism in the relationship between its contents and the context in which it makes its statement. In taking up the question of the harmony of the canon, whether of the rabbinic sources represented in this book by the Mishnah, or of the sources comprising the Pseudepigrapha, or of the writings of the Essenes of Qumran, or even of the Maccabean historians, we ask a theological question. And, in our context, that question elicits enormous interest: what after all was the Judaism of the Maccabean historians, or of the Essenes of Qumran, or of the authorship represented by Mark, or by the Mishnah?

By seeing the several components of the canons of the Judaisms of antiquity in sequence, first one by one, then one after the other in an orderly progression and sequence, and, finally, all together all at once, we may trace the histories of Judaisms. We may see a given document come into being on its own, in its context and circumstance. So we interpret the document at its site.

Since many documents relate to others prior to themselves or are brought into relationship to later writings, the issue of connectedness and connection demands attention. And, finally, all together and all at once, a given set of documents does form a whole, a canon, a frame that transcends the parts and imparts proportion, meaning, and harmony to the parts -- a Judaism (to resort to the "self-evident" category).

What do I hope to accomplish in the accurate description, to begin with through categories of its own devising, of a Judaism? The answer derives from the work on systemic analysis of Mary Douglas. Her stress is upon the conception that, "each tribe actively construes its particular universe in the course of an internal dialogue about law and order."[18] So, she says,

> Particular meanings are parts of larger ones, and these refer ultimately to a whole, in which all the available knowledge is related. But the largest whole into which all minor meanings fit can only be a metaphysical scheme. This itself has to be traced to the particular way of life which is realized within it and which generates the meanings. In the end, all meanings are social meanings.[19]

If I seek to state the large issues of that culture precisely as they are expressed through minute details of the way of life of those who stand within its frame, I have to start with the correct categories that encompass all the extant data of the culture at hand. These interrelate and define a coherent system. So at stake in category-formation is systemic description.

For once we have discerned the system which the compositors and framers of the books at hand evidently meant to create, we have the task before us of comparing that system to other systems, yielded both by Judaisms in their various stages and by other religious and cultural systems, in quite different contexts.[20] For a system described but not juxtaposed to, and compared with, other systems has not yet been interpreted. Until we realize what people might have done, we are not going to grasp the things they did do. We shall be unable to interpret the choices people have made until we contemplate the choices they rejected. And, as is clear, it is the work of comparison which makes that perspective possible. But how do we compare systems?[21] In fact, whenever we try to make sense for ourselves of what alien people do, we are engaged in a work of comparison, that is, an experiment of analogies. For we are trying to make sense specifically by comparing what we know and do to what the other, the alien culture before us, seems to have known and to have done. For this purpose we seek analogies from the known to the unfamiliar. I am inclined to think the task is to encompass everything deemed important by some one group, to include within, and to exclude from, its holy book, its definitive text: a

---

[18]Mary Douglas, *Implicit Meanings: Essays in Anthropology*, (London: Routledge & Kegan Paul, 1975), p. 5.

[19]p. 8.

[20]I experiment with comparison of systems in *Death and Birth of Judaism*.

[21]Much that is called 'comparative religions' compares nothing and is an exercise in the juxtaposition of incomparables. But it does not have to be that way.

system and its exclusions, its stance in a taxonomy of systems. For, on the surface, what they put in they think essential, and what they omit they do not think important.

VIII

Challenges to the Canonical Principle
of Category-Formation

Now in consequence of the theory at hand, we begin by describing, analyzing, and intrepeting the documents, not ideas held in a variety of documents. Our category derives not from *Judaism* but from *Torah*, that is, canon. But when we take up as our generative category a single book or document deriving from Jews of ancient times, without making theological judgments about whether the authors were "loyal" or "normative" or "authentic," we do something genuinely new. It is not only new, it also is secular. When we take up not a whole canonical, or official, literature but only a single book or document, and further, when we avoid judgments about normative or authentic or classical Judaism as against the heterodox or heretical kind, we set aside theological issues. Rather, we address descriptive and anthropological ones. That approach to the study of ancient Jewish writings still surprises believers of one kind or another.

When, furthermore, we approach the canon of that form of Judaism that did emerge as normative from late antiquity and did define the outlines of the history of the Judaism that was normative from the seventh to the nineteenth century, we commit a still more remarkable act. For, if some concede that all Jewish texts do not attest to a single Judaism, few grasp that to begin with we cannot treat as unified and harmonious all the texts preserved by rabbis from antiquity to the present time, that is, the canon, or, in common language, "rabbinic" or "Canon of Judaism in late antiquity" or simply "Judaism." Our work is to test, not to affirm at the outset, the premise that all books of the official canon of rabbinic Judaism form a single whole and harmonious "Torah." That fundamental dogma of the faith demands demonstration through the evidence itself. And the test must be a simple one. It is a test of description, analysis, and interpretation of the documents of the canon of Judaism, read, first, one by one, then, second, as connected to one another, and, third and finally as part of a single and harmonious system, a Judaism, thus, as a continuity. That test begins with my work and stands at its elementary stages even now. So, to return to the main point, when we take up a single book or document in the canon of Judaism as we know it, or in the canon of any other Judaism, and when we propose to describe, analyze, and interpret that book in particular, we violate the lines of order and system that have characterized earlier studies of these same documents. Not only so, but we open our question in a quite different way from earlier efforts to describe matters such as doctrine or belief. How so?

Until now canonical texts as testimonies to a single system and structure, that is, as I said, not to "*a Judaism*" or to a component of some larger Judaism, but to it, that is, to "*Judaism*." What sort of testimonies texts provide of course varies according to the interests of the scholars, students, and saints who study them. Scholars look for meanings of words and phrases or better versions of a text. For them, all canonical documents serve equally well as a treasury of philological facts and variant readings. Student look for the sense of words and phrases and follow a given phrase hither and yon as their teachers direct their treasure hunt. Saints study all texts equally, looking for God's will and finding testimonies to God in each component of the canon, in the case of Judaism, in each component of "the one whole Torah of Moses, our rabbi." And that is how it should be, for students, scholars, and saints within Judaism.

Among none of these circles, however, will the discrete description, analysis, and interpretation of a single text make sense. Why not? Because for them all texts ordinarily form a single statement in common, "Torah" in the mythic setting, "Judaism" in the philosophical and theological one. From that perspective people correctly expect each document to make its contribution to the whole, to the Judaism. If, therefore, we wish to know what "Judaism" or "the Torah" teaches on any subject, we simply open all the books equally. We draw freely on sayings relevant to that subject wherever they occur in the entire canon of Judaism. Guided only by the taste and judgment of the great "sages of the Torah" or, in formally-secular circumstances, Orthodox-Judaic professors at seminaries or ethnic-nationalist ones at universities, as they have addressed the question at hand, we do not merely describe "Judaism," we also declare dogma.

In the view of persons in these classifications, composites of sayings on a single topic (in our example, "Judaism," meaning "what the Jews believe") drawn from diverse books in no way violate the frontiers and boundaries that distinguish one part of the canon from some other part of the same canon. Why not? The theological conviction defines the established approach. Frontiers and boundaries stand only at the outer limits of "the whole Torah of Moses our rabbi." Within the bounds, "there is neither earlier nor later," that is to say, temporal (therefore all other differentiating) considerations do not apply.[22] If temporal distinctions make no difference, no others do either. For people who want to study in an inductive way the formation of Judaism in late antiquity as well as the setting in which Christianity took shape, however, the analysis of

---

[22]That view characterizes historians as much as theologians, historians of events, persons, or institutions and movements as much as historians of theology. These people just collect and arrange everything they find on the topic they have chosen and then make up history. That the younger and supposedly secular generation does the same sort of collecting and arranging -- but now by collecting things attributed to a single authority, without differentiating where and when and by whom the attribution is made -- is the burden of my *Ancient Judaism and Contemporary Fundamentalism: The Past Twenty-Five Years* (Lanham, 1986: University Press of America).

the literary evidence of the Jewish canon requires a different approach from the received Orthodox-scholarly one.

IX

The Integrity of a Document in the Canon of Judaism

To describe and analyze documents one by one violates the lines of order and system that have characterized all earlier studies of these same documents. But the hermeneutical issue dictated by the system -- hence, as I have argued, the canon and its components -- overall defines the result of description, analysis, and interpretation. Simple logic makes self-evident the proposition that, if a document comes down to us within its own framework, as a complete book with a beginning, middle, and end, in preserving that book, the canon presents us with a document on its own and not solely as part of a larger composition or construct. So we too see the document as it reaches us, that is, as autonomous.

If, second, a document contains materials shared verbatim or in substantial content with other documents of its classification, or if one document refers to the contents of other documents, then the several documents that clearly wish to engage in conversation with one another have to address one another. That is to say, we have to seek for the marks of connectedness, asking for the meaning of those connections. It is at this level of connectedness that we labor. For the purpose of comparison is to tell us what is like something else, what is unlike something else. To begin with, we can declare something unlike something else only if we know that it is like that other thing. Otherwise the original judgment bears no sense whatsoever. So, once more, canon defines context, or, in descriptive language, the first classification for comparative study is the document, brought into juxtaposition with, and contrast to, another document.

Finally, since the community of the faithful of Judaism, in all of the contemporary expressions of Judaism, concur that documents held to be authoritative constitute one whole, seamless "Torah," that is, a complete and exhaustive statement of God's will for Israel and humanity, we take as a further appropriate task, if one not to be done here, the description of the whole out of the undifferentiated testimony of all of its parts. These components in the theological context are viewed, as is clear, as equally authoritative for the composition of the whole: one, continuous system. In taking up such a question, we address a problem not of theology alone, though it is a correct theological conviction, but one of description, analysis, and interpretation of an entirely historical order.

In my view the various documents of the canon of Judaism produced in late antiquity demand a hermeneutic altogether different from the one of homogenization and harmonization, the ahistorical and anti-contextual one definitive for contemporary category-formation. As I showed in the opening unit of this chapter, it is one that does not harmonize but that differentiates. It is a hermeneutic shaped to teach us how to read the compilations of exegeses first of all one by one and in a particular context, and second, in comparison with one another.

X
From "Judaism" to *Torah*

Let us conclude with the point with which we began, the difficulty attached to generating categories for the present purpose out of theological or philosophical concepts. Why *Torah*, a literary principle of category-formation, not *Judaism*, a theological one? To answer that question, we briefly turn to the greatest work ever published in any language[23] under the title *Judaism,* namely, George Foot Moore, *Judaism. The Age of the Tannaim* (Cambridge, 1927: Harvard University Press). Here we shall gain acess to the main problem with the category at hand. The critical problem of definition is presented by the organizing category, "Judaism." Moore does not think definition is needed. But we now know that it is. Explaining what we propose to define when we speak about "Judaism" is the work of both contemporary philosophy of religion and history of religion. Moore fails to tell us also of whom he wishes to speak. So his repertoire of sources for the description of "Judaism" in the "age of the Tannaim" is awry. He makes use of sources which speak of people assumed to have lived in the early centuries of the Common Era, even when said sources derive from a much later or a much earlier time. What generates this error is a mistake in category-formation.

Specifically, Moore had to confront the problem of dealing with a category asymmetrical to the evidence. An essentially philosophical construct, "Judaism," is imposed upon wildly diverse evidence deriving from many kinds of social groups and testifying to the state of mind and way of life of many sorts of Jews, who in their own day would scarcely have understood one another, for instance, Bar Kokhba and Josephus, or the teacher of righteousness and Aqiba. So for Moore "Judaism" is a problem of ideas, and the history of Judaism is the history of ideas abstracted from the groups that held them and from the social perspectives of said groups. This seems to me a fundamental error, making the category "Judaism" a construct of a wholly fantastic realm of thought: a fantasy, I mean. In this regard matters are admirably summed up in Arthur Darby Nock's inquiry about the matter of "Gnosticism." He wanted to know where are the Gnostic churches, who are the Gnostic priests, and what are the Gnostic church's

---

[23] E. E. Urbach, *The Sages, Their Concepts and Beliefs* (Jerusalem, in Hebrew: 1969, English,1975: The Magnes Press) provides much valuable information but lacks intellectual cogency. It has not enjoyed a favorable reception. It has generated no studies beyond itself, no major books continuing its lines of inquiry. It marks the end, not the beginning, of research in its model.

books and doctrines.[24] What he meant was to point out that what we have are rather specific evidences of a single genus, the Gnostic one, e.g., of Manichaeism or Mandaism and now, of Nag Hammadi. Out of the agglutination and conglomeration of these diverse social groups and their writings scholars (not Jonas alone) formed (I should say invented) that higher idea, that "*the*" -- the Gnostic religion. That the forms the counterpart of the *ism*-izing of Juda-, thus: *Judaism*.

From a philosophical viewpoint the intellectual construct, Gnosticism, may bear scrutiny. From an historical viewpoint, it does not. The reason is that the -*ism* of *Gnostic*-, as much as the counterpart, the -*ism* of the *Juda*-, *ism*-izes too facilely. That is to say, Moore and other systematic theologians who have studied *Judaism* join together into harmonies data that derive from quite diverse groups at different times, and that were produced and preserved under different circumstances. So little is proved and much assumed. If we propose to present a cogent picture of how data deliver a single message, then the harmony and unity of the data demand demonstration. Before we know that the data derive from a single category, we can hardly undertake to form those data into a cogent statement about that category, describing, e.g., its ideas, analyzing its positions in comparison to the positions of other, related groups, interpreting those ideas in a still larger context. None of these routine activities of intellect can begin without a clear demonstratation that the *it* -- the -*ism* -- is an *it* to begin with, and not a *they*. History, rightly done, must err on the side of radical nominalism, as against the philosophical power for tolerance of something close to pure realism. In invoking these categories of medieval philosophy for analogical purposes, I mean only to explain why, for the present purpose, *"Juda"* + *"ism"* do not constitute self-evident, let alone definitive, categories. So, as I said, Judaism constitutes a category asymmetrical to the evidence adduced in its study. The category does not work because the principle of formation is philosophical and not historical. And to begin with historical category-formation, we start with the sources at hand: once more, the canon, or, in mythic terms, the Torah.

Second, Moore's work to begin with is not really a work in the history of religions at all -- in this instance, the developmental and formative history of a particular brand of Judaism. His research is in theology. It is organized in theological categories. That hardly presents a surprise, since Moore quite naturally took as the work of describing a religion the task of spelling out its ideas. For religion is faith, conviction, as the received datum, in theological words the tradition of salvation by faith, had taught him. This bias again derives from the faulty generative principle of category-formation: religion is belief, and the categories therefore are those of systematic theology.

---

[24]Arthur Darby Nock, *Essays on Religion and the Ancient World*, ed. Zeph Steward (Oxford, 1972: Clarendon Press), I, 444-51, in his review of Hans Jonas,*The Gnostic Religion*.

What Moore constructed therefore is a static exercise in dogmatic theology, not an account of the history of religious ideas and -- still more urgent -- their unfolding in relationship to the society of the people who held those ideas. Moore in no way describes and interprets the religious world-view and way of life expressed, in part, through the ideas under study. He does not explore the interplay between that world-view and the historical and political context of the community envisioned by that construction of a world. To state matters in the present context, my grandmother would not have understood Moore's picture of "Judaism," even if it had been translated into Yiddish.

But from our perspective, Moore's kind of classification, his "Judaism," and the continuators of that mode of description and analysis, prove equally alien. Why so? We who want to understand not only religions but religion ask ourselves a different set of questions, those that ask about religion as a social fact, a force in the shaping of human events. So far as history of religion (as distinct from histories of religions) attends to the material context of ideas and the class structure expressed by ideas and institutions alike, so far as ideas are deemed part of a larger social system and religious systems are held to be pertinent to the given political, social, and economic framework which contains them, Moore's account of dogmatic theology to begin with has nothing to do with religious history. His picture of Judaism bears no relationship to the history of Judaism in the first two centuries of the Common Era. So much for *Judaism* and for the principle of category formation that yields *Judaism*. As soon as we speak of Judaisms, not Judaism, we see the flaw and understand the hopeless impasse to which we have come in the Protestant ascendancy in the study of religion. The principle of category-formation derives from the wrong generative conception and premise.

This in conclusion brings us to the contrary principle of category-formation. Again I state with emphasis: it is this:

the principle of category-formation that commences with the sources, that is, in the case at hand, with the canon or the Torah -- that is, with an inductive inquiry originating in the data subject to categorization.

How do we proceed to form categories out of that principle of inductive formation out of data? One route to the interpretation of a system is to specify the sorts of issues it chooses to regard as problems, the matters it chooses for its close and continuing exegesis. When we know the things about which people worry, we have some insight into the way in which they see the world. So we ask, when we approach the canon of Judaism in late antiquity, about its critical tensions, the recurring issues which occupy its great minds. It is out of concern with this range of issues, and not some other, that the canon of Judaism in late antiquity defines its principal areas for discussion. Here is the point at which the great exercises of law and theology will be generated -- here and not somewhere else. This is a way in which we specify the choices people have made, the selections a system has effected. When we know what people have chosen, we also may speculate about the things they have rejected, the issues they regard as uninteresting or as closed. We then may describe the realm of thought and everyday life which they do not deem subject to tension and speculation. It is on these two sides -- the things people conceive to be dangerous and important, the things they set into the background as unimportant and uninteresting -- which provide us with a key to a Judaism -- that is to say, the culture of a community or, as I prefer to put it, to the system constructed and expressed by a given group of people.

The central issues, those questions which generate insight worth sharing and understanding worth having, therefore, find definition in these terms: what does the canon of Judaism in late antiquity, viewed item by item, by its components and then as a whole, define as its central problems? How does the canon of Judaism in late antiquity perceive the critical tensions of its world? We want to describe the solutions, resolutions, and remissions that the category of the canon poses for these tensions. We propose to unpack and then to put back together again the world-view of the canon as a whole, but first document by document. When we can explain how this system fits together and works, then we shall know something worth knowing, which is how to describe, analyze, and interpret *the Torah*.

Chapter Two

Description and the Category of System
An Exercise

My task here is to introduce "Judaism" to beginning students of religion. I can think of no more worthwhile assignment. In searching for simple and accessible language, categories, information, in aiming at giving a clear and correct account, I have to make those decisions that represent judgments on the whole, seen altogether and all at once: which categories, which facts, to what heuristic end? What I try to present is the "system" that is constituted by Judaism, meaning the way of life, world view and account of the social group that, all together, form the religion as a social entity and an intellectual construction -- a religion, seen whole.

Studying a Living Religion

Judaism traces its beginnings to the creation of the world. Following the biblical record, Judaism maintains that God created the world and for ten generations, from Adam to Noah, despaired of creation. Then for ten generations, from Noah to Abraham, God waited for humanity to acknowledge sovereignty of the one God, creator of heaven and earth. Through their children Sarah and Abraham founded Israel, the people of the Lord, to whom, later on, at Sinai, God revealed the Torah, the complete record of God's will for humanity, starting with Israel, the Jewish people. The biblical record goes on to speak of David, the king of Israel and founder of the ruling household, from which, at the end of time, the Messiah is destined to come forth. So Judaism tells the story of the world from creation in Adam and Eve, through the revelation of the Torah at Sinai, to the redemption of humanity through the Messiah at the end of time -- a picture of the world, beginning middle and end.

That account of the history of humanity and of all creation derives from a people that traces its origins to the beginnings of time and yet thrives in the world today. Let us begin with a simple statement of what interests us in any of the religions of the world today. We want to know why the world is the way it is, and we maintain that religion constitutes one of the principal forces in the formation of politics, economy, society and culture. Because of religion nations make war or peace. Because of religion people give their lives. Because of religion economic decisions favor one course of action and not some other. Because of religion politics, culture, social organization form a single cogent system in country after country -- or divide national societies along other than national or regional lines. Wherever we turn, from Europe to the Middle East to India, to the South Pacific, to the outer reaches of the Soviet Empire itself, religion turns out to form the single force that defines reality for humankind.

Religion is not private, not personal, not trivial, but public, political, and determinative. Most of the world is what it is today because of religion. You cannot understand the world today if you do not grasp the reality of religion as a powerful force in shaping politics and culture, economic action and social organization. No single object of study forms so public and social -- indeed, so measurable -- a presence as religion,. Nothing humanity has made constitutes a less personal, a less private, a less trivial fact of human life than religion. Some see religion as something private and interior, individual and subjective: how I feel all by myself, not what I do with other people. But religion is public, political, social, economic. It moves people to give their lives. Now to the example of Judaism, one of the world's oldest continuing and living religious traditions, and through Christianity and Islam, the single most influential religion in history.

Defining Judaism

We begin with a simple and clear definition of the Judaism predominant today and for twenty prior centuries. Judaism is the religion of the Torah, that is, of instruction of God's will, revealed by God to Israel through Moses at Mount Sinai. A further detail is critical to definition even at the outset. The definition of the Torah of Sinai encompasses more than the Pentateuch, or even the entirety of the Hebrew Bible or "Old Testament." In the view of Judaism, the Torah came to Moses in two media, one in writing, that is, the Scriptures, the other in the medium of memory, that is, orally, thus Judaism is comprised of "the written Torah," and "the Oral Torah." Judaism therefore is the religion of the dual Torah, and Judaists are people who believe in and practice Judaism, accept and follow the religion of the "one whole Torah of Moses, our rabbi."

The simple definition of Judaism as the religion of the "one whole Torah of Moses, or rabbi," derives from the formative period in the history of Judaism. It took shape in the centuries from before the destruction of the Jerusalem Temple in A.D. 70 to the end of Roman-Christian rule in the Middle East, in ca. A.D. 640. In those centuries the Judaism of the dual Torah reached its present definition. The holy books of that Judaism, beginning with the Mishnah, a law code of ca. A.D. 200, and ending with the Talmud of Babylonia of ca. A.D. 600, a systematic commentary on the Mishnah and on Scripture, came into being. That definition proved normative for the during which time nearly all Jews throughout the world believed in and practiced the Judaism of the dual Torah. That same definition moreover speaks today for nearly all those who affirm the classical teachings of Judaism, whether in the Orthodox, or the Reform, or the

Conservative, or the Reconstructionist expression of those teachings. But Judaism in the definition just given took shape only over a long period of time.

The Three Periods in the History of Judaism, 500 B.C. to A.D. 1900

There are three periods into which the history of Judaism is to be divided. The first was the age of diversity, in which many Judaic systems flourished, from the period of the formation of the Hebrew Scriptures, ca 500 B.C., to the destruction of the Second Temple, in 70. The second was the formative age, from 70 to closure of the Talmud of Babylonia, ca. A.D. 600. The third was the classical age, from late antiquity to the nineteenth century, in which that original definition dominated the lives of the Jewish people nearly everywhere they lived. That brings us to the modern age, from the nineteenth century to our own day, when an essentially religious understanding of what it means to be Israel, the Jewish people, came to compete among Jews with other views and other symbolic expressions of those views.

The Age of Diversity (500 B.C. - A . D. 70)

In the first period there were various Judaisms, that is, diverse compositions of a world view and a way of life that people believed represented God's will for Israel, the Jewish people. During that long age, nearly a five hundred years, a number of different kinds of Judaisms, that is, a system of world view and a way of life defining who is, and who is not, "Israel," or truly an heir to Scripture and its promises and blessings, came into being. During that time the roots of the Judaism of the dual Torah were put down.

The Formative Age of Judaism (70-640)

During the period at hand the canon of Judaism took shape. That canon consisted of the one whole Torah of Moses, our rabbi, reaching Israel in two forms, that is, through two media. One was the written Torah, which the world knows as the Hebrew Scriptures or the Old Testament. During the formative age sages selected those particular books of ancient Israel's library that Judaism would accept. During that same period the part of the Torah that came to Israel not in writing but orally, through the memory of Moses, the prophets, and the sages, down to the age at hand, also reached definition. The first of the documents that, in writing, preserved this memorized and orally-transmitted Torah was, as we have noted, the Mishnah, the last, the Talmud of Babylonia. In between writings of two kinds reached authoritative status, first, amplifications and commentaries for the Mishnah, second, the same sort of writing for Scripture. (All of these important books will be described in detail later on.) So the formative age saw the composition of a single, cogent canon, that one whole Torah of Moses our Rabbi, that constituted Judaism.

The Classical Period of Judaism (600-1900)

In the classical period, a single Judaism, the one teaching the dual Torah of Sinai, came to full definition and predominated. During that time whatever important ideas or issues developed Jews worked out within the categories of the Judaism of the dual Torah. For example a variety of mystical ideas and practices entered the world of Judaism and attained naturalization within the Torah.

The Contemporary Scene (1900 -)

In modern times, the diversity characteristic of the period of origins has come, once again, to prevail. Now the symbolic system and structure of the Judaism of the dual Torah competes for Jews' attention with other Judaic systems, on the one side, and with a wildly diverse range of symbols of other-than-Jewish origin and meaning, on the other. What of the Judaism of the dual Torah in relationship to the life of Israel, the Jewish people over time (not to be identified only with the contemporary State of Israel, which came into being in 1948)? That Judaism of the dual Torah endured and flourishes today as the religion of a small group of people.

Telling One Form of Judaism from Some Other:
The Symbolism of Judaism

What has been said indicates that over history more than a single version or Judaism has reached expression among Jews. So before we turn to the period of diversity, that is, the period in which the Hebrew Scriptures ("Old Testament") were taking shape, let us ask a question of method. How do we distinguish among "Judaisms"? What will tell us one system of Judaism from some other? Only when we know the answer to that quewstion can we approach the age of the formation of the Hebrew Scriptures and describe the types of Judaism (or "the Judaisms") of that age. We know one Judaism from another when we discover the definitive symbol adopted as characteristic by each.

Let us begin with the present. We may define Judaism today by asking whether there is a single symbol that speaks for all Jews who practice Judaic religion. Because in our own time there is such a single symbol everywhere deemed evocative, we may today speak not only of "Judaisms" but of a single, definitive Judaism. How shall we know what that symbol is? The way in which we know what stands at the center is to walk into a building put up by a group of Jews to serve as the focus of their collective religious life, for example, in our day, a synagogue.

Now if you walk into a synagogue anywhere in the world, your eye will be drawn to a contained space on the far wall which is called the ark. This contained space, ordinarily on the eastern wall, toward Jerusalem, forms the architectural and symbolic center and focus of the meeting room. That simple fact tells you what the community deems critical. If you know that within the ark are sacred objects, then the character and definition of those objects will dictate your judgment of what constitutes the central symbolic expression of the religion in the sanctuary in which you stand. Today, we realize, the visual, therefore also the doctrinal and symbolic, center of Judaism focuses upon the Torah. That simple fact takes on meaning when we realize that, in times past, other symbols, besides the Torah, served to express the whole, all at once and all together.

Three Kinds of Judaism Emerging from the Scriptures of Ancient Israel in the Formative Period (500 B.C. to 70 A.D.)

Today's Judaism, everywhere predominant, is not the only Judaism history has put forth.

The Torah-Scroll: The Judaism we know today comes to complete and whole expression in the symbol of the Torah, hence the Torah-scroll. But the Judaism of the Torah contrasts with other Judaisms. How do we know? Once again we ask about the symbols that served other groups of Jews to say, all at once and all together, what their particular version of Judaism -- their "Judaism" -- was.

The Holy Meal: If, in your mind's eye, you look into the buildings of the community of Jews who built a monastery community at what is now called Qumran, by the Dead Sea, the visual focus lies elsewhere. The central rite of the community focused on eating a meal. Christians, familiar with the Lord's supper, properly will expect that in the community of Judaism formed by the disciples of Christ in the early decades of Christianity, during which the disciples all saw themselves as Jews, that is, as part of Israel, the Jewish people, a table or a baptismal font will provide the visual center.

The Altar and its Sacrifices: If you review the biblical books that deal with the ancient Israelite Temple, for example, Leviticus and Numbers, Ezekiel Chapters Forty through Forty-Eight, various psalms and prophetic passages, you will imagine yet another visual center of another Judaic system, another Judaism. It is an altar. On it bonfires are kept burning; pieces of meat, loaves of bread, and other agricultural produce are burned up or displayed as "offerings" to God in heaven, that is, gifts, delivered by smoke. The Judaism at hand is one of sacrifice in a holy Temple by priests. So its definitive action is not study of the Torah but making offerings, and its leaders are not learned persons, called rabbis, but people permitted to carry out the sacrifice, called priests.

We thus can point to three central symbols, each definitive of a Judaism: a Torah-scroll, a table for a holy meal, and an altar for an offering. So, it is clear, the definitive symbol, both visual and verbal, tells us what is at the center of a Judaism, a world view and a way of life addressed to Israel, the Jewish people. If a Judaism comes to concrete expression in such a symbol, then to begin with we can identify at least three Judaisms, the three just now noted. One is represented by a Torah-scroll, a second by a table for a holy meal, a third by an altar for a sacrifice to God. Obviously, once we have come so far, we may stipulate that, through history, diverse groups of Jews have expressed their views of the world and symbolized their ways of life in yet another means besides those representative of Torah-learning, on the one side, a holy way of life climaxed by a sacred mealon the second, and acts of service through sacrifice to God.

But today, as I said, however diverse the Judaisms of the past, a single symbol stands for Judaism. That is the one with which we began, the Torah. So the history of Judaism as we now know it must sort out its facts in the story of the Torah, its contents and meaning, and how Israel, the Jewish people, became definitively and distinctively the people of the Torah.

Three Kinds of Judaism in the Age of Diversity

The Judaism of the dual Torah drew upon the Hebrew Scriptures, as did all the other Judaisms of that day and all other times. So in order to see in an appropriate framework the choices facing the Jews and to understand the selections that, all together, defined the Judaism that would predominate, we have to take into account the alternatives not selected.

How shall we find out what points of stress lay at hand? We have to turn back to Scripture, outlining the main alternatives laid forth in ancient Israel's days. Our task is to sort out the dominant strands of the inherited religion of the Hebrew Bible and to characterize each one. We now know how to do this work of description. We look for the definitive symbol, the critical point of stress. This we may discern in every detail of a system, whether in its leadership, or in its main mode of expression in action, or in its definition of what really matters in life. So we may ask about the definition of the hero, the specification of what people should do with their lives, or the kind of institution a given strand generated.

Priest, Scribe, Messiah: The principal strands of ancient Israelite life come to realization in the distinct types of holy men we identify as priests, scribes, and messiahs, and the definitive activities, cult, school and government offices, and (ordinarily) battlefield. Ancient Israel's heritage yielded the cult with its priests, the Torah with its scribes and teachers, and the prophetic and apocalyptic hope for meaning in history and an eschaton embodied in messiahs.

Altar, Torah-Scroll, Coin Celebrating: "Israel's Freedom, Year One:" The generative symbol of each mode were, first, an altar, for the priestly ideal; second, a scroll of Scripture, for the ideal of wisdom; and third, a coin marked "Israel's freedom: year one," for the messianic modality. The symbols captured everything in some one thing: the sheep for the sacrifice, the memorized aphorism for the disciple, the stout heart for the soldier of light. Priest, sage, soldier -- these figures stand for Israel, or part of the nation. When, as we now know, all would meld into one, that one would stand for a fresh and unprecedented Judaism.

The issues of the symbols under discussion, Temple altar, sacred scroll, victory wreath for the head of the King-Messiah, comprehended Jewish society at large. At the foundations, we deal with the organization of the people of Israel's society and the selection and interpretation of events that would constitute its history. The social groups for which these symbols stand are, first, the caste of priests, second, the profession of scribes, third, the calling of general or prophet.

The Ways of Life of Three Kinds of Judaism:
Priestly, Scribal, Messianic

The Priestly Ideal: The priest viewed society as organized through lines of structure emanating from the Temple. His caste stood at the top of a social scale in which all things were properly organized, each with its correct name and proper place. The inherent sanctity of Israel, the people, came through genealogy to its richest embodiment in him, the priest. Food set aside for his rations at God's command possessed that same sanctity; so too did the table at which he ate his food. To the priest the sacred society of Israel produced history as an account of what happened in, and (alas) on occasion to, the Temple.

Wisdom as a Way of Life: To the sage, the life of society demanded wise regulation. Relationships among people required guidance by the laws embodied in the Torah and best interpreted by the sage. Accordingly, the task of Israel was to construct a way of life in accordance with the revealed rules of the Torah. The sage, master of the rules, stood at the head.

Prophecy, History, and the End of Time: As for prophecy's insistence that the fate of the nation depended upon the faith and moral condition of society, history testified to the external context and inner condition of Israel, viewed as a whole. Both sage and priest saw Israel from the aspect of eternity. But the nation lived out its life in the history of this world, among other peoples coveting the very same land, within the politics of empires. The messiah's kingship would resolve the issues of Israel's subordinated relationship to other nations and empires, establishing once for all time the correct context for priest and sage alike.

The three modes of human existence expressed in the symbolic systems of cult, Torah, and messiah demand choices. If one thing is more important, then the others must be less important. History matters, or it happens "out there" without significance. The proper conduct of the cult of sacrifice in the Temple determines the course of the seasons and the prosperity of the land, or it is merely ritual. The messiah will save Israel, or he will ruin everything. So the way in which symbols are arranged and rearranged settles everything. Symbol change is social change. The particular way the three are bonded in a given system reflects an underlying human and social reality.

That is how it should be, since the three symbols with their associated myths, the world views they project, and the ways of life they define, stand for different views of what really matters. So let us translate the symbols we have surveyed -- the three points of emphasis of three "Judaisms," -- into the everyday life of ordinary people. What can we say about the existential foundations of the several symbolic systems available to Jews of antiquity? We seek to penetrate to the bedrock of Israel's reality.

The Points of Stress and Human Concern of the Three Kinds of Judaism in the Age of Diversity

In order to do so, we ask what made one particular focus, whether the priestly, the sagacious, or the messianic, appear more compelling and consequential than the others? The answer becomes obvious when we realize that each kind of piety addresses its point of concern and speaks about different things to different people. How so?

Priests and sages turn inward, toward the concrete everyday life of the community. They address the sanctification of Israel.

Messianists and their prophetic and apocalyptic counterparts turn outward, toward the affairs of states and nations. They speak of the salvation of Israel.

Priests see the world as a realm of life in Israel, and death beyond. They know what happens to Israel without requiring a theory about the place of Israel among the nations. The nations, for priests, form an undifferentiated realm of death.

Sages, all the more, speak of home and hearth, fathers and sons, husbands and wives, masters and disciples, the village and enduring patterns of life. What place in this domestic scheme for the disruptive realities of history, wars and threats of war, the rise and fall of empires? The messianic emphasis encompasses the consciousness of a singular society amidst other societies. So at issue for the priest is order, regularity, "being," for the prophet and Messiah, disruption, spontaneity, "becoming."

The Pharisees before 70 and Judaism after 70

Who were the Pharisees, and why do they matter? The Pharisees fall into the larger classification represented by the priests, the altar, the holy way of life. A sect who flourished in the period before the destruction of the Temple in 70, the Pharisees claimed to live as if they were priests, as if they had to obey the laws that applied to the Temple. To express that yearning for sanctification they tried to keep at home, in their private lives, the laws of cleanness most people thought applied only to the Temple. Those laws, deriving from the biblical book of Leviticus, defined for the priests how to conduct the Temple's work in a holy way. The Pharisees before 70 held that ordinary people were supposed to keep those laws as well. Emphasis on keeping that law of cleanness that others assigned only to the Temple meant that the Pharisees wanted everyone everywhere to live the life of priests in the holy place. So the Pharisees wanted Israel to be that "kingdom of priests and holy people" that the Torah, in the book of Leviticus, described.

Why do the Pharisees matter in the history of Judaism? Because they formed one of the principal groups in the formation of the Judaism that emerged after the destruction in 70. When the Temple itself was destroyed, it turned out that the Pharisees had prepared for that tremendous change in the sacred economy. Earlier, when the Temple stood, Pharisees had maintained that ordinary people, not priests, should eat everyday food, not shares of the Temple offerings, as if they were governed by the levitical rules applying to Temple priests eating holy things. So in Temple times the Pharisees were lay people pretending to be priests. Now, even after the destruction of the Temple to which those laws had applied, they maintained that same pretense, only with much better reason.

That is, they held that the holiness of the life of Israel, formerly centered on the Temple, endured and transcended the physical destruction of the building and the cessation of sacrifices. They therefore continued to live *as if*. They acted as if the Temple stood, as if there was a new Temple formed of the Jewish people. Joined to their mode of looking at life was the substance of the scribal ideal, the stress on learning of Torah and carrying out its teachings.

The Impact of the Destruction of the Temple in A.D. 70

In 66 A.D. a Jewish rebellion in the Land of Israel against Rome's rule of the country broke out in Jerusalem. Initially successful, the rebels in the end were pushed back into the holy city, which fell in August, 70. The Temple, destroyed in 586 B.C. and rebuilt three generations later, by the time of its second destruction had stood for five hundred years. In it the commandments of God to Moses concerning sacrifice reached fulfillment. With its destruction the foundations of Israel's national and social life in the Land of Israel were shaken. The Temple had constituted one of the primary, unifying elements in that common life. The structure not only of political life and of society, but also of the imaginative life of the country, depended upon the Temple and its worship and cult. It was there that people believed they served God. At the Temple the lines of structure -- both cosmic and social -- had converged. The Temple, moreover, had served as the basis for those many elements of autonomous self-government and political life left in the Jews' hands by the Romans. Consequently, the destruction of the Temple meant not merely a significant alteration in the cultic or ritual life of the Jewish people, but also a profound and far-reaching crisis in their inner and spiritual existence.

When the Temple was destroyed, two distinctive groups survived, the scribes with their learning, and the priests with their memories, their sense of what God required for service, and their notion that all Israel, every Jew, stood in relationship to all others within the grid of holiness. What happened was that, over the next half century or so, a viable cultural-religious existence was reconstructed. Between ca. 70 and ca. 120 a number of elements of the religious-cultural structure of the period before 70 were put together into a new synthesis. This synthesis, joining scribal, priestly, and (later on) the messianic points of emphasis, would come to expression in the writings of the rabbis of the first seven centuries A.D. We now know it as Judaism. We should call that synthesis by its own name, "the Torah." In more descriptive language, we may call it by the name of its ideal-type, the rabbi, hence Rabbinic Judaism.

In response to the disaster of the destruction therefore (Rabbinic, or Torah) Judaism took shape. Its success lay in its capacity to claim things had not changed at all -- hence the assertion that even at the start, Moses was "our rabbi." But the very destruction of the Temple itself served as the verification and vindication of the new structure. Rabbinic Judaism claimed, like the scribes of old, that it was possible to serve God not only through sacrifice, but also through study of Torah. So the question is the question of the priests and Pharisees: how to serve God? But the answer is the answer of the scribes: through Torah-learning.

The Scribe, the Priest, and the Rabbi: A priest is in charge of the life of the community, just as the priests had said. But now it was a new priest, the rabbi. The old sin-offerings still may be carried out. But today it would be the sacrifice of deeds of loving-kindness. In former times people revered the Temple. Now, if and when the whole Jewish people will fully carry out the teachings of the Torah, the rabbi, that is, the Pharisee-scribe promised, the Temple itself will be rebuilt. Like the prophets and historians in the time of the first destruction, in 586 B.C.E., the rabbis further claimed that it was because the people had sinned, had not kept the Torah, that the Temple had been destroyed. So the disaster itself was made to vindicate the rabbinic teaching and to verify its truth. When the people lived up to the teachings of the Torah as the rabbis expressed them, the Temple would be restored in response to the people's repentence and renewal.

The Judaism of the Dual Torah: The Formative Stage

So, to summarize the history of the formation of Judaism: two primary components in the synthesis then are to be discerned: first, the emphases of Pharisaism, and second, the values of the scribal profession. Pharisaism lay stress upon universal keeping of the law, obligating every Jew to do what only the elite -- the priests -- were normally expected to accomplish. The professional ideal of the scribes stressed the study of Torah and the centrality of the learned person in the religious system.

But there was something more. The unpredictable, final element in the synthesis of Pharisaic stress on widespread law, including ritual-law, observance and scribal emphasis on learning, is what makes Judaism distinctive. That is the conviction that the community now stands in the place of the Temple. The ruins of the cult did not mark the end of the collective, holy life of Israel. What survived was the holy people.

It was the genius of Judaism to recognize that the holy people might reconstitute the Temple in the sanctity of its own community life. Therefore the people had to be made holy, as the Temple had been holy. The people's social life had to be sanctified as the surrogate for what had been lost. That is why the rabbinic ideal for Judaism further maintained that the rabbi served as the new priest, the study of Torah substituted for the Temple sacrifice, and deeds of loving-kindness were the social surrogate for the sin-offering -- personal sacrifice instead of animal sacrifice. All things fit together to construct out of the old Judaisms the world-view and way of life of the new and enduring Judaism of the Torah.

The Formative Period: Summary

Thus the Judaism of the dual Torah came into being as the amalgam of two of the three strands of the period of diversity, specifically, the priestly and the sagacious. Among three main choices, the messianic, priestly, and scribal, the Judaism of the two Torahs began with the priestly, now represented by the Pharisees and their method, and the scribal, now represented by the scribes, or sages and rabbis, and their Torah-teachings. The third, the Messianic, would become important as the Judaism of the two Torahs developed, but not at the outset.

Wherever Jews lived in times past, whether in Christian Europe or Moslem Africa and the Middle East, they worked out both their private lives and their collective and social existence through the system of Judaism involving the two media of the Torah, or the two Torahs, of Sinai, written and oral. Now let us conclude this portrait of the beginning of Judaism by answering some narrowly historical questions about the Judaism of the dual Torah.

1. **When:**

When, exactly, did the Judaism of the two Torahs originate? While drawing on much older materials, beginning with the Scriptures themselves, the Judaism of the dual Torah began to take shape as we now know it only in the first century of the Common Era (C.E. = A.D.)

2. **Who:**

What particular groups made their contribution to this Judaism? The Scribes, a profession, and the Pharisees, a sect, contributed the contents and the method of Judaism, respectively.

3. **Why:**

Above all, under what circumstances was this union of established elements in a striking new way accomplished? It was in the aftermath of the destruction of the second Temple, in Jerusalem, in 70 that the two groups coalesced and began that process that in the next six centuries would yield Judaism in the form in which we now know it.

Judaism in the Encounter with Christianity: The Crisis of the Triumph of Christianity as the Religion of Rome

During this same period, between the first and the seventh centuries, Christianity came into being. Christianity took shape in the matrix of the Judaism of the first century, a period of flux, as we have seen. It initially laid its emphasis upon the messianic component of the diverse Judaisms of the period, though, in due course, absorbed within its system the priestly and scribal ones as well. Did the advent of Christianity make an impact on Judaism? Not in the first four centuries, during which Christianity was not an important force in the Greco-Roman world.

But from the conversion of Constantine, in the early part of the fourth century, to the establishment of Christianity as the religion of the Roman Empire, at the end of the fourth century, Christianity began to define issues for the Judaic sages of the age. For the triumph of Christianity also represented a powerful shift in human history, of which the sages of Judaism took full account.

The one whole Torah of Moses, our rabbi, confronted the challenge of the Cross of Christianity and, later on, the sword and crescent of Islam as well. Within Israel, the Jewish people, the Torah triumphed. If we understand how rabbinic Judaism met the crisis of Christianity in its triumphant form, as ruler of the world from the time of Constantine in the fourth century, we also will grasp why Judaism as the rabbis defined it succeeded through history from that time to this. For when Christianity arose to define the civilization of the West, then Judaism met and overcame it greatest crisis. It held. As a result, Jews remained within the system. They continued for the entire history of the West to see the world through the world-view and conduct life in accord with the way of life of the Torah as the rabbis explained it.

To state matters simply, with the triumph of Christianity through Constantine and his successors in the West. Christianity's explicit claims, now validated in world-shaking events of the age, demanded a reply. The sages of the Talmud provided it. At those very specific points at which the Christian challenge met head-on old Israel's world-view, sages' doctrines responded. What did Israel's sages have to present as the Torah's answer to the cross? It was the Torah. This took three forms. The Torah was defined in the doctrine, first, of the status, as oral and memorized revelation, of the Mishnah, and, by implication, of other rabbinical writings. The Torah, moreover, was presented as the encompassing symbol of Israel's salvation. The Torah, finally, was embodied in the person of the Messiah who, of course, would be a rabbi. The Torah in all three modes confronted the cross, with its doctrine of the triumphant Christ, Messiah and king, ruler now of earth as of heaven.

We deal with three important changes that first emerge in the writings of sages of the Land of Israel that reached closure at the end of the fourth and the beginning of the fifth century, one a massive commentary to the Mishnah, as I shall explain, and others equally impressive commentaries to books of Scripture. All these changes constitute shifts in the symbolic system and structure of the Judaism then taking shape. What I propose is not merely that things changed, but that things took the particular changes that they did because of a critical challenge.

The Torah and the Cross: The symbolic system of Christianity, with Christ triumphant, with the cross as the now-regnant symbol, with the canon of Christianity now defined and recognized as authoritative, called forth from the sages of the Land of Israel a symbolic system strikingly responsive to the crisis: the coming of the Messiah set as the teleology of the system of Judaism as they defined that system, the symbol of the Torah expanded to encompass the whole of human existence as the system laid forth the limns of that existence, the canon of Sinai broadened to take account of the entirety of the sages' teachings, as much as of the written Torah everyone acknowledged as authoritative. Did the sages say these things in order to answer the challenge of Christianity? No one can claim that they did. We cannot speculate on motive, since we have no evidence by which to test our speculation.

The Triumph of the Torah in Israel, the Jewish People: What was the outcome? A stunning success for that society for which, to begin with, sages, and, in sages' view, God, cared so deeply: eternal Israel after the flesh. For Judaism in the rabbis' statement did endure in the Christian West, imparting to Israel the secure conviction of constituting that Israel after the flesh to which the Torah continued to speak. How do we know sages' Judaism won? Because when, in turn, Islam gained its victory, Christianity throughout the Middle East and North Africa gave way. But sages' Judaism in those same vast territories retained the loyalty and conviction of the people of the Torah. The cross would rule only where the crescent and its sword did not. But the Torah of Sinai everywhere and always sanctified Israel in time and promised secure salvation for eternity. So Israel believed and so does faithful Israel, those Jews who also are Judaists, believe today. The entire history of Judaism is contained within these simple propositions.

So the Judaism of the dual Torah, written and Oral, began its long historical life in a moment of crisis and renewal. It solved a problem that proved perennial, namely, how to deal with disaster and nurture rebirth in a small, vanquished nation. The solution to the problem, as we shall see at the very end, lay in helping the individual Judaic woman or man to identify the private life and inner feeling and anguish with the public history and destiny of the Jewish nation. People therefore found a close correspondence between the immediate and everyday life they lived -- a life of birth, maturing, marriage, raising children, and dying -- with the collective and social world of Israel, the Jewish people. When the individual suffered, he or she could appeal to the condition of all reality. When the individual encountered hope, love, or small and private salvation, these too represented a foretaste of the redemption of Israel, the Jewish people. So public history and private destiny came together. This perfect union, fostered by the Judaic world view and way of life of the Judaism of the dual Torah, enjoyed the status of being self-evidently true and right to the Jews who saw the world in the Judaic way and lived out their years within the disciplines of the Torah.

Ideas, Practices, Ethics

What is the one important idea of Judaism? Central to Judaism is the belief, to which we have referred already, that the ancient Scriptures constituted divine revelation, but only a part of it. At Sinai, God had handed down revelation in two media: the written part widely known, and the oral, memorized part preserved by the great scriptural heroes, passed on by prophets in the obscure past, finally and most openly handed down to the rabbis who ultimately created the Palestinian and Babylonian Talmuds. The "whole Torah" thus consisted of both written and oral parts. The rabbis taught that "whole Torah" was studied by David, augmented by Ezekiel, legislated by Ezra, and embodied in the schools and by the sages of every period in Israelite history from Moses to the present. It is a singular, linear conception of a revelation, preserved only by the few, pertaining to the many, and in time capable of bringing salvation to all. The rabbinic conception of Torah further regards Moses as "our rabbi," the first and prototypical figure of the ideal Jew. It holds that whoever embodies the teachings of Moses "our rabbi" thereby conforms to the will of God -- and not to God's will alone, but also to God's way. In heaven, Rabbinic Judaism teaches, God and the angels study Torah just as rabbis do on earth. God dons phylacteries like any Jew. He prays in the rabbinic mode. He carries out the acts of compassion called for by Judaic ethics. He guides the affairs of the world according to the rules of Torah, just as does the rabbi in his court. One exegesis of the creation legend taught that God had looked into the Torah and, guided by the Torah, had created the world.

The symbol of Torah is multidimensional. It includes the striking detail that whatever the most recent rabbi is destined to discover through proper exegesis of the tradition is as much a part of the Torah revealed to Moses as is a sentence of Scripture itself. It is therefore possible to participate even in the giving of the law by appropriate, logical inquiry into the law. God himself, studying and living by Torah, is believed to subject himself to these same rules of logical inquiry. When an earthly court overruled the testimony, delivered through miracles, of the heavenly one, God rejoiced, crying out, "My sons have conquered me!" -- so the sages believed.

In a word, before us is a mythicoreligious system in which earth and heaven correspond to one another, with Torah -- in place of Temple -- model of both.

The heavenly paradigm is embodied upon earth in Moses "our rabbi." Moses then sets the pattern for the ordinary sage. And God himself participates in the system, for, as is clear, it is God's image which, in the end, forms that cosmic paradigm. The faithful Jew constitutes the projection of the divine on earth. That is why honor is due to the learned rabbi even more than to the holy scroll of the Torah, for through his learning and logic the sage may alter the very content of Mosaic revelation. The sage is Torah, not merely because he lives by it, but because at his best he forms as compelling an embodiment of the heavenly model as does a Torah scroll itself.

The critical idea in the rabbinic conception of Torah concerns salvation. Through learning and living by the Torah, Israel will be saved. This idea takes many forms. One salvific teaching holds that had Israel not sinned -- that is, disobeyed the Torah -- the Scriptures would have closed with the story of the conquest of Palestine. From that time forward, the sacred community would have lived in eternal peace under the divine law. Keeping the Torah was therefore the veritable guarantee of salvation. The opposite is said in many forms as well. Israel had sinned, therefore God had called the Babylonians in 586 B.C., then Romans in A.D. 70, to destroy the Temple of Jerusalem. But in his mercy he would restore the fortunes of the people when they, through their suffering and repentance, had expiated the result and the cause of their sin.

So in both negative and positive forms, the rabbinic idea of Torah tells of a necessary connection between the salvation of the people and the state of Torah among them. It is at this point that the Messiah-strand of ancient Israelite tradition came into play. The coming of the Messiah, meaning the end of the difficult world that Israel endured, was tied up to the system of the Torah. So if people wanted the Messiah to come -- and they surely did -- they should study the Torah and carry out its teachings.

For example, if all Israel properly keep a single Sabbath, the Messiah will come. Of special interest here is the rabbinic saying that the rule of the pagans depends upon the sin of Israel. If Israel constitutes a full and complete replication of "Torah," that is, of heaven, then pagan rule will come to an end. It would end because all Israel then, like some few rabbis even now, would attain to the creative powers inherent in Torah. Just as God had created the world through Torah, so saintly rabbis could create a sacred community. When Israel makes itself worthy through its embodiment of Torah, that is, through its perfect replication of heaven, then the end will come.

Learning thus finds a central place in the Judaic program of religious practices because of the belief that God had revealed his will to humankind through the medium of a written revelation, given to Moses at Mount Sinai, accompanied by oral traditions taught in the rabbinical schools and preserved in the Talmuds and related literature. The text of the written Torah without the oral traditions of the memorized part of the Torah might have led elsewhere than into the academy. But belief in the text was coupled with the belief that oral traditions also were revealed. Only from masters, rabbis, could these oral traditions be learned. In the books composed in the rabbinical academies, as much as in the Hebrew Bible itself, was contained God's will for humanity. So learning defined a principal practice of Judaism, a ritual act, and learning meant serving as a disciple to a master

The act of study, memorization, and commentary upon the sacred books is holy. The study of sacred texts therefore assumes a central position in Judaism. Other traditions had their religious virtuosi whose virtuosity consisted in knowledge of a literary tradition; but few held, as does Judaism, that everyone must become such a virtuoso. The central ritual of Judaism, therefore, is study. Study as a natural action entails learning traditions and executing them -- in this context, in school or in court. Study becomes a ritual action when it is endowed with values extrinsic to its ordinary character, when set into a mythic context. When disciples memorize their masters' traditions and actions, they participate in the rabbinic view of Torah as the organizing principle of reality. Their study is thereby endowed with the sanctity that ordinarily pertains to prayer or other cultic matters. Study loses its this-worldly focus on merely learning things or acquiring information. The act of study itself becomes holy. Its original purpose, which is mastery of particular information, ceases to matter. What matters is the spirit of the act, the piety expressed through the rites of studying. Repeating the words of the oral revelation, even without comprehending them, might produce reward, just as imitating the masters matters, even if the pious person cannot explain the reasons for sages' actions. The separation of the value, or sanctity, of the act of study from the natural, cognitive result of learning therefore transforms studying from a natural to a ritual action. That separation is accomplished by the rabbis' conception of Torah.

If the principal practice of Judaism as rabbis define it is to study the Torah, then what, beyond Scriptures, did and do people actually study? The first document of the Torah beyond the Hebrew Scriptures is the Mishnah, ca. A.D. 200. The Mishnah is studied paragraph by paragraph in the light of the commentary of the Babylonian Talmud, ca. A.D. 600. So if we wish to know the contents of Judaism, we turn first of all to the topical program of the Mishnah, and second to the exegetical approach of the Babylonian Talmud. The Mishnah is a book that expresses its authors' ideas through statements of halakhah, meaning rules or laws. It follows that the characteristic way in which Judaism speaks its great ideas is through what we call "laws." By "law," you probably understand such things as not stealing, or "no parking," or not lying under oath. But to the ethics of Judaism, expressed as laws, law is meant to express, to encompass, all of reality. Law is too small a word to make room for all which, in Judaism, we know as halakhah, the way things are and should be. The ethos and ethics of Judaism are contained in the halakhah.

Precisely what are the topics important to the halakhah of the Mishnah and the Talmud? Into what components do the sages of the halakhah divide this "reality" of which we have spoken? Let us consider the major divisions of Mishnah and, translated into our own terms, their topics and subject matter.

First, comes the section on "Seeds," that is, on agricultural laws. Farming comes first because the Jews made their living by farming. "If there is no bread, there is no Torah." But what is it about farming that interested the rabbis? Their primary topic encompasses the ways in which farmers should do their work in accord with Torah. The Torah contains many "laws" about farming, and the purpose of most of these laws is to teach people how to express their thanks to God for what God gives. The way thought appropriate, both in the Written Torah and in the Oral Torah which is Mishnah, is to give, for sacred purposes, a part of the yield of the field and the farm, to observe those rites and restrictions revealed in the Torah about how farming was to be carried on. The halakhah encompassed planting which seeds with which, defining what proportion of the crop is given to the poor (for helping the poor is serving God), what proportion to the priest, the teacher of Torah, keeping one sort of seed separate from another sort of seed, and so on.

The second division of the Mishnah is called "Seasons" or -- to use the language of the anthropologists -- "taboos" about holy days. On this day, one does so and so, on that day one does not. So the halakhah lays down the rites and rituals of dividing time into "holy" and "profane." Naturally, the Sabbath comes first, for it is the Sabbath which is The Holy Day. This topic is divided into two sides or aspects: (1) the meaning of Sabbath-holiness for labor, and (2) the meaning of holiness of time for space. That last point is difficult. The Written Torah says that, on the Sabbath, Israelites should stay home. ["Let no man leave his place on the seventh day." (Exodus 16:29)] The Mishnah, the Oral Torah, takes up this rule and asks, "How far away is still home?" What is the effect of the Sabbath upon the space we occupy? "Seasons" then proceeds to various holy days, Passover, Sukkot, the Day of Atonement, the New Year, and other topics concerning the Jewish calendar.

The third division concerns the family. Here the rabbis express a very simple conception of the family. They call the division of the Mishnah dealing with family affairs "Women." Their idea is that women are the foundation of the home and family. Their deepest concern is to protect, define, and defend the rights of women. How does a family begin? It begins with a document which defines the rights and duties of women and of their husbands. How does a family end? It ends with a document which effects divorce, freeing the woman to build a new house and a new family, providing for her maintenance in the interval between the divorce and the (taken for granted) remarriage.

The fourth division of the Mishnah is called "Damages." The halakhah here deals with conflict, aggression, and property rights which have to be worked out in an orderly way. At this point the rabbis of the Mishnah introduce how we transfer property from one person to another, how we adjudicate conflicting claims of all sorts. Here what we understand by "law" and what Mishnah gives us as halakhah come together. How so? If in law school, one would study a great deal about torts and damages, property an the transfer of property, the rights of individuals to own and to dispose of the fruit of their labor, not to mention the way courts are set up and how they do their business (in the Mishnah, Tractate Sanhedrin), oaths in court and oaths for other purposes, and the like. There is nothing surprising here except for one fact: To Judaism, all of this is part of Torah, a matter of religion. Indeed, in a yeshivah, an academy where the Talmud is studied, one of the first tractates to learn will be selected from this fourth division of the Mishnah. And the reason is that holiness is not merely rite, ritual, or "taboo" -- something in our minds and imagination -- but, especially, holiness governs the conduct of everyday life, of law in the commonplace practical sense.

The fifth division is on "Sacrifices" and how they are to be offered, the sixth on "Purity" and impurity. Both relate to the Temple and its cult. The fifth division takes up those many biblical laws on how God is served through sacrifice.

The sixth division, on purities, deals with the rules of Leviticus 1-15 on unclean and clean things. To understand the purity-laws, we turn to an analogy. There are things which we cannot see but which we know are present. Take, for instance, radiation. If you were to go into an area contaminated by radiation, you might see nothing and feel nothing, but that does not mean you are not affected. You are contaminated; and if you do not wash or wear protective clothing against severe radiation, you will become very sick and may die. Further, things which you wear may be contaminated and they may, in turn, infect others with contamination. Now, in the books of Leviticus and Numbers, the written Torah tells about various sources and modes of contamination, of things which make a person unclean. In all ways, the result is the same: A person who is "unclean" cannot come into the holy place. These various sources of contamination have one thing in common: They break the order of nature, the wholeness and completeness of life. Death breaks the balance of life. The corpse is unclean. Various sorts of animals or insects are conceived -- for reasons that do not concern us -- as "unclean." If you touch them, you are unclean. Since it is in the sanctuary, the holy temple, that the wholeness or completeness of life is most fully realized, the person who has somehow broken with the natural balance and order of creation cannot go there. The rabbis of the Mishnah take up this conception and work it out in exquisite detail.

Let us now turn to a passage of Mishnah and consider its literary traits and legal substance. The passage concerns personal damages: What is the law if Peter breaks John's leg? The answer follows. We assess Peter with monetary damages, and we have to reckon how to translate the breaking of a leg into fair compensation. The Mishnah paragraph is the first in the Eighth Chapter of tractate *Baba Qamma*, The First Gate, laws on civil damages. It is given in the translation by E.W. Kirzner, published by The Soncino Press, London (pp. 473-

474), as part of *The Babylonian Talmud,* a complete and reliable translation into English of that fundamental document of Judaism.

A Paragraph of the Mishnah:

One who injures a fellow man becomes liable to him for five items: (1) For depreciation, (2) for pain, (3) for healing, (4) for loss of time and (5) for degradation.

M. Baba Qamma 8:1

How is it with (1) "depreciation"? If he put out his eye, cut off his arm or broke his leg, the injured person is considered as if he were a slave being sold in the market place, and a valuation is made as to how much he was worth [previously], and how much he is worth [now].

(2) "Pain" -- if he burnt him either with a spit or with a nail, even though on his [finger] nail which is a place where no bruise could be made, it has to be calculated how much a man of equal standing would require to be paid to undergo such pain.

(3) "Healing" -- if he has struck him, he is under obligation to pay medical expenses. Should ulcers [meanwhile] arise on him as a result of the wound, the offender would be liable, not as a result of the wound, he would be exempt. Where the wound was healed but reopened, healed again but reopened, he would still be under obligation to heal him. If, however, it had completely healed [but had subsequently reopened] he would no more be under obligation to heal him.

(4) "Loss of time" -- the injured person is considered as if he were a watchman of cucumber beds [as even a lame or one-armed person could be employed in this capacity] [so that the loss of such wages(but not of the previous employment on account of the reason which follows) sustained by him during the period of illness may be reimbursed to him], for there has already been paid to him the value of his hand or the value of his leg through which deprivation he would no more be able to carry on his previous employment].

(5) "Degradation" -- all to be estimated in accordance with the status of the offender and the offended.

Babylonian Talmud Baba Qamma 83a

The passage of the Mishnah specifies the five sorts of damages one has to pay if he or she damages someone else. In the Talmud we ask how to assess "depreciation"; then we want to know how to translate "pain" into dollars and cents. Third comes healing, which of course means the payment of medical expenses. But we forthwith have to ask about expenses for secondary costs, that is, for healing an ailment not directly caused by the original act of damage. This is relatively easy to calculate, as is the fourth item, loss of time. Finally, we include a peculiarly human matter, embarrassment or degradation.

Before we proceed, let us make a few observations about the paragraph of Mishnah we have just read.

First, does the Mishnah follow the literary style of the Hebrew Scriptures or "the written Torah"? The answer quite obviously is that it does not. While this may be "Oral Torah" or "the second Torah" in some important way, no effort has been made to copy the biblical modes of formulation and expression. The second Torah is stylistically independent and autonomous of the first.

Second, what is the presupposition of this law? It is that a person who injures someone must compensate him or her, and is not punished -- as Scripture explicitly states -- by having to suffer an equivalent punishment. The one thing Mishnah ignores is: An eye for an eye, a tooth for a tooth (Exod. 21:24). What sort of Torah is this, which takes as its basic assumption the exact opposite of what the written Torah explicitly demands? It is one prepared to complement the text at hand by reading that basic document in a fresh and original way.

Third, when we turn to the substance of the law, we find a careful effort to supply guidelines applicable everywhere. We do not specify compensation in terms likely to be relevant to one country or one brief period of time. We calculate in terms relative to all times. "How much a man of equal standing would require to be paid..." "Loss of Wages..." "The status of the offender and the offended" -- these all are efforts to avoid such specificity as would make the Oral Torah useless three years after its promulgation or two hundred miles from its home base.

And this leads us to the final, most important observation: "Torah" -- written and oral -- is hardly a "Jewish" document. Why not? We find remarkably little attention to the "Jewishness" of the society -- the victim or the injurer. On the contrary, the frame of reference is not only neutral as to a particular place or time. It is also indifferent to the ethnic origin of the participants. It speaks of society, time, man and woman, family, home, and metaphysical world. We find no stress on the particularity or ethnic distinctiveness of the individuals who form the society and demarcate the time. What is most distinctive about Judaism is the belief in the dual revelation, written and oral Torah. Yet when we come to the substance of that dual revelation, we find ourselves in a world of universals, not particular and distinctively Jewish at all.

Now let us turn to the second component of the Oral Torah, the commentary to the Mishnah, which explains the meaning and significance of Mishnah's law. The great and authoritative commentary to the Mishnah is called the Talmud. This is a compilation of materials relevant to a given paragraph of Mishnah, developed from the third through the seventh centuries A.D. In point of fact, two Talmuds exist for the same Mishnah. One was edited in Palestine at ca. 400 A.D. and is called the Palestinian or Jerusalem Talmud; the other was edited in Babylonia at ca. A.D. 600 and is called the Babylonian Talmud. The latter is widely studied to this day and supplies the authoritative interpretation of Mishnah. Let us now proceed to the Talmud's problem in interpretation of the Mishnah we have just read, regarding the laws or civil damages? It is the obvious one: How do we link the Oral Torah, which assumes we pay monetary damages for personal injury, to the Written Torah, which is clear that we punish personal injury by inflicting an equivalent injury, an eye for an eye. We read the passage in Dr. Kirzner's translation (pp. 474-480). I have inserted his footnotes into the text of the translation, in brackets.

> Why [pay compensation]? Does the Divine Law not say "Eye for eye"[Exod. 21:24]? Why not take this literally to mean [putting out] the eye [of the offender]?

The Talmud begins with the obvious question. It asks why Mishnah ignores the Scriptural law.

> Let this not enter your mind, since it has been taught: You might think that where he put out his eye, the offender's eye should be put out, or where he cut off his arm, the offender's arm should be cut off, or again where he broke his leg, the offender's leg should be broken. [Not so; for] it is laid down, "He that smiteth any man..." "And he that smiteth a beast..." [Lev. 24:18, 21]. Just as in the case of smiting a beast compensation is to be paid, so also in the case of smiting a man compensation is to be paid [but no resort to Retaliation].

The first proof is before us. Scripture refers to smiting a beast, and, if you look up the relevant passage, you will see that Scripture then says you pay monetary damages. The passage similarly refers to injuring a person. It follows that Scripture has in mind the payment of monetary damages in both cases. But this proof may not please everyone. So we are given another -- and another, and another. That is to say, virtually every conceivable argument in behalf of monetary damages instead of physical retaliation is going to be laid before us.

> And should this [reason] not satisfy you, note that it is stated, "Moreover ye shall take no ransom for the life of a murderer, that is guilty of death" [Num. 35:31], implying that it is only for the life of a murderer that you may not take "satisfaction" [i.e., ransom, and thus release him from capital punishment], whereas you may take "satisfaction" [even] for the principal limbs, though these cannot be restored.

The second proof depends upon a close reading of the cited passage. The Scripture says you do not take a ransom -- a monetary payment -- for the life of a murderer. This is then turned around. For the life of a murderer, you may not take a ransom, but you do so for the destruction of limbs.

> How [do you know that it refers] to pecuniary compensation? Why not say that it really means capital punishment? [As indeed appears fromthe literal meaning of the text.]

Let not this enter your mind; first, because it is compared to the case dealt with in the text, "He that smiteth a beast mortally shall make it good," and furthermore, because it is written soon "as he hath done so shall it be done to him" [Lev. 24:19] thus proving that it means pecuniary compensation.

But what is meant by the statement, "If this reason does not satisfy you"? [Why should it not satisfy you?] The difficulty which further occurred to the Tanna [Mishnah-teacher] was as follows: What is your reason for deriving a law of man injuring man from the law of smiting a beast and not from the law governing the case of killing man [where retaliation is the rule]?

This is the right question. We have now reviewed two proofs. Both of them in one way or another depend upon the analogy between man and beast. But perhaps such an analogy is false. This is the answer.

I would answer: It is proper to derive [the law of] injury [Lev.24:19] from [the law governing another case of] injury [i.e., where man injured beast], and not to derive [the law of] injury [Lev. 24:19] from [the law governing the case of] murder.

It could, however, be argued to the contrary: [that it is proper] to derive [the law of injury inflicted upon] man from [another case of] man but not to derive [the law of injury inflicted upon] man from [the case of] beast.

This was the point of the statement, "If, however, this reason does not satisfy you." [The answer is as follows:] 'It is stated:

Moreover ye shall take no ransom for the life of a murderer who is guilty of death; but he shall surely be put to death, implying that it was only 'for the life of a murderer' that you may not take ransom whereas you may take ransom [even] for principal limbs though these cannot be restored.

We have concluded that line of argument. We thus have examined an example of the method of Judaism, that is, its modes of thinking, its ways of deriving religious beliefs and conceptions, and the centrality of Torah study. It is time to ask about the substance of Judaism, its conceptions of God and humankind, history and eternity, Israel -- the Jewish people -- and the nations.

One must first ask, How do we find these conceptions? Do we have now to consider two thousand years of theological writings, the decrees of councils of rabbis, or the conceptions of philosophers and authoritative theologians? The answer is negative. The best place in which to discover and study the religious beliefs of Judaism is in the Jewish prayerbook, the Siddur. The accepted prayerbook is a document of public piety. In its main outlines, it begins with Rabbinic Judaism. But in its contents it goes back to still more ancient times. As we shall see, the Siddur contains descriptions and interpretations of Judaism's view of the world.

The Siddur thus is the document of piety characteristic of, believed in, shared and understood by the masses of Jews, not merely by the religious elite. To be sure, it may have been the creation of religious virtuosi. But it speaks to and for the common folk. That is why we may confidently describe the religious beliefs of Judaism out of the materials of worship. These materials contain and express a vast conception of reality, and a detailed interpretation of everyday affairs. The great teaching, the dogma, of Judaism is that God is one. That is not meant as a philosophical declaration, alleging the unity of the Divinity as against the claim of the plurality of Divinity. It is a religious affirmation, to be discerned from the language of the prayer. It is to this majestic proclamation of faith that we now turn. Evening and morning, the Judaist -- the Jew who practices Judaism -- proclaims the unity and uniqueness of God. The proclamation is preceded and followed by blessings. The whole constitutes the credo of the Judaic tradition. Components recur everywhere. Let us first examine the prayer, called Shema, "Hear." The Shema begins with a celebration of God as creator of the world. In the morning, one says (in the translation of Rabbi Jules Harlow):

> Praised are You, O Lord our God, King of the universe.
> You fix the cycles of light and darkness;
> You ordain the order of all creation.
> You cause light to shine over the earth;
> Your radiant mercy is upon its inhabitants.
> In Your goodness the work of creation
> Is continually renewed day by day...
> O cause a new light to shine on Zion;
> May we all soon be worthy to behold its radiance.
> Praised are You, O Lord, Creator of the heavenly
>   bodies.

The corresponding prayer in the evening refers to the setting of the sun:

> Praised are You...
> Your command brings on the dusk of evening.
> Your wisdom opens the gates of heaven to a new day.
> With understanding You order the cycles of time;
> Your will determines the succession of seasons;
> You order the stars in their heavenly courses.
> You create the day, and You create night.
> Rolling away light before darkness. Praised are You,
>   O Lord, for the evening dusk.

Morning and evening, the Judaist responds to the natural order of the world with thanks and praise of God who created the world and who actively guides the daily events of nature. Whatever happens in nature gives testimony to the sovereignty of the creator. And that testimony is not in unnatural disasters, but in the most ordinary events, sunrise and sunset. These, especially, evoke the religious response. God is purposeful. The works of creation serve to justify -- to testify to Torah -- the revelation of Sinai. Torah is the mark not merely of divine sovereignty, but of divine grace and love, source of life here and now and in eternity. So goes the second blessing:

> Deep is Your love for us, O Lord our God;
> Bounteous is Your compassion and tenderness.
> You taught our fathers the laws of life.
> And they trusted in You, Father and King.
> For their sake be gracious to us, and teach us,
> That we may learn Your laws and trust in You.
> Father, merciful Father, have compassion upon us;
> Endow us with discernment and understanding.
> Grant us the will to study Your Torah,
> To heed its words and to teach its precepts...
> Enlighten our eyes in Your Torah,
> Open our hearts to Your commandments...
> Unite our thoughts with singleness of purpose
> To hold You in reverence and in love...
> You have drawn us close to You;
> We praise You and thank You in truth.
> With love do we thankfully proclaim Your unity,
> And praise You who chose Your people Israel in love.

Here is the way in which revelation takes concrete and specific form in the Judaic tradition; God, the creator, revealed his will for creation through the Torah, given to Israel his people. That Torah contains the "laws of life."

This is the mark of the relationship between God and humankind, and Judaic man or woman in particular, that a person's eyes are open to Torah and that his or her heart is open to the commandments. These are the means of divine service, of reverence and love for God. Israel sees itself as "chosen," close to God, because of the Torah, and it finds its devotion to the Torah the mark of its chosenness. The covenant made at Sinai, a contract on Israel's side to do and hear the Torah, on God's side to be the God of Israel -- that covenant is evoked by natural events, then confirmed by human deeds and devotion. Torah, revelation, leads Jews to enunciate the chief teachings of revelation:

Hear O Israel, the Lord our God, the Lord is One.

This proclamation is followed by three Scriptural passages. First, Deuteronomy 6:4-9:

You shall love the Lord your God with all your heart, with all your soul, and with all your might.

And further, one must diligently teach the children these words and talk of them everywhere and always, and place them on one's forehead, doorposts, and gates. The second Scripture is Deuteronomy 11:13-21, which emphasizes that if the people keep the commandments, they will enjoy worldly blessings, but if they do not, they will be punished and disappear from the good land God gives them. The third is Numbers 15:37-41, the commandment to wear fringes on the corners of one's garments, today attached to the prayer shawl worn at morning services. The fringes remind the Jew of all the commandments of the Lord. Redemption, the third element in the tripartite world view, resolves the tension between what people are told to do and what they are able actually to accomplish. In the end it is the theme of God not as creator or revealer, but God as redeemer, that concludes the twice daily drama:

You are our King and our father's King,
Our redeemer and our father's redeemer.
You are our creator...
You have ever been our redeemer and deliverer
There can be no God but You...
You, O Lord our God, rescued us from Egypt;
You redeemed us from the house of bondage...
You split apart the waters of the Red Sea,
The faithful You rescued, the wicked drowned...
Then Your beloved sang hymns of thanksgiving...
They acclaimed the King, God on high,
Great and awesome source of all blessings,
The everliving God, exalted in His majesty.
He humbles the proud and raises the lowly;
He helps the needy and answers His people's call...
Then Moses and all the children of Israel
Sang with great joy this song to the Lord:
Who is like You O Lord among the mighty?

Who is like You, so glorious in holiness?
So wondrous Your deeds, so worthy of praise!
The redeemed sang a new song to You;
They sang in chorus at the shore of the sea,
Acclaiming Your sovereignty with thanksgiving:
The Lord shall reign for ever and ever.
Rock of Israel, arise to Israel's defense!
Fulfill Your promise to deliver Judah and Israel.
Our redeemer is the Holy One of Israel.
The Lord of hosts is His name.
Praised are You, O Lord, redeemer of Israel.

Redemption is both in the past and in the future. That God not only creates but also redeems is attested by Israel's redemption from Egyptian bondage. The congregation repeats the exultant song of Moses and the people at the Red Sea, not as scholars making a learned allusion, but as participants in the salvation of old and of time to come. Then the people turn to the future and ask that Israel once more be redeemed. But redemption is not only past and future. When the needy are helped, when the proud are humbled and the lowly are raised -- in such commonplace, daily events, redemption is already present. Just as creation is not only in the beginning, but occurs daily, so redemption is not only at the Red Sea, but every day, in humble events. Just as revelation was not at Sinai alone, but takes place whenever people study Torah, whenever God opens their hearts to the commandments, so redemption and creation are daily events.

When, however, we reflect upon the language of the *Shema*, we realize that that unity which is affirmed is the oneness of nature and history, the conviction that all reality is the creation of God and finds unity in the oneness of the Creator. Above all things, behind all things, is the one God who made heaven and earth, who regulates nature and history. The rising and the setting of the sun testify to the oneness, the orderliness of creation. The Torah contains and expresses the orderliness of human history. Redemption, at the end of days, will complete the unity of being. We now turn from the great issue of being to the seemingly trivial but far more relevant question: How does Judaism express the condition of the individual man and woman? What prayers reveal the context of private life? And what ideals for everyday life, what interpretation of the human condition of the Jewish man and the Jewish woman, are shaped by these prayers? The answers to these questions tell us about more than the shape and substance of Judaic piety. They tell us, too, what manner of man or woman would take shape, for the constant repetition of the sacred words and moral and ethical maxims in the setting of everyday life was bound to affect the personality and character of the individual and the quality of communal life as well. Prayer expresses the most solemn aspirations of the praying community; it is what gives that community a sense of oneness, of shared hopes; and it embodies the values of the community. But it is the community at its least particular and self-aware moment, for in praying people stand before God without the mediation of ethnic consciousness. That does not mean in Judaic prayer one does not find an acute awareness of history and collective destiny. These are present.

In the morning, noon, and evening prayers of praise and petition are found, called the Eighteen Benedictions. Some of these, in particular at the beginning and the end, recur in Sabbath and festival prayers. Each individual prays by and for himself or herself, but together with other silent, praying individuals. To contemplate the meaning of these prayers, one should imagine a room full of people, each alone, yet in close proximity to the next, some swaying this way and that, all addressing themselves directly and intimately to God, in a whisper or in a low tone. They do not move their feet, for they are now standing before the King of kings, and it is not mete to shift and shuffle. If spoken to, they will not answer. Their attention is fixed upon the words of supplication, praise, and gratitude. When they begin, they bend their knees; so too toward the end, and at the conclusion, they step back and withdraw from the presence. These, on ordinary days, are the words they say:

Wisdom -- Repentance
You graciously endow man with intelligence;
You teach him knowledge and understanding.
Grant us knowledge, discernment, and wisdom.
Praised are You, O Lord, for the gift of knowledge.

Our Father, bring us back to Your Torah;
Our King, draw us near to Your service;
Lead us back to You truly repentant.
Praised are You, O Lord who welcomes repentance.

Forgiveness -- Redemption
Our Father, forgive us, for we have sinned;
Our King, pardon us, for we have transgressed;
You forgive sin and pardon transgression.
Praised are You, gracious and forgiving Lord.

Behold our affliction and deliver us.
Redeem us soon for the sake of Your name,
For You are the mighty Redeemer.
Praised are You, O Lord, Redeemer of Israel.

Heal us -- Bless our years

Heal us, O Lord, and we shall be healed;
Help us and save us, for You are our glory.
Grant perfect healing for all our afflictions,
O faithful and merciful God of healing.
Praised are You, O Lord, Healer of His people.

O Lord our God! Make this a blessed year;
May its varied produce bring us happiness.

Bring blessing upon the whole earth.
Bless the year with Your abounding goodness.
Praised are You, O Lord, who blesses our years.

Gather our exiles -- Reign over us

Sound the great shofar to herald man's freedom;
Raise high the banner to gather all exiles;
Gather the dispersed from the corners of the earth.
Praised are You, O Lord, who gathers our exiles.

Restore our judges as in days of old;
Restore our counsellors as in former times;
Remove from us sorrow and anguish.
Reign over us alone with loving kindness;
With justice and mercy sustain our cause.
Praised are You, O Lord, King who loves justice.

Humble the arrogant -- Sustain the righteous

Frustrate the hopes of those who malign us;
Let all evil very soon disappear;
Let all Your enemies be speedily destroyed.
May You quickly uproot and crush the arrogant;
May You subdue and humble them in our time.
Praised are You, O Lord, who humbles the arrogant.

Let Your tender mercies, O Lord God, be stirred
For the righteous, the pious, the leaders of Israel,
Toward devoted scholars and faithful proselytes.
Be merciful to us of the house of Israel;
Reward all who trust in You;
Cast our lot with those who are faithful to You.

May we never come to despair, for our trust is in You.
Praised are You, O Lord, who sustains the righteous.

Favor Your City and Your People

Have mercy, O Lord, and return to Jerusalem, Your
  city;
May Your Presence dwell there as You promised;
Rebuild it now, in our days and for all time;
Re-establish there the majesty of David Your servant.
Praised are You, O Lord, who rebuilds Jerusalem.

Bring to flower the shoot of Your servant David.
Hasten the advent of the Messianic redemption;
Each and every day we hope for Your deliverance.
Praised are You, O Lord, who assumes our deliverance.

O Lord, our God, hear our cry!
Have compassion upon us and pity us;
Accept our prayer with loving favor.
You, O God, listen to entreaty and prayer.
O King, do not turn us away unanswered,
For You mercifully heed Your people's supplication.
Praised are You, O Lord, who is attentive to prayer.

O Lord, our God, favor Your people Israel;
Accept with love Israel's offering of prayer;
May our worship be ever acceptable to You.
May our eyes witness Your return in mercy to Zion.
Praised are You, O Lord, whose Presence returns to
  Zion.

Our Thankfulness

We thank You, O Lord, our God and God of our
  fathers,
Defender of our lives, Shield of our safety;
Through all generations we thank You and praise You.
Our lives are in Your hands, our souls in Your charge.

We thank You for the miracles which daily attend us,
For Your wonders and favor morning, noon, and
  night.
You are beneficent with boundless mercy and love.

From of old we have always placed our hope in You.

For all these blessings, O our King.

We shall ever praise and exalt You.

Every living creature thanks You, and praises You in
    truth.

O God, You are our deliverance and our help. Selah!

Praised are You, O Lord, for Your goodness and Your
    glory.

Peace and well-being

Grant peace and well-being to the whole house of
    Israel;

Give us of Your grace, Your love, and Your mercy.

Bless us all, O our Father, with the light of Your
    Presence.

It is Your light that revealed to us Your life-giving
    Torah,

And taught us love and tenderness, justice, mercy, and
    peace.

May it please You to bless Your people in every
    season,

To bless them at all times with Your gift of peace.

Praised are You, O Lord, who blesses Israel with
    peace.

The Individual: The first two blessings pertain to intelligence. Man or woman thanks God for mind: knowledge, wisdom, discernment. But knowledge is for a purpose, and the purpose is knowledge of Torah. Such discernment leads to the service of God and produces a spirit of repentance. Judaists cannot pray without setting themselves right with God, and that means repenting for what has separated them from God. Torah is the way to repentance, to return. So knowledge leads to Torah, Torah to repentance, and repentance to God. Logically, the next is the prayer for forgiveness. That is the sign of return. God forgives sin; God is gracious and forgiving. Once man and woman discern what they have done wrong through the guidance of Torah, they seek to be forgiven. Sin leads to affliction. Affliction stands at the beginning of the way to God; once people have taken that way, they task for their suffering to end, they beg redemption. Man and woman ask for healing, salvation, a blessed year. Healing without prosperity means one may suffer in good health, starve (if not for long) in a robust body. So along with the prayer for healing goes the supplication for worldly comfort.

The Community or Nation: The individual's task is done. But what of the community? Health and comfort are not enough. The world is unredeemed. People are enslaved, in exile, and alienated. At the end of the day a great shofar will sound to herald the Messiah's coming. This is now besought. The Jewish people at prayer asks first for the proclamation of freedom, then for the ingathering of the exiles to the promised land. Establishing the Messianic kingdom, God needs also to restore a wise and benevolent government, good judges, good counsellors, loving justice.

History and Redemption: Meanwhile, Israel, the Jewish people, finds itself maligned. Arrogant people hating Israel hate God as well. They should be humbled. And the pious and righteous, the scholars, the faithful proselytes, the whole House of Israel, that trusts in God -- these should be rewarded and sustained. Above all, remember Jerusalem. Rebuild the city and dwell there. Set up Jerusalem's king, David, and make him to prosper. These are the themes of the daily prayer: personal atonement, good health and good fortunes; collective redemption, freedom, the end of alienation, good government and true justice; the final and complete salvation of the land, Jerusalem, the Messiah.

At the end comes the supplication that prayer may be heard and found acceptable, then an expression of thanksgiving not for what may come, but for the miracles and mercies already enjoyed morning, noon, and night. And at the end is the prayer for peace, a peace that consists of wholeness for the sacred community.

The Modern and Contemporary Period: 1900 to the Present

The Demography of Contemporary Judaism
Calvin Goldscheider

Brown University

The demography of Judaism encompasses two broad topics -- the distribution of the Jewish population in places around the world and the variation and intensity of their Judaism in those places. There is some statistical documentation available to estimate the demography of Jews; issues associated with the definition and quality of Judaism are more complex and less amenable to simpler description.

There are an estimated 13 million Jews in the world as of 1985. The largest concentration of Jewish population is in the United States, where an estimated 5.7 million Jews live. In the State of Israel, the only country where the Jewish population is a numerical majority, there are 3.4 million Jews; the Soviet Union has an estimated 1.6 million Jews. Together, these three countries contain over 80 percent of all world Jewry.

There are over one million Jews in Western Europe; most live in France (530,000) and Great Britain (350,000). Canada has a Jewish population of 308,000; Argentina follows in Jewish population size with 233,000 Jews. South Africa with 120,000 Jews and Brazil with 100,000 Jews are the only other countries with at least 100,000 Jews. These nine countries account for 95 percent of the world Jewish population. Jews are therefore highly concentrated in a few but very diverse societies. There are small Jewish communities in a wider range of countries within Europe (East and West), Asia, North and South America.

The Jewish population in the United States, as true of Jews in other countries, is not evenly spread throughout its regions, states, and cities. Most Jews everywhere live in urban places and usually in the largest metropolitan areas of their countries. The majority of American Jews live in the Northeast (54 percent of the Jews, twice the proportion of non-Jews). About the same percent of Jews and non-Jews live in the Western region of the United States (17 percent of each group) but Jews are significantly underrepresented in the South (17 percent of Jews compared to 34 percent of non-Jews) and in the North Central region (12 percent of Jews compared to 26 percent of non-Jews). A closer inspection of the distribution of Jews by states within the United States reveals a disproportionate geographic spread. There are only 10 states where Jews have a population size of over 100,000. Together these account for 87 percent of all U.S. Jewry. By size, the largest five Jewish population sizes by state are (in thousands):

New York	1,870
California	790
Florida	479
New Jersey	425
Pennsylvania	408

Within states, Jews are heavily concentrated in the largest cities.

The extent and variation of contemporary Judaism -- the religiosity and religious commitments of Jews -- defy simple definition and classification. For most Jews there is limited evidence on the degree of Jewish identification, religious practice, ritual observance, or other indicators of Judaism. This is true despite the highly organized character, e.g., congregational, institutional, of Jewish communities and synagogue and Rabbinical associations. An examination of some rough indicators of Judaism reveals the following profile for the largest communities in the United States, Israel, and the Soviet Union.

National American data show that about 85 percent of the adult Jewish population in the United States identify themselves with one of the three major religious denominations -- Orthodox, Conservative or Reform, which are generally ranked from higher to lower intensity of religious observances. Overall, about 11 percent identify with the Orthodox, 42 percent with Conservative Judaism and 33 percent with Reform Judaism. There is, of course, variation in denominational identification within the United States. In 1981, for example, the distribution in New York, the largest Jewish community in the world, was 13 percent Orthodox, 35 percent Conservative and 29 percent Reform. About one-fourth of New York Jews define themselves denominationally as either "other" or "none." In St. Louis, there were fewer Conservative Jews but more Reform Jews. In the western states the proportion Reform and "other-none" tends to be higher.

Variation in this identification and practice of Judaism is also reflected in ritual practices and synagogue attendance. Nationally, data from a 1970-71 survey showed that about 30 percent of the Jews observed the dietary rules, 13 percent attended synagogue frequently, 24 percent were members of two or more Jewish organizations. Data (1981) from New York show that about 90 percent of adult Jews attend a Passover Seder, 80 percent light Hannukah lights, 70 percent have a Mezuzah on the doorpost, 67 fast on Yom Kippur, 36 percent buy only kosher meats and 30 percent keep two sets of dishes for meat and dairy. Few Jews attend services weekly (14 percent of the men in New York); most attend a few times a year. About 30 percent of the men never attend. Again, Jews in other American communities, particularly in the west have lower levels of ritual observance and synagogue attendance.

The State of Israel is also a secular society and religious observances tend to parallel the patterns found in the United States. Religious divisions in Israel are not along Orthodox, Conservative or Reform lines or synagogue membership. National data in Israel show that between 10 and 15 percent of the population define themselves as "very religious." Almost half are "religious" or "traditional," 36 percent define themselves as not religious and an additional 9 percent are totally secular. About 47 percent keep separate meat and dairy dishes. Synagogue attendance in Israel is as low as in New York -- about 26 percent never attend and most attend a few times a year. Ethnic Jewish variation, particularly between those of western (or European) origins and those of oriental (or Asian-African) origins, divide the population in terms of religiosity. The orientals, who now form a majority of the Jewish population, tend to be more traditional than western Jews but have rapidly become secularized. Despite the large proportion secular in Israel (about one-third the adult Jewish population), most of 6,000-8,000 synagogues in Israel are Orthodox. Only about 40 congregations in Israel with a total membership of 2,000 families are affiliated with Reform or Conservative Judaism. This undoubtedly reflects the association between politics and religion in Israel society and the power of various Orthodox political parties within the government coalition.

In the Soviet Union, there are constraints on religious observances and practices among Jews. There are no communal Jewish organizations except for approximately 60 synagogues, half of which are located in the Caucasus and Asiatic Republics. In Great Britain, Canada and Europe, most of the formal and centralized institutions are nominally Orthodox. Most of the population tends to be secular in orientation.

Meaning Yesterday, Today, and Tomorrow

When we ask what Judaism means to the individual Judaist, we turn from the public affirmations of the community at prayer to the private feelings of the individual. How does the human being at the most personal relate his or her life to the on-going and enduring life of Israel, the Jewish people, viewed as the people of God? That question is joined by a second: how does Judaism so define the inner life of the individual as to impart the values of the Torah to the shape not only of the society of the Torah but of the individual heart and soul? The answers to these questions about the teachings about emotions and the deep recesses of the heart of the individual will guide us toward a clear picture of the meaning of Judaism in the lives of Judaists.

The canonical writings, from the Mishnah through the Talmud of Babylonia, lay down a set of rules and judgments about the affective life. What we deal with here encompasses what we might call virtue, though some would speak of emotions. How we feel as much as what we do or believe, that is to say, emotions as much as deeds, on the one side, and convictions or opinions or deliberations, on the other, constitute a central category of the religious life. One may sin by feeling as much as by action or affirmation. One may serve God in the heart -- and in the heart alone without regard to conviction or action -- as much as in the mind and in the workaday life of doing what is commanded and not doing what is forbidden. Not only so, but the doctrine of virtue remains remarkably stable from the beginning to the end. So if we want to know what meaning inheres in the life of Judaism, we turn at the end to the issue of virtue.

Mishnah-tractate Avot, which means "the founders," presents the single most comprehensive account of religious emotions or affections. The reason is that, in that document above all, how one feels defines a critical aspect of virtue. A simple catalogue of permissible feelings comprises humility, generosity, self-abnegation, love, a spirit of conciliation of the other and eagerness to please. A list of impermissible emotions is made up of envy, ambition, jealousy, arrogance, sticking to one's opinion, self-centeredness, a grudging spirit, vengefulness, and the like. People should aim at eliciting from others acceptance and good will and should avoid confrontation, rejection, and humiliation of the other. This they do through conciliation and giving up their own claims and rights. So both catalogues form a harmonious and uniform whole, aiming at the cultivation of the humble and malleable person, one who accepts everything and resents nothing.

God favors those who please others. The virtues appreciated by human beings prove identical to the ones to which God responds as well. And what single virtue of the heart encompasses the rest? Restraint, the source of self-abnegation, humility, the antidote for ambition, vengefulness, and, above all, for arrogance. It is restraint of our own interest that enables us to deal generously with others, humility about ourselves that generates a liberal spirit towards others. So the emotions prescribed in tractate Avot turn out to provide variations of a single feeling, which is the sentiment of the disciplined heart, whatever affective form it may take. And where does the heart learn its lessons, if not in relationship to God? So: "Make his wishes yours, so that he will make your wishes his" (Avot 2:4). Applied to the relationships between human beings, this inner discipline of the emotional life will yield exactly those virtues that the framers of tractate Abot spell out in one example after another. Imputing to Heaven exactly those responses felt on earth -- "Anyone from whom people take pleasure, God takes pleasure" (Avot 3:10) makes the point at the most general level.

The basic motif -- theological as much as affective -- encompassing all materials is simple. Israel is estranged from God, therefore should exhibit the traits of humility and uncertainty, acceptance and conciliation. When God recognizes in Israel's heart, as much as in the nation's deeds and deliberation, the proper feelings, God will respond by ending that estrangement that marks the present age. So the single word encompassing the entire affective doctrine of the canon of Judaism is alienation. No contemporary can miss the psychological depth of the system, which joins the human condition to the fate of the nation and the world, and links the whole to the heart of God.

How shall we characterize people who see things this way? They constitute the opposite of ones who call a thing as it is. Self-evidently, they have become accustomed to perceiving more -- or less -- than is at hand. Perhaps that is a natural mode of thought for the Jews, so long used to calling themselves God's first love, yet seeing others with greater worldly reason claiming that same advantaged relationship. Not in mind only, but still more, in the politics of the world, the people that remembered its origins along with the very creation of the world and founding of humanity, that recalled how it alone served, and serves, the one and only God, for centuries confronted a quite different existence. The radical disjuncture between the way things were and the way Scripture said things were supposed to be -- and in actuality would some day become -- surely imposed an unbearable tension. It was one thing for the slave born to slavery to endure. It was another for the free man sold into slavery to accept that same condition. The vanquished people, the broken-hearted nation that had lost its city and its temple, that had, moreover, produced another nation from its midst to take over its Scripture and much else, could not bear too much reality. That defeated people then found refuge in a mode of thought that trained vision to see other things otherwise than as the eyes perceived them. Among the diverse ways by which the weak and subordinated accommodate to their circumstance, the one of iron-willed pretense in life is most likely to yield the mode of thought at hand: things never are, because they cannot be, what they seem. This trait of mind characterized the founders and all who followed, to see the world as if it were other than what it is, then to try to make it so. The uniform tradition on emotions persisted intact because the social realities of Israelite life remained constant.

The Judaist in the model of the Torah thus accepts, forgives, conciliates, makes the soul like dirt beneath other people's feet. Why sages counseled a different kind of courage we need hardly ask. Given the situation of Israel, vanquished on the battlefield, broken in the turnings of history's wheel, we need hardly wonder why wise men advised conciliation and acceptance. Exalting humility made sense, there being little choice. Whether or not these virtues found advocates in other contexts for other reasons, in the circumstance of the vanquished nation, for the people of broken heart, the policy of forebearance proved instrumental, entirely appropriate to both the politics and social condition at hand. How so? If Israel produced a battlefield hero, the nation could not give him an army. If Jewry cultivated the strong-minded individual, it sentenced such a person to a useless life of ineffective protest. The nation required not strong-minded leadership but consensus. The social virtues of conciliation reenforced the bonds that joined the nation lacking frontiers, the people without a politics of its own. For all there was to hold Israel together to sustain its life as a society would have to come forth out of the sources of inner strength. Bonding emerged only from within. So consensus, conciliation, self-abnegation and humility, the search for acceptance within the group -- these defined appropriate emotions because to begin with they dictated wise policy and shrewd politics.

Israel could survive only on the sufferance of others. Israel therefore would nurture not merely policies of subordination and acceptance of diminished status among nations. Israel also would develop, in its own heart, the requisite emotional structure. The composition of individuals' hearts would then comprise the counterpart virtues. A policy of acceptance of the rule of others dictated affections of conciliation to the will of others. A defeated people meant to endure defeat would have to get along by going along. How to persuade each Jew to accept what all Jews had to do to endure? Persuade the heart, not only the mind. Then each one privately would feel what everyone publicly had in any case to think. The human condition finds its match in a religion that lends dignity to defeat and emphasizes the power of acceptance and the courage of endurance. For the human condition begins in the destiny of death, the ultimate defeat for humanity's frail hope, and the circumstance of nations, the story of history, ultimate ends in defeat. Israel, the Jewish people, endured for most of the history of humanity and lives today. The story of Israel is the tale of slaves who overcame degradation, of a nation that survived one disaster after another, even the Holocaust of our own day, in which six million children, men, and women were put to death because they were Israel, the Jewish people, and for that reason alone. So Judaism's claim upon the attention of the world, the reason that it records a religion worth studying, in the end is simple. Judaism claims to attend to the human condition of Israel. Its message of survival, endurance, courage, patience, above all discipline and hope -- that message proves remarkably congruent to the human condition of humanity.

Chapter Three

Description and the Category of History
Another Exercise

Describing a religion by tracing its formative history represents no innovation. By pointing to definitive developments, important books seen in their initial context, events of the formative age, we set forth an array of facts that form cogent patterns of meaning: a description. In many ways description through historical narrative of the formative age of a religion exacts its costs. We get no clear statement of a system of beliefs and a way of life. But, in compensation, we do get a sense of where it all began. In this exercise I attempt to put together the results of several distinct projects of mine, working my way, in succession, through the first, second and third, and, finally, fourth centuries, showing the important events in the formation of Judaism over that critical period. I wrote this paper for *Biblical Review*, which will publish a much abbreviated version of it, of course. My concern at the outset was to get everything down on paper and in one place. Beyond that point, the editor takes over and produces what, in the magazine at hand, actually may serve the readership.

Everyone knows that Judaism gave birth to Christianity. But the formative centuries of Christianity also tell us much about the development of Judaism as we know it. So formative Christianity demands to be studied in the context of formative Judaism, and formative Judaism in the context of formative Christianity. For throughout the history of the West, these two religious traditions, along with Islam, have struggled in competition with one another. While in numbers the competing parties were scarcely equal, in theological and moral power, each met its match in the other. What perpetually drew the one into competition with the other? Why could they not let one another be? These questions draw attention in our own setting, in modern times, after the Holocaust in particular, because, at last, the two great faiths of the West join together to confront a common challenge of renewal. So Judaism and Christianity work together in mutual respect, as never before, in the service of one humanity in the image of one God. We are able to ask these questions because the spirit of our own age permits us to discuss them irenically, in ways utterly without precedent in the centuries before our own so-tragic times.

Both Judaism and Christianity claim to be the heirs and products of the Hebrew Scriptures -- Tanakh to the Jews, Old Testament to the Christians. Yet both great religious traditions derive not solely or directly from the authority and teachings of those Scriptures, but rather from the ways in which that authority has been mediated, and those teachings interpreted, through other holy books. The New Testament is the prism through which the light of the Old comes to Christianity. The canon of rabbinical writings is the star that guides Jews to the revelation of Sinai, the Torah. That canon consists of the Mishnah, a law code, ca. 200 C.E., the Talmud of the Land of Israel, ca. 400 C.E., a systematic exegesis of the Mishnah, the various collections of exegeses of Scriptures called midrashim, ca. 400-600 C.E., and the Talmud of Babylonia, also a systematic explanation of the Mishnah, ca. 500-600 C.E. All together, these writings constitute "the Oral Torah," that is, that body of tradition assigned to the authority of God's revelation to Moses at Mount Sinai. The claim of these two great Western religious traditions, in all their rich variety, is for the veracity not merely of Scriptures, but also of Scriptures as interpreted by the New Testament or the Babylonian Talmud (and associated rabbinical writings).

The Hebrew Scriptures produced the two interrelated, yet quite separate groups of religious societies that formed Judaism and Christianity. Developed along lines established during late antiquity, these societies in modern times come near to each other in the West. Here they live not merely side by side, but together. However, while most people are familiar with the story of the development of Christianity, few are fully aware that Judaism constitutes a separate and distinctive religious tradition. The differences are not limited to negations of Christian beliefs -- "Jews do not believe in this or that" -- but also extend to profound affirmations of Judaic ones. To understand the Judaic dissent, one must comprehend the Judaic affirmation in its own terms.

What is it that historical Judaism sought to build? What are its primary emphases, its evocative symbols? What lies at the heart of the human situation, as constructed and imagined by classical Judaism? The answers come first of all from the pages of the rabbinic canon and related literature. From late antiquity onward, the rabbis of the Torah, written and oral, supplied the prooftexts, constructed the society, shaped the values, occupied the mind, and formed the soul of Judaism. For all the human concerns brought by Christians to the figure of Christ, the Jews looked to Torah. Torah means revelation: first, the five books of Moses; later, the whole Hebrew Scriptures; still later, the Oral and Written Revelation of Sinai, embodied in the Mishnah and the Talmuds. Finally it comes to stand for, to symbolize, what in modern language is called "Judaism": the whole body of belief, doctrine, practice, patterns of piety and behavior, and moral and intellectual commitments that constitute the Judaic version of reality.

However, while Christ stands at the beginning of the tradition of Christianity, the rabbinic canon comes at the end of the formation of the Judaism contained in it. It is the written record of the constitution of the life of Israel, the Jewish people, long after the principles and guidelines of that constitution had been worked out and effected in everyday life. Moreover, the early years of Christianity were dominated first by the figure of the Master, then his disciples and their followers bringing the gospel to the nations; the formative years of rabbinic Judaism saw a small group of men who were not dominated by a single leader but who effected an equally far-reaching revolution in the life of the Jewish nation.

Both the apostles and the rabbis thus reshaped the antecedent religion of Israel, and both claimed to be Israel. That pre-Christian, pre-rabbinic religion of Israel, for all its variety, exhibited common traits: belief in one God, reverence for and obedience to the revelation contained in the Hebrew Scriptures, veneration of the Temple in Jerusalem (while it stood), and expectation of the coming of a Messiah to restore all the Jews to Palestine and to bring to a close the anguish of history. The Christian Jews concentrated on the last point, proclaiming that the Messiah had come in Jesus; the rabbinic Jews focused on the second, teaching that only through the full realization of the imperatives of the Hebrew Scriptures, Torah, as interpreted and applied by the rabbis, would the people merit the coming of the Messiah. The rabbis, moreover, claimed alone to possess the whole Torah of Moses. This is central to their doctrine: Moses had revealed not only the message now written down in his books, but also an oral Torah, which was formulated and transmitted to his successors, and they to theirs, through Joshua, the prophets, the sages, scribes, and other holy men, and finally to the rabbis of the day. For the Christian, therefore, the issue of the Messiah predominated; for the rabbinic Jew, the issue of Torah; and for both, the question of salvation was crucial.

What form would Western civilization have taken had the Judaic, rather than the Christian, formulation of the heritage of Hebrew Scriptures come to predominate? What sort of society would have emerged? How would people have regulated their affairs? What would have been the shape of the prevailing value systems? Behind the immense varieties of Christian life and Christian and post-Christian society stand the evocative teachings and theological and moral convictions assigned by Christian belief to the figure of Christ. To be a Christian in some measure meant, and means, to seek to be like him, in one of the many ways in which Christians envisaged him. To be a Jew may similarly be reduced to the single, pervasive symbol of Judaism: Torah. To be a Jew meant to live the life of Torah, in one of the many ways in which the masters of Torah taught.

We know what the figure of Christ has meant to the art, music, and literature of the West; the church to its politics, history, and piety; Christian faith to its values and ideals. It is much harder to say what Torah would have meant to creative arts, the course of relations among nations and people, the hopes and aspirations of ordinary folk. For between Christ, universally known and triumphant, and Torah, the spiritual treasure of a tiny, harassed, abused people, seldom fully known and never long victorious, stands the abyss:

mastery of the world on the one side, the sacrifice of the world on the other. Perhaps the difference comes at the very start when the Christians, despite horrendous suffering, determined to conquer and save the world and to create the new Israel. The rabbis, unmolested and unimpeded, set forth to transform and regenerate the old Israel. For the former, the arena of salvation was all humankind, the actor was a single man. For the latter, the course of salvation began with Israel, God's first love, and the stage was that singular but paradigmatic society, the Jewish people.

To save the world the apostle had to suffer in and for it, appear before magistrates, subvert empires. To redeem the Jewish people the rabbi had to enter into, share, and reshape the life of the community, deliberately eschew the politics of nations and patiently submit to empires. The vision of the apostle extended to all nations and peoples. Immediate suffering therefore was the welcome penalty to be paid for eventual, universal dominion. The rabbi's eye looked upon Israel, and, in his love for Jews, he sought not to achieve domination or to risk martyrdom, but rather to labor for social and spiritual transformation which was to be accomplished through the complete union of his life with that of the community. The one was prophet to the nations, the other, priest to the people. No wonder then that the apostle earned the crown of martyrdom, but prevailed in history; while the rabbi received martyrdom, when it came, only as one of and wholly within the people. He gave up the world and its conversion in favor of the people and their regeneration. In the end the people hoped that through their regeneration, if need be through their suffering, the world also would be redeemed. But the people would be the instrument, not the craftsmen, of redemption, which God alone would bring.

That is how things look when we turn backward, from the present. But what do we see when we place ourselves squarely into the formative centuries of Christianity and of Judaism? Let us move in three stages, first, Jerusalem before 70, second, the following two centuries (principally from the angle of Judaism and its history), third, the final stage, the fourth century, at which the two traditions reached that definition that would mark their shared life for the next fifteen hundred years of coexistence.

I. The First Century

Jerusalem and the Temple

From near and far pilgrims climbed the paths to Jerusalem. Distant lands send their annual tribute, taxes imposed by a spiritual rather than a worldly sovereignty. Everywhere Jews turned to the Temple mountain when they prayed. Although Jews differed about matters of law and theology, the meaning of history, and the timing of the Messiah's arrival, most affirmed the holiness of the city Isaiah called Ariel, Jerusalem, the faithful city. It was here that the sacred drama of the day must be enacted. And looking backward, we know they were right. It was indeed the fate of Jerusalem which in the end shaped the faith of Judaism for endless generations to come -- but not quite in the ways that most people expected before 70 C.E.

How had Jerusalem cast its spell upon the Jews of far-off lands, to bring them together in their hearts' yearning? For centuries Israel had sung with the psalmist, "Our feet were standing within thy courts, O Jerusalem." They had exulted, "Pray for the peace of Jerusalem! May all prosper who seek your welfare!" Jews long contemplated the lessons of the old destruction. They were sure that by learning what Jeremiah, Ezekiel, and (Second) Isaiah taught about the meaning of the catastrophe of 586 B.C.E., by keeping the faith that prophecy demanded, they had ensured the city's eternity. Even then the Jews were a very old people. Their own records, translated into the language of all civilized people, testified to their antiquity. They could look back upon ancient enemies now forgotten by history, and ancient disasters, the spiritual lessons of which illumined current times. People thought that they kept the faith by devotion to the holy city, to the sacred Temple, to divinely ordained rites of service, to the priesthood, to the altar. And many a Jew yearned to see the priests upon their platform, to hear the Levites in their great choir singing the songs of David, to receive the blessing of the Lord in the Temple in Jerusalem. If people thought they kept the faith, they had good reason. What had the Lord commanded of old, which now they did not do? For three sins the ancient temple had fallen in 586 B.C.E. -- murder, adultery, and idolatry. Now, five centuries later, idolatry was a grotesque memory. Murder and adultery were surely not so common among those whom God had instructed as elsewhere, they supposed. As to ancient Scriptures, were these not studied in the synagogues Sabbath upon Sabbath? But the most certain testimony of all to the enduring covenant was the Temple, which stood as the nexus between Jew and God. Its services bore witness to Israel's enduring loyalty to the covenant and the commandments of Sinai. They saw Jerusalem with the eye of faith, and that vision transformed the city.

The activity was endless. Priests hurried to and fro, important because of their tribe, sacred because of their task, officiating at the sacrifices morning and eventide, busying themselves through the day with the Temple's needs. They were always careful to keep the levitical rules of purity which God decreed, they thought, for just this place and hour. Levites assisting them and responsible for the public liturgies could be seen everywhere. In the outer courts Jews from all parts of the world, speaking many languages, changed their foreign money for the Temple coin. They brought up their *sheqel*, together with the free will, or peace, or sin, or other offerings they were liable to give. Outside, in the city beyond, artisans created the necessary vessels or repaired broken ones. Incense makers mixed spices. Animal dealers selected the most perfect beasts. In the schools young priests were taught the ancient law, to which in time they would conform as had their ancestors before them, exactly as did their fathers that very day. All the population either directly or indirectly was engaged in some way in the work of the Temple. The city lived for it, by it, and on its revenues. In modern terms, Jerusalem was a center of pilgrimage, and its economy was based upon tourism.

But no one saw things in such a light. Jerusalem had an industry, to be sure, but if a Jew were asked, "What is the business of this city?" he would have replied without guile, "It is a holy city, and its work is the service of God on high." Only a few people doubted it. For reasons of their own, those who formed the commune at the Dead Sea abandoned the Temple, regarding it as hopelessly impure, its calendar as erroneous. Others, the Pharisees, thought that the priests should conduct themselves in accordance with the oral tradition they believed God had revealed to Moses at Sinai, that Moses had transmitted to the prophets, and the prophets to sages, down to that very day and to their own group. But even they were among the Temple's loyal servants. The Temple was the center of the world. They said the mount was the highest hill in the world. To it in time would come the anointed of God. In the meantime, they taught, the Temple sacrifice was the way to serve God, a way he himself in remotest times had decreed. True, there were other ways believed to be more important, for the prophets had emphasize that sacrifice alone was not enough to reconcile the sinner to a God made angry by unethical or immoral behavior. Morality, ethics, humility, good faith -- these, too, he required. But good faith meant loyalty to the covenant which had specified, among other things, that the priests do just what they were doing. The animal sacrifices, the incense, the oil, wine, and bread were to be arrayed in the service of the Most High.

"Because of Their Sins"

Later, people condemned this generation of the first Christian century. Christians and Jews alike reflected upon the destruction of the great sanctuary. They looked to the alleged misdeeds of those who lived at the time for reasons to account for the destruction. No generation in the history of Jewry had been so roundly, universally condemned by posterity as that of the destruction of the Temple. Christians remembered, in the tradition of the church, that Jesus wept over the city and said a bitter, sorrowing sentence:

> O Jerusalem, Jerusalem, killing the prophets and stoning those who are sent to you! How often would I have gathered your children together as a hen gathers her brood under her wings, and you would not! Behold, your house is forsaken and desolate. For I tell you, you will not see me again, until you say, "Blessed is he who comes in the name of the Lord" (Matt. 23:37-39). "And when the disciples pointed out the Temple buildings from a distance, he said to them, "You see all these, do you not? Truly, I say to you, there will not be left here one stone upon another, that will not be thrown down" (Matt. 24:2; cf. Luke 21:6).

So for twenty centuries, Jerusalem was seen through the eye of Christian faith as a faithless city, killing prophets, and therefore desolated by the righteous act of a wrathful God.

But Jews said no less. From the time of the destruction, they prayed: "On account of our sins we have been exiled from our land, and we have been removed far from our country. We cannot go up to appear and bow down before you, to carry out our duties in your chosen Sanctuary, in the great and holy house upon which your name was called." It is not a great step from "our sins" to "the sins of the generation in whose time the Temple was destroyed." It is not a difficult conclusion, and not a few have reached it. The Temple was destroyed mainly because of the sins of the Jews of that time, particularly "causeless hatred." Whether the sins were those specified by Christians or by talmudic rabbis hardly matters. This was supposed to be a sinning generation.

It was not a sinning generation, but one deeply faithful to the covenant and to the Scripture that set forth its terms, perhaps more so than many who have since condemned it. First-century Israelites sinned only by their failure. Had they overcome Rome, even in the circles of the rabbis they would have found high praise, for success indicates the will of Providence. But on what grounds are they to be judged sinners? The Temple was destroyed, but it was destroyed because of a brave and courageous, if hopeless, war. That war was waged not for the glory of a king or for the aggrandizement of a people, but in the hope that at its successful conclusion, pagan rule would be extirpated from the holy land. This was the articulated motive. It was a war fought explicitly for the sake and in the name of God. The struggle called forth prophets and holy men, leaders whom the people did not kill or stone, but courageously followed past all hope of success. Jews were not demoralized or cowardly, afraid to die because they had no faith in what they were doing, fearful to dare because they did not want to take risks. The Jerusalemites fought with amazing courage, despite unbelievable odds. Since they lost, later generations looked for their sin, for none could believe that the omnipotent God would permit his Temple to be destroyed for no reason. As after 586 B.C.E., so after 70 C.E., the alternative was this: "Either our fathers greatly sinned, or God is not just." The choice thus represented no choice at all. "God is just, but we have sinned -- we, but mostly our fathers before us. Therefore, all that has come upon us -- the famine, the exile, the slavery to pagans -- these are just recompense for our own deeds."

Herod and Roman Rule

The Jews were ruled, just before the turn of the first century, by King Herod, a Roman ally and a strong and able monarch. Herod's sons took over after his death, just before the turn of the century. What was Herod's position within the larger Roman context, and why did he, as a native Jew, enjoy Roman support and allegiance? It was imperial policy in Herod's time to exert authority through territorial monarchs, petty kings who ruled frontier territories still too

unruly to receive a Roman viceroy. Rome later came to govern the protectorates
through its own agents. It finally incorporated the subjugated lands into the
normal provincial structure. Thus in Armenia, Cilicia, and other territories on
the Parthian frontier Rome established or supported friendly kings, ethnarchs,
and tetrarchs, thereby governing through subservient agents in lands where Rome
itself did not choose to rule. Honored by Rome with the titles *Socius et Amicus
Populi Romani,* "associate and friend of Roman people," and, in the East, *Philo-
Romaios* and *Philo-Kaiser,* "friend of Rome," "Friend of Caesar," Herod
governed efficiently. He collected revenues, contrived public works to develop
vast tracts of land and eliminate unemployment, and, as we have seen,
constructed a magnificent temple in Jerusalem. He also built several large cities,
fortresses, and palaces including Herodion in the south, Sebaste in Samaria, and
Caesarea, a seaport in the Sharon. Herod stabilized political life, which had been
in turmoil during the reign of the last Hasmonean monarchs. Indeed, under him
there were no politics at all, only palace intrigue and slaughter of potentially
dangerous wives, sons, and servants. Most Jews simply could not participate in
public affairs. Many retired from the stage of political history. Earlier
institutions of political life were either transformed into instruments of state,
like the high priesthood, or apparently ignored, like the Sanhedrin. Under Herod,
official culture came more and more under Hellenistic domination. Court history
was written in Greek by able Syrians such as Nicholaus of Damascus. The
Temple cult was managed by agents of the monarchy, men who purchased the
high priesthood at a price, held it at the king's pleasure, and, enriched by the
priestly dues, handed it in the accepted Greek manner to the next appointee. It
was a brilliant reign, but in the wrong time and over the wrong people.

After Herod's death in 6 B.C.E., the people begged for direct Roman
government. "They implored the Romans to unite their country to Syria and to
entrust its administration to Roman governors. The Jews would then show that,
though people said they were factious and always at war, they knew how to obey
equitable rulers." The Romans tried to keep Herod's sons in power, but when
this led to further difficulties, they acquiesced and appointed the first in a line of
procurators. The procurators did not share Herod's interest in developing the
economy by building port cities and roads. They were mainly concerned with
the imperial welfare, if not, first of all, with their own. They lived in
Hellenistic Caesarea, went up to Jerusalem when masses of pilgrims came up to
celebrate the festivals, and were glad to return to the cosmopolitan capital as
soon as possible. When, in the spring of 66 C.E., one of them, Cestius, did not
survive a bloody ambush on the road back, the revolution began. The
procuratorial government ended as abruptly as it had begun.

Economic Life

The first act of the procuratorial government was normally to divide the
conquered territory into municipal districts; the second was to take a census,

determining the rate at which cities could be expected to contribute to the treasury. Taxes were applied to men, houses, animals, sales, imports, and exports (at a moderate rate) and were collected by an efficient bureaucracy. Besides these taxes, Jews paid dues to another sovereignty as well, that imposed by the ancestral faith. The Bible had detailed many kinds of priestly and levitical offerings and animal sacrifices to support the expensive Temple cult. Under a priestly government these taxes would certainly have supported a large administration. This doubtless was the economic rationale for the multitudinous tithes and offerings. Although the priests had ceased to rule, they still claimed their dues. With Roman help they obtained some of them from the majority of Jews and all from the very pious. Throughout these years Jews thus were paying a twofold tax. The extent of civil and religious taxation has been estimated at from thirty to forty percent of the gross national income, but it was probably considerably lower since the majority of the Jews paid only a small part of the religious imposts.

In any event the Jews never regarded Roman rule as legitimate. Taxes were therefore seen to be robbery. The Pharisaic sages made no distinction between a tax collector and a thief or an extortioner. Sages regarded gentile rulers in Palestine as robbers, without any rights whatsoever either in the land or over its inhabitants. No pagan power whatever had any right in the land. No land acquisition could free a field user from the obligation to pay the tithes. Even if a gentile bought land from a Jew, he was held to be a sharecropper. No gentile could ever take valid, legal possession of any part of the land. This attitude to the rightful ownership of the land affected collection of taxes and much else, as we shall see. But religious imposts were something else again. The Pharisees believed they must be paid. Pharisees therefore separated themselves from Jews who neglected the tithes and heave-offerings or paid only part of them. It was one of the main distinctions between the Pharisaic masters and disciples, on the one hand, and the common people on the other. The former were meticulous in paying the priestly and levitical dues, and the latter were not.

Roman rule was advantageous for some. It opened the way for the adventurous to undertake vast enterprises in commerce and travel. Many took advantage of the opportunities of the Roman Empire to move to more prosperous lands. Throughout this period one discovers Jews settling in the most remote corners of the empire and beyond. Those who stayed at home benefited from economic stability.

Situated on the trade routes to the east and south, the coastal cities, which contained large Jewish minority populations, imported new wares for sale in the bazaars and markets of back country towns like Jerusalem. The Jewish economy in the land flourished. Roman peace, Herodian enterprise, the natural endowments of the land, and broad economic opportunities combined to yield an adequate subsistence in a relatively stable economy for a very large population.

Living standard nonetheless were modest. Archaeologists have not turned up pretentious synagogues, treasures of gems, rich pottery, furnishings, or costly sarcophagi dating from the first century. Life was simple. People at cheap foods such as salted fish, bread made from low grades of local wheat, low quality grain imported from Egypt, or barley. They drank beer or wine diluted with water and sweetened their food with honey. Meat was eaten mostly on festival occasions, fish on the Sabbath. Judea was famed for its date palms, and the palm tree was sometimes engraved on coins as the emblem of the land. Most lived by farming or handicrafts. Contemporary parables borrow the imagery of fishing, agriculture, and petty trade. Few related to large-scale commerce, since Jews were mainly farmers and craftsmen. Riches meant a long-term food supply or a good wife. No parables refer to sophisticated problems of government, but many allude to a majestic, exalted monarch much magnified from the viewpoint of the mute populace.

Education

Many of the people, rich and poor alike, received an education in the main disciplines of Jewish tradition. This education, centering on religious learning, was sufficiently broad to impart civilizing and humanizing lessons. What did ordinary people study? They learned the Holy Scriptures. They, therefore, considered the history of the world from creation onward. They were taught in lessons about their forefathers, Abraham, Isaac, and Jacob, to emulate patriarchal hospitality to others and faithfulness to God. They studied about the life and laws of Moses. From those laws they gained an idea of how a covenanted community should conduct its affairs. They were instructed about their obligations to the poor, weak, orphaned, homeless, the stranger, and the outsider. They were educated to say that God is one, and that there are no other gods. They were told about the prophets whom God had sent to warn before ancient disasters and to exhort afterward. Those prophets had said that what God wanted of people was that they do justice, lover mercy, and walk humbly before God. The people learned that Providence guided their fate and that nothing happened but that God decreed it. So they were taught to look for the meaning of daily and cosmic events alike. A comet, drought, broken leg, or earthquake -- all could equally convey a truth. In the biblical writings they studied the wisdom of ancient sages, learning prudence, piety, and understanding.

In modern terms their curriculum included much attention to matters of metaphysics, law and morality, ethics and history. Such lessons were intended to create a decent human being. Perhaps everyday conduct revealed something of their impact but it was the historical lesson that seems to have had the greatest effect. God had given the land to Israel. Pagans had held it for a time, because in ancient days the people had sinned. But Israel had gotten it back after God had purified the people through suffering. In time, God again would set things straight and send a king like David of old, anointed in the manner of the ancient monarchy, to sit upon Mount Zion and dispense justice and revelation to all nations.

Social Classes

Class divisions were complicated by the regional variations of the land. Jerusalem was the metropolis of the Jews. Its populace included a significant number of wealthy people, both absentee landlords and great merchants, as well as many priests who lived on the priestly dues and Temple endowments. The city also contained a smaller class of Levites, who performed certain nonsacrificial tasks in the sanctuary and managed the buildings. Artisans whose skills were indispensable in the building and maintenance of the Temple, petty traders, a large urban proletariat, and unskilled laborers filled the crowded streets. Jerusalemites tended to separate themselves from the Judean provincials for both social and ritual reasons. Living in close proximity to the sanctuary, the inhabitants of the city were more concerned about observing the requirements of ritual cleanness, imposed by residence in the holy place, than were the provincials who purified themselves mainly for the festal pilgrimages. The provincials often did not have the benefit of much advanced education. Animosities between urban and rural residents were bitter. The provincials themselves were by no means united. The country gentry, landowners holding considerable property in the fertile lowland plains, had less in common with their highland neighbors than with the urban upper bourgeoisie.

On the other hand, the rural farmers and proletarian submerged classes were divorced from the main issues of national life. They welcomed the ministry of powerful personalities, sometimes sages empowered by learning, but more often wonderworkers able to heal mind and body. Jericho and the Southern Plain were the main centers of the rural gentry. On the rocky Judean hills lived the rural yeomanry and proletariat. In Galilee class divisions between wealthier and poor peasants likewise were manifest. Hundreds of rural villages, large and small, clustered in the fertile hills and valleys of the north. Only Sepphoris and Tiberias were large urban centers, and they did not dominate the province as Jerusalem did Judea.

The Sects: Essenes, Sadducees, Pharisees

The main social and religious events of this period held little interest for contemporary historians. Josephus, for one, paid very little attention to the inner life of Israel in his rich narrative of politics and war. His histories provide evidence that the masses had turned away from public affairs. They may have responded to changes in their political situation. They may have felt growing impatience with social inequity or with the alien government whose benefits were not obvious to them. Only in the riots and continuous unrest toward the end of this period, however, does their response become entirely evident. A few indicated their disapproval of the course of events by withdrawing from the common society. Some became hermits; some fled to other lands or entered monastic communities in which contact with the outside world was minimal.

The monastic commune near the shores of the Dead Sea was one such group. To the barren heights came people seeking purity and hoping for eternity. The purity they sought was not from common dirt, but from the uncleanness of this world, symbolized by contact with the impure insects or objects Scripture had declared unclean. In their minds that uncleanness carried a far deeper meaning. This age was impure and therefore would soon be coming to an end. Those who wanted to do the Lord's service should prepare themselves for a holy war at the end of time. The commune at the Dead Sea, therefore, divided by ranks under captains, lived under military discipline and studied the well-known holy books as well as books others did not know about. These books specified when and how the holy war would be fought and the manner of life of those worthy to fight it. Men and women came to Qumran with their property, which they contributed to the common fund. There they prepared for a fateful day, not too long to be postponed, scarcely looking backward at those remaining in the corruption of this world. These Jews would be the last, smallest, "saving remnant" of all. Yet through them all humankind would come to know the truth. They prepared for Armageddon, and their battle against forces of ritual impurity, evil, and sin alike was for the Lord. The Qumran commune ordained: "This is the regulation for the men of the commune, who devote themselves to turn away from all evil, and to hold fast to all that he has commanded as his will, to separate themselves from the congregation of men of iniquity to be a commune in Torah and property." Likewise the psalmist of Qumran prayed:

> Only as you draw a man near will I love him.
> And as you keep him far away, so will I abominate him.

The members of wilderness communes described by Philo as Essenes avoided the settled society of town and city "because of the inequities which have become inveterate among city dwellers, for they know that their company would have a deadly effect upon their own souls." The communards sanctified themselves by meticulous observance of the rules of ritual purity and tried to found such a society as they thought worthy of receiving God's approval. Strikingly, they held that God himself had revealed to Moses the very laws they now obeyed.

Pharisees, probably meaning Separatists, also believed that all was not in order with the world. But they chose another way, likewise attributed to mosaic legislation. They remained within the common society in accordance with the teaching of Hillel, "Do not separate yourself from the community." The Pharisaic community therefore sought to rebuild society on its own ruins with its own mortar and brick. The Pharisees actively fostered their opinions on tradition and religion among the whole people. According to Josephus, "They are able greatly to influence the masses of people. Whatever the people do about divine worship, prayers, and sacrifices, they perform according to their direction. The cities give great praise to them on account of their virtuous conduct, both in the actions of their lives and their teachings also." Though Josephus exaggerated the extent of their power, the Pharisees certainly exerted some influence in the religious life of Israel before they finally came to power in 70 C.E.

Among those sympathetic to the Pharisaic cause were some who entered into an urban religious communion, a mostly unorganized society known as the fellowship (havurah). The basis of this society was meticulous observance of laws of tithing and other priestly offerings as well as the rules of ritual purity outside the Temple where they were not mandatory. The members undertook to eat even profane foods (not sacred tithes or other offerings) in a state of rigorous levitical cleanness. At table, they compared themselves to Temple priests at the altar. These rules tended to segregate the members of the fellowship, for they ate only with those who kept the law as they thought proper. The fellows thus mediated between the obligation to observe religious precepts and the injunction to remain within the common society. By keeping the rules of purity the fellow separated from the common man, but by remaining within the towns and cities of the land, he preserved the possibility of teaching others by example. The fellows lived among, but not with, the people of the land. With neither formal structure nor officers and bylaws as at Qumran, the fellowship represented the polity of people who recognized one another as part of the same inchoate community. They formed a new, if limited, society within the old. They were the few who kept what they held to be the faith in the company of the many who did not.

Upper-class opinion was expressed in the viewpoint of still another group, the Sadducees. They stood for strict adherence to the written word in religious matters, conservatism in both ritual and belief. Their name probably derived from the priesthood of Zaddoq, established by David ten centuries earlier. They differed from the Pharisees especially on the doctrine of revelation. They acknowledge Scripture as the only authority, themselves as its sole arbiters. They denied that its meaning might be elucidated by the Pharisees' allegedly ancient traditions attributed to Moses or by the Pharisaic devices of exegesis and scholarship. The Pharisees claimed that Scripture and the traditional oral interpretation were one. To the Sadducees such a claim of unity was spurious and masked innovation. They differed also on the eternity of the soul. The Pharisees believed in the survival of the soul, the revival of the body, the day of judgment, and life in the world to come. The Sadducees found nothing in Scripture that to their way of thinking supported such doctrines. They ridiculed both these ideas and the exegesis that made them possible. They won over the main body of officiating priests and wealthier men. With the destruction of the Temple their ranks were decimated. Very little literature later remained to preserve their viewpoint. It is difficult indeed to compare them to the other sects. They may have constituted no social institution like the Pharisaic and

Essenic groups. In their day, however, the Sadducees claimed to be the legitimate heirs of Israel's faith. Holding positions of power and authority, they succeeded in leaving so deep an impression on society that even their Pharisaic, Essenic, and Christian opponents did not wholly wipe out their memory.

The Sadducees were most influential among landholders and merchants, the Pharisees among the middle and lower urban classes, the Essenes among the disenchanted of both these classes. These classes and sectarian divisions manifested a vigorous inner life, with politics revolving about peculiarly Jewish issues such as matters of exegesis, law, doctrine, and the meaning of history. The vitality of Israel would have astonished the Roman administration, and when it burst forth, it did.

Conversion: "Normative Judaism"?

The rich variety of Jewish religious expression in this period ought not to obscure the fact that for much of Jewish Palestine, Judaism was a relatively new phenomenon. Herod was the grandson of pagans. Similarly, the entire Galilee had been converted to Judaism only one hundred and twenty years before the Common Era. In the later expansion of the Hasmonean kingdom, other regions were forcibly brought within the fold. The Hasmoneans used Judaism imperially, as a means of winning the loyalty of the pagan Semites in the regions of Palestine they conquered. But in a brief period of three or four generations the deeply rooted practices of the Semitic natives of Galilee, Idumea, and other areas could not have been wiped out. They were rather covered over with a veneer of monotheism. Hence the newly converted territories, though vigorously loyal to their new faith, were no more Judaized in so short a time than were the later Russians, Poles, Celts, or Saxons Christianized within a century.

It took a great effort to transform an act of circumcision of the flesh, joined with a mere verbal affirmation of one God, done under severe duress, into a deepening commitment to faith. And yet in the war of 66 C.E. the Jews of newly converted regions fought with great loyalty. While the Galileans had proved unable to stand upon the open battlefield, many of them together with Idumeans retreated to the holy city. There they gave their lives in the last great cataclysms of the war. The exceptional loyalty of the newly converted regions would lead one to suppose that it was to the Temple cult, to the God whom it served, and to the nation that supported it that the pagan Semites were originally converted. They could have known little of the more difficult service of the heart through study of Torah and ethical and moral action which the Pharisees demanded.

While the central teachings of the faith were very ancient, adherence of many who professed it was therefore only relatively recent and superficial. The Pharisaic party, dating at least from the second century B.C.E., if not much earlier, never solidly established itself in Galilee before the second century C.E.

The religious beliefs of recently converted people could not have encompassed ideas and issues requiring substantial study, elaborate schooling, and a well-established pattern of living. Conversion of one group to another faith never obliterates the former culture, but rather entails the translation of the new into the idiom of the old, so that in the end it results in a modification of both. The newly Judaized regions similarly must have preserved substantial remnants of their former pagan Semitic and Hellenistic cultures. The inhabitants could not have been greatly changed merely be receiving "Judaism," which meant in the beginning little more than submitting to the knife of the circumcizer rather than to the sword of the slaughterer. Only after many generations was the full implication of conversion realized in the lives of the people in Galilee, and then mainly because great centers of tannaitic law and teaching were established among them.

For this period, however, no such thing as "normative Judaism" existed, from which one or another "heretical" group might diverge. Not only in the great center of the faith, Jerusalem, do we find numerous competing groups, but throughout the country and abroad we may discern a religious tradition in the midst of great flux. It was full of vitality, but in the end without a clear and widely accepted view of what was required of each individual, apart from acceptance of mosaic revelation. And this could mean whatever you wanted. People would ask one teacher after another, "What must I do to enter the kingdom of heaven?" precisely because no authoritative answer existed. In the end two groups emerged, the Christians and the rabbis, heirs of the Pharisaic sages. Each offered an all-encompassing interpretation of Scripture, explaining what it did and did not mean. Each promised salvation for individuals and for Israel as a whole. Of the two, the rabbis achieved somewhat greater success among the Jews. Wherever the rabbis' views of Scripture were propagated the Christian view of the meaning of biblical, especially prophetic, revelation and its fulfillment made relatively little progress. This was true, specifically, in Jewish Palestine itself, in certain cities in Mesopotamia, and in central Babylonia. Where the rabbis were not to be found, as in Egyptian Alexandria, Syria, Asia Minor, Greece, and in the West, Christian biblical interpretation and salvation through Christ risen from the dead found a ready audience among the Jews. It was not without good reason that the gospel tradition of Matthew saw in the "scribes and Pharisees" the chief opponents of Jesus' ministry. Whatever the historical facts of that ministry, the rabbis proved afterward to be the greatest stumbling block for the Christian mission to the Jews.

Self-Government

It was a peculiar circumstance of Roman imperial policy that facilitated the growth of such a vigorous inner life and permitted the development of nonpolitical institutions to express it. Rome carefully respected Jewish rights to limited self-government. The populace was subject to its own law and quarrels were adjudicated by its own judges. Rome had specific and clearly defined purposes for the empire. Her policies could be adequately effected without totalitarian interference in the inner affairs of the conquered peoples. The same indifference to local sensitivities that very occasionally permitted a procurator to bring his military standards into a city pure of "graven images" likewise encouraged him to ignore territorial affairs of considerable weight.

The national tribunal, called variously the Sanhedrin or High Court, acted with a measure of freedom to determine internal policy in religion, ritual, cult, and local law. The Sanhedrin lost authority to inflict capital punishment, it is generally assumed, shortly after Judea became a part of the Syrian provincial administration. Whether, in fact, it had administered the death penalty in Herod's reign is not entirely clear. The court certainly maintained the right to direct Temple affairs. It decided matters of civil and commercial law and torts and defined personal and family status and marriage procedure. The court also collected the biblical levies and determined the sacred calendar. It thus represented the one abiding institutional expression of Israel's inner autonomy during the procuratorial regime. Both the Pharisees and Sadducees took an active interest in the religious, social, and economic administration of Israel's life. The Sanhedrin provided a means to formulate and effect these interests. The leaders of both major viewpoints played a considerable part in the nation's autonomous affairs. The exact nature of Jewish self-government and the institutions that embodied it has not yet been finally clarified. The sources are difficult; no body of sources presents a picture that can be wholly verified in some other independent tradition.

Women

While women play a prominent part in the Gospels' lives of Jesus, they constituted a subordinated caste. In important ways they took second place. First of all, the Temple cult, so critical in the nation's understanding of the world, lay entirely in the hands of men. Women could not enter the innermost parts of the Temple or actually share in the cult by serving as priests. Accordingly, when it came to the processes of sanctification carried on in the Temple, women stood along the sides but never at the center; the women's court was set away from the holy altar itself, and that fact captured the position of women in society as a whole. Yet Scripture, for its part, knew women in numerous roles of leadership and influence, beginning with Miriam, sister of Moses, extending through prophets and savior figures, for example, Huldah, in the time of Jeremiah, and Esther, later on. Women played a central role in the political life of the country, both in ancient Israel and also in the century before the coming of Jesus, as well as at points in between.

Accordingly, in politics and in religion, women found for themselves important places everywhere but in the Temple itself. Yet, it surely is a fact that God was imagined, in general, as male, not female, and man, not woman, dominated. In the later laws of the Mishnah, preserving both rules and attitudes of the period at hand, woman is regarded as anomalous, man the norm and normal. In all, therefore, the position of women in first-century Israelite society exhibited those contradictory trends we find earlier and later. Where the priestly tradition dominated, there women were excluded. Perhaps, to begin with, the ancient pagan traditions of women as cult prostitutes led the framers of the Israelite priestly code to keep women out of the cult and Temple altogether. Whatever the original motive, the result, for centuries to come, proved disastrous.

The Irrepressible Conflict

Jesus came into a world of irrepressible conflict. That conflict was between two pieties, two universal conceptions of what the world required. On the one hand, the Roman imperialist thought that good government, that is, Roman government, must serve to keep the peace. Rome would bring the blessings of civil order and material progress to many lands. For the Roman that particular stretch of hills, farmland, and desert that Jews called "the Land of Israel" meant little economically, but a great deal strategically. No wealth could be hoped for, but to lose Palestine would mean to lose the keystone of empire in the East. We see Palestine from the perspective of the West. It appears as a land bridge between Egypt and Asia Minor, the corner of a major trade route. But to the imperial strategist, Palestine loomed as the bulwark of the eastern frontier against Parthia. The Parthians, holding the Tigris-Euphrates frontier, were a mere few hundred miles from Palestine, separated by a desert no one could control. It the Parthians could take Palestine, Egypt would fall into their hands. Parthian armies moreover were pointed like a sword toward Antioch and the seat of empire established there. Less than a century earlier they had actually captured Jerusalem and seated upon its throne a puppet of their own. For a time they thrust Roman rule out of the eastern shores of the Mediterranean.

For Rome, therefore, Palestine was too close to the most dangerous frontier of all to be given up. Indeed, among all the Roman frontiers only the oriental one was now contested by a civilized and dangerous foe. Palestine lay behind the very lines upon which that enemy had to be met. Rome could ill afford such a loss. Egypt, moreover, was her granary, the foundation of her social welfare and wealth. The grain of Egypt sustained the masses of Rome herself. Economic and military considerations thus absolutely required the retention of Palestine. Had Palestine stood in a less strategic locale, matters might have been different. Rome had a second such frontier territory to consider -- Armenia. While she fought vigorously to retain predominance over the norther gateway to the Middle East, she generally remained willing to compromise on joint suzerainty with Parthia in Armenia -- but not in Palestine.

For the Jews, the Land of Israel meant something of even greater import. They believed that history depended upon what happened in the Land of Israel.

They thought that from creation to end of time the events that took place in Jerusalem would shape the fate of all humankind. Theirs, no less than Rome's, was an imperial view of the world, but with this difference: the empire was God's. If Rome could not lose Palestine, the Jew was unwilling to give up the Land of Israel. Rome scrupulously would do everything possible to please Jewry, permitting the Jews to keep their laws in exchange only for peaceful acquiescence to Roman rule. There was, alas, nothing Rome could actually do to please Jewry but evacuate Palestine. No amiable tolerance of local custom could suffice to win the people's submission.

II. From the First Century to the Fourth in Judaism
The Events of the Second and Third Centuries

Two important events defined the history of the Jews in the Land of Israel from the first century to the fourth, the destruction of the Temple of Jerusalem in 70, and the catastrophic failure of the rebellion against Rome led by Bar Kokhba in 132-135. These two events formed, in reality, a single historical moment. For, in the mind of many, the first set in motion the expectations that led to the second. When the Temple was destroyed, Jews naturally looked to Scripture to find the meaning of what had happened and, more important, to learn what to expect. There they di+scovered that when the Temple had been destroyed earlier, a period of three generations -- seventy years -- intervened. Then, in the aftermath of atonement and reconciliation with God, Israel was restored to its Land, the Temple to Jerusalem, the priests to the service of the altar. So, many surmised, in three generations the same pattern will be reenacted, now with the Messiah at the head of the restoration. So people waited patiently and hopefully. But whether or not Bar Kokhba said he was the Messiah, he was to disappoint the hopes placed in him. The Jews, possessed of a mighty military tradition then as now, fought courageously, but lost against overwhelming force. The result: Jerusalem was closed to the Jews, except on special occasions, much Jewish settlement in the southern part of the country was wiped out. Deep disappointment settled over the people.

In ancient Israelite times the history of Israel defined the issues of faith, and the prophets in God's name interpreted events as statements of God's will to Israel. So it was perfectly natural that, in the period at hand, the Judaism that took shape should respond in a direct and immediate way to the momentous events of the day. In many ways Judaism, from age to age, forms God's commentary on the text that is formed by the events of the history of the Jewish people, and the holy books of Judaism contain that commentary. So too in the history of Judaism from the first to the fourth century. We work out way back from the books sages wrote to the Judaism that, through those books, they constructed in God's service. Of those books, the first and most important, the foundation for all else, the basis for Judaism from then to now, was the

Mishnah. So let us consider the historical setting for that book and its message for the moment at which it came forth.

The Mishnah is a work of philosophy expressed through laws. That is to say, it is a set of rules, phrased in the present tense: "one does this, one does not do that." But when we look closely at the issues worked out by those laws, time and again we find such profound essays on philosophical questions as being and becoming, the acorn and the oak, the potential and the actual. The topical program of the document, as distinct from the deep issues worked out through discussion of the topics, focuses upon the sanctification of the life of Israel, the Jewish people. Four of the six principal parts of the Mishnah deal with the cult and its officers. These are, first, Holy Things, which addresses the everyday conduct of the sacrificial cult; second, Purities, which takes up the protection of the cult from sources of uncleanness specified in the book of Leviticus (particularly Leviticus Chapters Twelve through Fifteen); third, Agriculture, which centers on the designation of portions of the crop for the use of the priesthood (and others in the same classification of a holy caste, such as the poor), and so provides for the support of the Temple staff; and, fourth, Appointed Times, the larger part of which concerns the conduct of the cult on such special occasions as the Day of Atonement, Passover, Tabernacles, and the like (and the rest of which concerns the conduct in the village on those same days, with the basic conception that what you do in the cult forms the mirror image of what you do in the village). Two further divisions of the document as a whole deal with every day affairs, one, Damages, concerning civil law and government, the other, Women, taking up issues of family, home, and personal status. That, sum and substance, is the program of the Mishnah.

When did the document take shape, why did it endure, and what accounts for its importance? The document was completed -- the consensus of scholarship holds -- around the year 200. That is to say, approximately two long generations after the defeat of Bar Kokhba's armies, the Mishnah came forth. It lasted and proved influential because it served as the basic law book of the Jewish government of the Land of Israel, the authority of the patriarchate, as well as the Jewish government of the Jewish minority in Babylonia, a western province of the Iranian Empire. That empire allowed its many diverse ethnic groups to run internal affairs on their own, and the Jews' regime, in the hands of a "head of the exile," or exilarchate, employed sages who had mastered the Mishnah and therefore imposed the pertinent laws of the Mishnah within its administration and courts. So the Mishnah rapidly became not a work of speculative philosophy, in the form of legal propositions or rules, but a law code for the concrete and practical administration of the Jewish people in its autonomous life. Why was the Mishnah important? It was important because of two considerations, first, the political, but, second, the intellectual.

Before we speak of the Mishnah's future, as the foundation for Judaism from then to now, we have to take one last look backward, at the Mishnah's message on the recent past. If we were to ask the framers of the document to tell us where, in their writing, they speak of what has happened in their own century, they will direct our attention to a few episodic allusions to the destruction of the Temple, on the one side, and the repression after the war of 132-135, on the other. But if we were to ask them to give us their comment on the catastrophe — the radical turning — of their day, they will direct us to look not at bits and pieces, but at the whole of their document. For the Mishnah focuses upon the sanctification of Israel, the Jewish people, and its message is that the life of the people, like the life of the cult, bears the marks of holiness. One important aspect of how critical to the Mishnah is the dimension of holiness is the role of women.

The law of the Mishnah repeatedly uses the language of sanctification when it speaks of the relationship between man and woman, and it regards marriage as a critical dimension of the holiness of Israel, the Jewish people. Building on the scriptural rules, the sages point to the holiness of the marital bed, conducted as it is in accord with the laws of Leviticus Chapter Fifteen, the holiness of the women to the man, and of the man to the woman, as effected when a union between the two is sanctified under God's rule, the holiness of the table and the heart, where food that accords with the levitcal requirements, e.g., of Leviticus Chapter Eleven, is served, and the holiness of the rhythm of time and circumstance, as a holy day comes to the home and transforms the home into the model of the Temple. In all these ways, therefore, the message of the Mishnah comes through: the holy Temple is destroyed, but holy Israel endures, and will endure until, in God's time, the holy Temple is restored. That focus upon sanctification therefore imparts to the Mishnah remarkable relevance to the question on peoples' mind: if we have lost the Temple, have we also lost our tie to God? No, the Mishnah's authors reply, Israel remains God's holy people. The Mishnah then outlines the many areas of sanctification that endure: land and priesthood, in Agriculture, time, in Appointed Times, not to mention the record of the Temple, studied and restudied in the mind's reenactment of the cult. But the Mishnah stressed sanctification, to the near-omission of the other critical dimension of Israel's existence, salvation. Only later on would Scripture-exegetes complete the structure of Judaism, a system resting on the twin-foundations of sanctification in this world and salvation in time to come. But we have, first, to see what happened then, that is, why did the Mishnah make a difference?

We turn now to the future. Why did the Mishnah matter to generations to come. The Mishnah mattered, on the near term, because of its importance to the Jewish state(s) of the day. But it mattered on the long term because of its centrality in the intellectual life of the Jews' sages. These sages, many of them clerks in the Jewish governments, believed, and persuaded many, that the Mishnah formed part of the Torah, God's will for Israel revealed to Moses at Sinai. So the Mishnah, originally not a work of religion in a narrow sense, attained the status of revelation. How did this happen? A look at the first great apologetic for the Mishnah, the Sayings of the Founders (Pirqé Avot) tells us the answer. It begins, "Moses received Torah on Sinai and handed it on to Joshua...," and, the chain of tradition goes on, the latest in the list turn out to be authorities of the generations who form the named authorities of the Mishnah itself. So what these authorities teach they have received in the chain of tradition from Sinai. And what they teach is Torah. Now the Mishnah, which is their teaching, enjoys its standing and authority because it comes from sages, and, it follows, sages' standing and authority comes from God.

Such a claim imparted to the Mishnah and its teachers a position in the heart and mind of Israel, the Jewish people, that would insure the long-term influence of the document. What happened beyond 200 and before 400? Two processes, one of which generated the other. The first of the two was that the Mishnah was extensively studied, line by line, word by word. The modes of study were mainly three. First, the sages asked about the meanings of words and phrases. Then they worked on the comparison of one set of laws with another, finding the underlying principles of each and comparing, and harmonizing, those principles. So they formed of the rather episodic rules a tight and large fabric. Third, they moved beyond the narrow limits of the Mishnah into still broader and more speculative areas of thought. So, in all, the sages responsible to administer the law also expounded, and, willy nilly, expanded the law. Ultimately, in both countries, the work, of Mishnah-commentary developed into two large-scale documents, each called a Talmud. We have them as the Talmud of the Land of Israel, which I have translated into English, completed by about 400, and the Talmud of Babylonia, completed by about 600.

The second process -- besides the work of Mishnah-commentary -- drew attention back to Scripture. Once the work of reading the new code got under way, an important problem demanded attention. What is the relationship between the Mishnah and the established Scripture of Israel, the written Torah? The Mishnah only occasionally adduces texts of the Scriptures in support of its rules. Its framers worked out their own topical program, only part of which intersects with that of the laws of the Pentateuch. They followed their own principles of organization and development. They wrote in their own kind of Hebrew, which is quite different from biblical Hebrew. So the question naturally arose, Can we through sheer logic discover the law? Or must we tease laws out of Scripture through commentary, through legal exegesis? The Mishnah represented an extreme in this debate, since so many of its topics to begin with do not derive from Scripture, and, further, a large part of its laws ignores Scripture's pertinent texts in that these texts are simply not cited. When, moreover, the framers of the Sayings of the Founders placed sages named in the Mishnah on the list of those who stand within the chain of tradition beginning at Sinai, they did not assign to those sages verses of Scripture, the written Torah (except in one or two instances). Rather, the Torah-saying assigned to each of the named sages is not scriptural at all. So the sages enjoy an independent standing and authority on their own, they are not subordinate to Scripture and their sayings enjoy equal standing with sentences of Scripture.

The work of exegesis of the Mishnah therefore drew attention, also, to the relationship of the Mishnah to Scripture. Consequently, important works of biblical commentary emerged in the third and fourth centuries. In these works, focused on such books as Leviticus (Sifra), Numbers (Sifré to Numbers) and Deuteronomy (Sifré fo Deuteronomy), a paramount issue is whether law emerges solely on the basis of processes of reasoning, or whether only through looking inverses of Scripture are we able to uncover solid basis for the rules of the Mishnah. In that discourse we find the citation of a verse of Scripture followed by a verbatim citation of a passage of the Mishnah. Since this mode of reading Scripture is not apt to be familiar to many readers, let me give a concrete example of how the process of Mishnah-exegesis in relationship to Scripture-exegesis was carried forward in the third and fourth centuries. What follows is from Sifré to Numbers:

Pisqa VI:II

1. A. "...every man's holy thing shall be his; whatever any man gives to the priest shall be his" (Num. 5:10).
    B. On the basis of this statement you draw the following rule:
    C. **If a priest on his own account makes a sacrificial offering, even though it falls into the week [during which] another priestly watch than his own [is in charge of the actual cult, making the offerings and dues], lo, that priest owns the priestly portions of the offering, and the right of offering it up belongs to him [and not to the priest ordinarily on duty at that time, who otherwise would retain the rights to certain portions of the animal] [T. Men. 13:17].**

What we have is simply a citation of the verse plus a law in a prior writing (in this case not the Mishnah, but the Tosefta, a compilation of supplements to the Mishnah's laws) which the verse is supposed to sustain. The formal traits require [1] citation of a verse, with or without comment, followed by [2] verbatim citation of a passage of the Mishnah or the Tosefta. What we have is a formal construction in which we simply juxtapose a verse, without or with intervening words of explanation, with a passage of the Mishnah or the Tosefta. So we see that, when sages proposed to provide for Scripture a counterpart, a commentary, to what they were even then creating for the Mishnah, they sought to build bridges from the Mishnah to Scripture. In doing so, they vastly articulated the theme of the Mishnah, the sanctification of Israel.

But what of salvation? Where, when, and how did sages then shaping Judaism address that other and complementary category of Israel's existence? And, we further ask, is the work of linking the Mishnah to Scripture the only kind of scriptural commentary sages produced between the first and the fourth century? Not at all. Sages turned to Scripture to seek the laws of Israel's history, to ask the questions of salvation, of Israel's relationship to God, that, in the Mishnah and in the works of amplification of the Mishnah, they tended to neglect. When did they do so?

The answer to that question brings us to the fourth century. For that is when the sages produced the great works on Genesis, in Genesis Rabbah, and on Leviticus, in Leviticus Rabbah, which answered the questions of salvation, of the meaning and end of Israel's history, that the Mishnah and its continuator-writings did not take up. Why in the fourth century? Because the historical crisis precipitated by Christianity's takeover of the Roman Empire and its government demanded answers from Israel's sages: what does it mean? what does history mean? Where are we to find guidance to the meaning of our past -- and our future? Sages looked, then, to Genesis, maintaining that the story of the creation of the world and the beginning of Israel would show the way toward the meaning of history and the salvation of Israel. They further looked to Leviticus, and, in Leviticus Rabbah, they accomplished the link between the sanctification of Israel through its cult and priesthood, which is the theme of the book of Leviticus, and the salvation of Israel, which is the concern of the commentators to that book. What they did was to place Israel, the people, at the center of the story of Leviticus, applying to the life of the people of Israel those rules of sanctification that, when observed, would prepare Israel, holy Israel, for salvation. So, in a nutshell, the framers of Leviticus Rabbah imparted to the book of Leviticus the message, in response to the destruction of the Temple, that the authors of the Mishnah had addressed two hundred years earlier: Israel's holiness endures. Sanctifying the life of Israel now will lead to the salvation of Israel in time to come: sanctification and salvation, the natural world and the supernatural, the rules of society and the rules of history all become one in the life of Israel.

But I have gotten ahead of my story. We take a step back. Let me prepare the way for our consideration of Genesis Rabbah and Leviticus Rabbah, works of the end of the fourth century, by completing this picture of the principal work of sages, the main kinds of books they wrote in the formation of Judaism in the second, third, and, as we shall shortly see, fourth centuries. For up to now I have omitted reference to a second sort of creative effort. That concerns Scripture not in relationship to the Mishnah, but on its own, and it further concerns that dimension of Israel's life to which, in the aggregate, the Mishnah scarcely turns. You will recall that I represented the Mishnah as an essentially philosophical book, which rapidly came to serve other than speculative purposes. But where is the other side to things, not the philosophy of life, the rules of natural and social existence, such as the Mishnah gives? Can we find the theology of life, the rules of supernatural and historical existence? Indeed we can and do, and they are in the other great area of commentary to Scripture. That other area required the reading of the books of Genesis and Leviticus in precisely the same way in which sages read the Mishnah: same modes of exegesis, episodic and then generalizing. But the sages raised new questions, and, as we shall now see, it was an event as momentous as the destruction of the Temple that precipitated and defined those questions. When Constantine declared Christianity a legal religion, then favored the Church, and finally converted, from 312 onward, and when his heirs and successors made Christianity the religion of the Roman Empire, sages and Israel in general had to negotiate a very difficult and critical moment. The crisis was not so much political and legal, though it bore deep consequences in both politics and the Jews' standing in law, was it was spiritual. If the Messiah is yet to come, then how come Jesus, enthroned as Christ, now rules the world? Christians asked Israel that question, but, of greater consequence, Israel asked itself. And one more event of the fourth century, besides the triumph of Christianity, demands attention even as we turn to that critical age. In 362-363 a pagan, Julian, regained the throne and turned the empire away from Christianity. He further invited the Jews to rebuild the Temple. But the project proved a fiasco, and Julian was killed in battle against Iran. Consequently, the succeeding emperors, Christians all, restored the throne to Christ (as they would put it) and secured for the Church and Christianity the control of the State through law. So -- and Chrysostom so argued in the aftermath of Julian's brief reign -- the destruction of the Temple in 70 now has proved definitive. Three hundred years later, the Temple was supposed to be rebuilt, but God prevented it. What hope for Israel now -- or ever? What meaning for Israel in history now -- or at the end of time? The events of the day made urgent these essentially theological questions. So we come to the critical time, when Judaism as we know it reached the definition it would have for fifteen hundred years, and, in matters of politics and culture and the institutions of society, Christianity too would emerge as it would build the West.

III. The Fourth Century:
Judaism and Christianity in The First Century of Western Civilization

The West as we have known it from Constantine to the nineteenth century carried forward three principal elements of the heritage of antiquity and made of them one. These were, first, Roman law and institutions, second, the legacy of ancient Israel, the Hebrew Scriptures, and, third, Christianity as religion of the state and formative force in culture. The West was what it was because of Christianity. So the history of the West began when Christianity attained that position in politics and culture that it was to occupy for the history of the West, until nearly the present day.

The shift from pagan to Christian Rome took place in the fourth century, from the initial moment at which Constantine accorded to Christianity the status of licit, favored religion, at the outset, to the moment, by the end, at which Christianity became the official and governing religion of the state. Judaism and Christianity in late antiquity, we realize, present histories that mirror one another. When Christianity began, in the first century, Judaism was the dominant tradition in the Holy Land and framed its ideas within a political framework until the early fifth century. Christianity there was subordinate and had to work out against the background of a politically definitive Judaism. From the fourth century, the time of Constantine onward, matters reversed themselves. Now Christianity predominated, expressing its ideas in political and institutional terms. Judaism, by contrast, had lost its political foundations and faced the task of working out its self-understanding in terms of a world defined by Christianity, now everywhere triumphant and in charge of politics. The important shift came in the early fourth century, the West's first century. That was when the West began in the union of Christian religion and Roman rule. It also was when the Judaism that thrived in the West reached the definition it was to exhibit for the next fifteen centuries, until, as I shall note at the end, our own time.

Historians of Judaism take as dogma the view that Christianity never made any difference to Judaism. Faith of a "people that dwells apart," Judaism went its splendid, solitary way, exploring paths untouched by Christians. Christianity -- people hold -- was born in the matrix of Judaism, but Judaism, beginning to now, officially ignored the new "daughter" religion and followed its majestic course in aristocratic isolation. But the Judaism expressed by the writings of the sages of the Land of Israel in the fourth century -- the age of Constantine -- not only responded to issues raised for Israel by the political triumph of Christianity but did so in a way that, intellectually at least, made possible the entire future history of Judaism in Europe and beyond.

The importance of the age of Constantine in the history of Judaism derives from a simple fact. It was at this time that important Judaic documents undertook to deal with agenda defined, for both Judaism and Christianity, by the triumph of Christianity. Important Christian thinkers reflected on issues presented by the political revolution in the status of Christianity. Issues of the rewriting of human history, the canonization of the Bible as the Old and New Testaments, the restatement of the challenge and claim of Christ the King as Messiah against the continuing "unbelief" of Israel (phrased from the Christian viewpoint, Jews would refer to their continuing belief in God's power to save the world at the end of time), the definition of who is Israel -- these make their appearance in Christian writings of the day. And these issues derive from the common agenda of both Judaism and Christianity, namely, the Holy Scriptures of Ancient Israel, received in Judaism as the written half of the One Whole Torah of Moses, our Rabbi, and in Christianity as the Old Testament.

What in fact do the sages of the fourth century say to Israel? They turned back to Scripture, rereading the two books that mattered, first, the one on the Creation of the world and of the children of Israel, Genesis, second, the one on the sanctification of Israel. So they proposed to explain history by rereading the book of Genesis. There they found the lesson that what happened to the patriarchs in the beginning signals what would happen to their children later on. And Jacob then is Israel now, just as Esau then is Rome now. And Israel remains Israel: bearer of the blessing. They explained the status and authority of the traditions -- now two hundred years old -- of the Mishnah and related writings by assigning to them a place in the Torah. Specifically, in the canonical documents of the period at hand for the first time we find clear reference to the notion that when God revealed the Torah to Moses at Sinai, part of the Torah was in the medium of writing, the other part, in the medium of memory, hence oral. And, it would later be explained, the Mishnah (and much else) enjoyed the status of Oral Torah. They explain the Messiah-claim of Israel in very simple terms. Israel indeed will receive the Messiah, but salvation at the end of time awaits the sanctification of Israel in the here and now. And that will take place through humble and obediant loyalty to the Torah. They counter the claim that there is a new Israel in place of the old, and this they do by rereading the book of Leviticus, with its message of sanctification of Israel, and finding in that book a typology of the great empires -- Babylonia, Media, Greece, Rome. And the coming, the fifth and final sovereign, will be Israel's messiah. So, in all, the points important to Christianity in the advent of Constantine and the Christian empire -- history vindicates Christ, the New Testament explains the Old, the Messiah has come and his claim has now been proved truthful, and the Old Israel is done for and will not have a messiah in the future -- all those points were countered, for the Jews in a self-evidently valid manner, by the writings of the fourth century sages. The rabbinic system, which laid stress on the priority of salvation over sanctification, on the dual media by which the Torah came forth from Sinai, on the messinaic dimension of Israel's everyday life, and on the permanence of Israel's position as God's first love -- that system came to first articulate expression in the Talmud of the Land of Israel and related writings -- there, and not in the Mishnah and in its companions in which priorities were reversed. And the reason is clear: the system responded to a competing system, one heir of the ancient Israelite Scripture answering another heir and its claims. The siblings would struggle, like Esau and Jacob, for the common blessing. For the Jewish people, in any event the system of the fourth century sages would endure for millenia as self-evidently right and persuasive.

Christians had a great deal on their minds, much of which had no bearing at all on the public history of Christianity as worked out in the theories of history, Messiah, and Israel -- topics so important to sages and to some of the great intellects of the Church of the fourth century. The quest for a unifying creed, for example, absorbed the best efforts of generations of Christian theologians. But identifying these questions, -- the meaning of history, the identification of the Messiah, the definition of Israel, God's people -- deriving from Scripture in particular, does not represent an act of anachronism. The questions at hand did demand attention and did receive it. And the shape of Judaism as laid forth in documents redacted in the fourth and early fifth century exhibits remarkable congruence to the contours of the same intellectual program. Specifically, in the

Judaism of the sages of the Land of Israel who redacted the principal documents at hand both a doctrine and an apologetic remarkably relevant to the issues presented to both Christianity and Judaism by the crisis of Christianity's worldly triumph.

Jews and Christians alike believed in the Israelite Scriptures, and so understood that major turnings in history carried a message from God. That message bore meaning for questions of salvation and the Messiah, the identification of God's will in Scripture, the determination of who is Israel and what it means to be Israel, and similar questions of a profoundly historical and social character. So it is no wonder that the eneormous turning represented by the advent of a Christian empire should have precipitated deep thought on these issues, important as they are in the fourth century thought of both Judaic sages and Christian theologians. The specification of the message at hand, of course, would produce long-term differences between the Christianity of the age and the Judaism of the time as well.

The success of the Judaism shaped in this place, in this time, is clear. Refined and vastly restated in the Talmud of Babylonia, two hundred years later, the system of Judaism worked out here and now enjoyed the status of self-evidence among Jews confronted with Christian governments and Christian populations over the next fifteen hundred years. So far as ideas matter in bonding a group -- the success among the people of Israel in Europe, west and east alike, of the Judaism defined in the fourth century writings of the sages of the Land of Israel derives from the power and persuasive effect of the ideas of that Judaism. Coming to the surface in the writings of the age, particularly the Talmud of the Land of Israel, Genesis Rabbah, and Leviticus Rabbah, that Judaism therefore secured for despairing Israel a long future of hope and confident endurance.

Prior to the time of Constantine, the documents of Judaism that evidently reached closure -- the Mishnah, Pirqé Abot, the Tosefta -- scarcely took cognizance of Christianity and did not deem the new faith to be much of a challenge. If the scarce and scattered allusions do mean to refer to Christianity at all, then sages regarded it as an irritant, an exasperating heresy among Jews who should have known better. But, then, neither Jews nor pagans took much interest in Christianity in the new faith's first century and a half. The authors of the Mishnah framed a system to which Christianity bore no relevance whatsoever; theirs were problems presented in an altogether different context. For their part, pagan writers were indifferent to Christianity, not mentioning it until about 160. Only when Christian evangelism enjoyed some solid success, toward the later part of that century, did pagans compose apologetic works attacking Christianity. Celsus stands at the start, followed by Porphyry in the third century. But by the fourth century, pagans and Jews alike knew that they faced a formidable, powerful enemy. Pagan writings speak explicitly and accessibly. The answers sages worked out for the intellectual challenge of the hour do not emerge equally explicitly and accessibly. But they are there, and, when we ask the right questions and establish the context of discourse, we hear the answers in the Talmud of the Land of Israel, Genesis Rabbah, and Leviticus Rabbah, as clearly as we hear pagans' answers in the writings of Porphyry and Julian, not to mention the Christians' answers in the rich and diverse writings of the fourth-century fathers, such as Eusebius, Jerome, John Crysostom, and Aphrahat, to mention just four. So, as Rosemary Radford Reuther pointed out nearly fifteen years ago, the fourth century was the first century of Christianity and Judaism as the West would know them both (see her article in *Studies in Religion* 1972, 2:1-10).

The Judaism of the sages of the Land of Israel who redacted the principal documents at hand therefore framed both a doctrine and an apologetic remarkably relevant to the issues presented to both Christianity and Judaism by the crisis of Christianity's worldly triumph. Why the common set of questions? Because Jews and Christians alike believed in the Israelite Scriptures, and so understood that major turnings in history carried a message from God. The specification of the message at hand, of course, would produce long-term differences between the Christianity of the age and the Judaism of the time as well. But the shared program brought the two religions into protracted confrontation on an intersecting set of questions. The struggle between the one and the other -- a struggle that would continue until our own time -- originated in the simple fact that, to begin with, both religions agreed on pretty much everything that mattered. They differed on little, so made much of that little. Scripture taught them both that vast changes in the affairs of empires came about because of God's will. History proved principles of theology. In that same Torah prophets promised the coming of the Messiah, who would bring salvation. Who was, and is, that Messiah, and how shall we know? And that same Torah addressed a particular people, Israel, promisng that people the expression of God's favor and love. But who is Israel, and who is not Israel? So Scripture defined the categories that were shared in common. Scripture filled those categories with deep meaning. That is why to begin with a kind of dialogue -- made up, to be sure, of two monologues on the same topics -- could commence. The dialogue continued for centuries because the conditions that to begin with precipitated it, specifically the rise to political dominance of Christianity and the subordination of Judaism, remained constant for fifteen hundred years.

That is not to suggest that only the three topics at hand dominated sages' thought and the consequent shape of their writings. I do not claim that all of Genesis Rabbah deals with the meaning of history, though much of it does that; all of the Talmud of the Land of Israel takes up the Messianic question, though important components do; or that all of Leviticus Rabbah asks about who is Israel, though the question is there. None, indeed, can presently claim to assess matters of proportion, importance, or, therefore, predominance, in so sizable a canon as that of the sages before us. Characterizing so large and complex a corpus of writings as theirs poses problems of its own, which need not detain us. For we cannot readily settle to everyone's satisfaction the questions of taste and judgment involved in determination of proportion and identification of points of stress. That is why none can claim that just these questions took a paramount role in the documents I cite. Just as the formative figures of Christianity had more on their minds than the issues I lay out, so the creative and authoritative intellects of Judaism thought about many more things than those I take up.[1] But that is not the point. The point is simple. The topics, dictated by politics, before us did matter, and both sides did confront them. We know that is the fact, because we find in the writings of the age clear and important evidence that Judaic sages, as much as Christian theologians, answered these questions. Moreover, when they did address these questions, they defined the issues at hand in pretty much the same terms. So, sharing the premises that generated the questions and agreeing upon the source of facts that would settle them -- Scripture in both cases -- the two sets of intellectuals did agree as well on a common topic of argument. Having so much in common, they could differ, and the differences prove instructive. So Judaism and Christianity in the fourth century entered that initial confrontation that would define the terms for the next fifteen hundred years.

So if we ask, when did people actually enter a confrontation on the same issues, defined in the same way? The answer is that it was not in the first century. Christians and Jews in the first century did not argue with one another. Each set of groups -- the family of Christianities, the family of Judaisms -- went its way, focusing upon its own program. When Christianity came into being, in the first century, one important strand of the Christian movement laid stress on issues of salvation, in the Gospels maintaining that Jesus was, and is, Christ, come to save the world and impose a radical change on history. At that same time, an important group within the diverse Judaic systems of the age, the Pharisees, emphasized issues of sanctification, maintaining that the task of Israel is to attain that holiness of which the Temple was a singular embodiment. When, in the Gospels, we find the record of the Church placing Jesus into opposition with the Pharisees, we witness the confrontation of different people talking about different things to different people. But in the fourth century, by contrast, different people addressing different groups really did talk about exactly the same things. That is the point, therefore, at which the Judaic and Christian conflict reached the form in which, for fifteen hundred years, it would come to intellectual expression. People really did differ about the same issues. These issues -- the meaning of history, the identity of the Messiah, and the definition of Israel, or of God's instrument for embodying in a social group God's will, -- would define the foundations of the dispute from then on. So we find for the

[1] And that is not to ignore the vast internal agenda requiring discussion, questions of no interest whatsoever to the relationship between the two groups. The internal agenda in the writings of both parties to the debate surely predominated.

first time a genuine confrontation: people differing about a shared agendum in exactly the same terms.

What about the moment at which Judaism in important documents did deal in a significant way with the existence of Christianity? Once more, I maintain, it was in the fourth century. How so? The issues presented to Jews by the triumph of Christianity do inform the documents shaped in the Land of Israel in the period of that triumph. The three largest writings, the great commentary to Genesis called Genesis Rabbah, the Talmud of the Land of Israel, and the commentary to Leviticus called Leviticus Rabbah take up and systematically work out important components of the intellectual program of the age, once more: the meaning of history, the Messianic crisis, the identification of Israel. These issues do not play an important role in prior components of the unfolding canon of Judaism, in particular, the Mishnah and the Tosefta and Sifré to Numbers, all of which, it is generally held, reached closure before the fourth century. So the contrast in each case suggests that a new set of issues has compelled attention, in documents of the age, to questions neglected in earlier compilations. And these issues proved pressing for other intellectuals, the Christian ones, of the same period. On the basis of the confluence of discourse on precisely the same questions, in precisely the same terms, I think we may fairly argue that the two groups talked about the same things at the same time and so engaged in whatever genuine debate proved possible. So, in all, in many ways the fourth century marks the point of intersection of trajectories of the history of the two religions, Judaic and Christian.

IV. A Final Word

The ancient rabbis look out upon a world destroyed and still smoking in the aftermath of calamity, but they speak of rebirth and renewal. The holy Temple lay in ruins, but they ask about sanctification. The old history was over, but they look forward to future history. Theirs, as we see, is a message that what is true and real is the opposite of what people perceive. God stands for paradox. Strength comes through weakness, salvation through acceptance and obedience, sanctification through the ordinary and profane, which can be made holy. Now to informed Christians, the mode of thought must prove remarkably familiar. For the cross that stands for weakness yields salvation, and the crucified criminal is king and savior. That is the foolishness to which the apostle Paul makes reference. Yet the greater the "nonsense" -- life out of the grave, eternity from death -- the deeper the truth, the richer the paradox! So here we have these old Jews, one group speaking of sanctification of Israel, the people, the other of salvation of Israel and the world. Separately, they are thinking along the same lines, coming to conclusions remarkably congruent to one another, affirming the paradox of God in the world, of humanity in God's image, in the rabbinical framework; of God in the flesh, in the Christian. Is it not time for the joint heirs of ancient Israel's Scripture and hope to meet once more, in humility, before the living God? Along with all humanity, facing backward toward Auschwitz and total destruction, and forward toward complete annihilation of the world as we know it -- is it not time?

Judaism and Christianity in the age of holocaust come together as they have not since the beginning, and as they have not been able to since the fourth century. The relationship of subordinated, patient Judaism, always at the border of despair, and world-possessing Christianity, forever on the edge of celebrating this world alone, -- that relationship which began in the age of Constantine, has ended. In their contemporary encounter Judaism and Christianity have entered a new epoch of relationship. For that, at least, we have, all of us, to give thanks. Why at just this time, in just this dreadful way, God has brought us to the threshhold of mature reconciliation, no one now knows. If it is to wipe us out, all together, all at once, for the sins of fifteen hundred years of sibling hatred, we do not now know. But perhaps it is for a blessing, held back until, mourning unspeakable tragedy, in shame, sadness, silence, we rejoined ranks, before not "Auschwitz" or Golgotha but Sinai -- there alone. There in a cleft in the rock we shall shelter before the Presence. There we shall hear, after the mighty noise, a voice of silence.

V. Bibliography

This article for the first time draws together into a single picture the results of a number of different studies of mine. These include the following:

A Life of Yohanan ben Zakkai. Leiden, 1962: Brill. Awarded the Abraham Berliner Prize in Jewish History, Jewish Theological Seminary of America, 1962. Second edition, completely revised, 1970. Japanese translation: Yamamoto Shoten Publishing House, Tokyo. Expected in 1986.

Aphrahat and Judaism. The Christian Jewish Argument in Fourth Century Iran. Leiden, 1971: Brill.

The Rabbinic Traditions about the Pharisees before 70. Leiden, 1971: Brill. I-III.

The Tosefta. Translated from the Hebrew. N.Y., 1977-1986: Ktav. I-VI.

The Talmud of the Land of Israel. A Preliminary Translation and Explanation. Chicago: The University of Chicago Press: 1982-1989.

Judaism and Scripture: The Evidence of Leviticus Rabbah. Chicago, 1985: The University of Chicago Press.

Genesis Rabbah. The Judaic Commentary on Genesis. A New American Translation. Atlanta, 1985: Scholars Press for Brown Judaic Studies.

Sifra. The Judaic Commentary on Leviticus. A New Translation. The Leper. Leviticus 13:1-14:57. Chico, 1985: Scholars Press for Brown Judaic Studies. Based on the translation of Sifra Parashiyyot Negaim and Mesora in A History of the Mishnaic Law of Purities. VI. Negaim. Sifra. [With a section by Roger Brooks.]

Sifré to Numbers. An American Translation. I. 1-58 Atlanta, 1986: Scholars Press for Brown Judaic Studies.

Sifré to Numbers. An American Translation . II. *59-115*. Atlanta, 1986: Scholars Press for Brown Judaic Studies. [III. *116-161*: William Scott Green].

A *History of the Mishnaic Law of Purities.* Leiden, 1977: Brill. XXI. *The Redaction and Formulation of the Order of Purities in the Mishnah and Tosefta.* And XXII. *The Mishnaic System of Uncleanness. Its Context and History.*

A *History of the Mishnaic Law of Holy Things.* Leiden, 1979: Brill. VI. *The Mishnaic System of Sacrifice and Sanctuary.*

A *History of the Mishnaic Law of Women.* Leiden, 1980: Brill. V. *The Mishnaic System of Women.*

A *History of the Mishnaic Law of Appointed Times.* Leiden, 1981: Brill. V. *The Mishnaic System of Appointed Times.*

A *History of the Mishnaic Law of Damages.* Leiden, 1985: Brill. V. *The Mishnaic System of Damages*

The Integrity of Leviticus Rabbah. The Problem of the Autonomy of a Rabbinic Document. Chico, 1985: Scholars Press for Brown Judaic Studies.

Comparative Midrash: The Plan and Program of Genesis Rabbah and Leviticus Rabbah. Atlanta, 1986: Scholars Press for Brown Judaic Studies.

Judaism. The Evidence of the Mishnah . Chicago, 1981: University of Chicago Press. Paperback edition: 1984. *Choice*, "Outstanding academic book list" 1982-3. Second printing, 1985. Hebrew translation: Tel Aviv, 1986: Sifriat Poalim. Italian translation: Casale Monferrato, 1987: Editrice Marietti.

Judaism in Society: The Evidence of the Yerushalmi. Toward the Natural History of a Religion. Chicago, 1983: The University of Chicago Press. *Choice* , "Outstanding Academic Book List, 1984-1985."

Judaism: The Classical Statement. The Evidence of the Bavli. Chicago, 1986: University of Chicago Press.

Ancient Israel after Catastrophe. The Religious World-View of the Mishnah. The Richard Lectures for 1982. Charlottesville, 1983: The University Press of Virginia.

The Foundations of Judaism. Method, Teleology. Doctrine. Philadelphia, 1983-5: Fortress Press. I-III. I. *Midrash in Context. Exegesis in Formative Judaism.* II. *Messiah in Context. Israel's History and Destiny in Formative Judaism.* Italian translation: Casale Monferrato, 1988: Editrice Marietti. III. *Torah: From Scroll to Symbol in Formative Judaism.*

The Oral Torah. The Sacred Books of Judaism. An Introduction. San Francisco, 1985: Harper & Row.

Vanquished Nation, Broken Spirit. The Virtues of the Heart in Formative Judaism. New York, 1986: Cambridge University Press.

Judaisms and their Messiahs in the beginning of Christianity . New York, 1986: Cambridge University Press. [Edited with William Scott Green, Jonathan Z. Smith, and Ernest S. Frerichs.]

Judaism in the Matrix of Christianity. Philadelphia, 1986: Fortress Press.

Judaism and Christianity in the Age of Constantine. The Initial Confrontation. Chicago, 1987: University of Chicago Press.

The Death and Birth of Judaism. Self-Evidence and Self-Consciousness in Modern Times. New York, 1987: Basic Books.

Method and Meaning in Ancient Judaism. Missoula, 1979: Scholars Press for Brown Judaic Studies. Second printing, 1983.

Method and Meaning in Ancient Judaism . Second Series. Chico, 1980: Scholars Press for Brown Judaic Studies.

Method and Meaning in Ancient Judaism. Third Series. Chico, 1980: Scholars Press for Brown Judaic Studies.

Ancient Judaism. Disputes and Debates. Chico, 1984: Scholars Press for Brown Judaic Studies.

The Pharisees. Rabbinic Perspectives. N.Y., 1985: Ktav Publishing House

The Jews in Talmudic Babylonia. A Political History. N.Y., 1986: Ktav.

Judaism, Christianity, and Zoroastrianism in Talmudic Babylonia. N.Y., 1986: Ktav.

Early Rabbinic Judaism. Historical Studies in Religion, Literature, and Art. Leiden, 1975: Brill.

From Politics to Piety. The Emergence of Pharisaic Judaism. Englewood Cliffs, 1973: Prentice-Hall. Second printing, N.Y., 1978: Ktav. Japanese translation: Tokyo, 1985: Kyo Bun Kwan.

Editor: *Contemporary Judaic Fellowship. In Theory and in Practice.* N.Y., 1972: Ktav.

Invitation to the Talmud. A Teaching Book. N.Y., 1973: Harper & Row. Second printing, 1974. Paperback edition, 1975. Reprinted: 1982. Second edition, completely revised, San Francisco, 1984: Harper & Row. Japanese translation: Tokyo, 1986: Yamamoto Shoten.

First Century Judaism in Crisis. Yohanan ben Zakkai and the Renaissance of Torah. Nashville, 1975: Abingdon. Second printing, N.Y., 1981: Ktav.

Torah from Our Sages: Pirke Avot. A New American Translation and Explanation . Chappaqua, 1983: Rossel.

Our Sages, God, and Israel. An Anthology of the Yerushalmi . Chappaqua, 1984: Rossel. 1985 selection, Jewish Book Club.

Judaism in the Beginning of Christianity. Philadelphia, 1983: Fortress. British edition, London, 1984: SPCK. German translation, Stuttgart, 1984: Calwerverlag. Dutch translation, Kampen, 1986: J. H. Kok. French translation: Editions du Cerf. Expected in 1986. Presently under consideration: translations into Norwegian and Suomi (Finnish).

Genesis and Judaism: The Perspective of Genesis Rabbah. An Analytical Anthology. Atlanta, 1986: Scholars Press for Brown Judaic Studies.

Judaism: The First Two Centuries. Abbreviated version of *Judaism : The Evidence of the Mishnah.* Chicago, 1987: University of Chicago Press.

Part Two

CONTEXT AND ANALYSIS

Chapter Four

Analysis of a Text in the Context of its Literary Structures
The Case of Sifré to Numbers

1. The Problem of Defining Sifré to Numbers

Were we to face the task of writing an encyclopaedia article on Sifré to Numbers, we should want to answer these questions: [1] where, when, and by whom was the book written? [2] what is the book about? [3] does the author propose to argue a particular case, and, if so, what polemic does he propose to advance? Yet another range of questions -- is it a book or a scrapbook, a cogent statement or a composite? -- might also attract our attention. For defining the document demands classifying it, and describing the document requires stating its main points of emphasis. In other words, just what is Sifré to Numbers, what sort of a book is it, and what particular example of that sort of book is it? These questions define the work of introducing a book -- any book. The answers to these and other questions constitute the definition of our book as of any other. They tell us what it is: its context, composition, and contents. The character and contents of Sifré to Numbers permit answering none of these questions. To deal with all of them, we have to moved beyond the limits of the book itself, through an exercise of comparison and contrast. But even reaching the point of comparison and contrast will require considerable preliminary analysis. Let us speak first of context. The book reaches us under particular auspices, so we turn first to the institutional medium by which Sifré to Nuimbers has come down from antiquity to our own day: the medium of Judaism. Sifré to Numbers is a holy book. Let us start there. There too we shall conclude.

Books such as Sifré to Numbers, that form part of the canon of Judaism, that is, of "the one whole Torah of Moses our rabbi revealed by God at Sinai," do not contain answers to questions of definition that ordinarily receive answers within the pages of a given book. In antiquity books or other important writings, e.g., letters and treatises, bore the name of the author or at least an attribution, e.g., Aristotle's or Paul's name, or the attribution to Enoch or Baruch or Luke. For no document in the canon of Judaism produced in late antiquity is there a named author, let alone a clearcut date of composition, a defined place or circumstance in which a book is written, a sustained and on-going argument to which we readily gain access, or any of the other usual indicators by which we define the authorship, therefore the context and the circumstance, of a book. Internal evidence alone testifies; there is nothing on the surface to tell us who is telling us these things and why: what is at issue? So the canon of which our document forms a part presents single books as episodes in a timeless, ahistorical setting: Torah revealed to Moses by God at Mount Sinai, but written down long afterward. That theological conviction about the canon overall denies us information to introduce the book at hand, that is, to say, what it is. Without the usual indicators, then, how then are we to read our document on its own terms, so as to answer the question: what is this book? When, where, why was it written? What does it mean?

Lacking clear answers to these questions, we turn to the evidence the document does provide: its salient traits of plan and program. By plan I mean simply the literary traits before us. The intellectual program, so far as we can define it, derives from those same literary traits: from *how* the book's authorship presents its messages, we hope to learn *what* important points that authorship proposed to impart. So these two go together: form and meaning, structure and sustained polemic. Proposing to define the document at hand, we begin from the outside, with formal traits, and work our way inwards, toward the deciphering of the messages contained within those recurrent points of interest and stress, to begin with signified in form.. Only by seeing the document whole and all at once shall we gain the rudiments of a definition. Describing and so defining bits and pieces would yield no encompassing description of the whole. If we ask, therefore, what is this book, we begin with the entirety of the document.

If, as we must, we focus on intrinsic traits, exhibited within the words of the document itself, we do not know much more than that the book forms part of a canon of books. That we know because Sifré to Numbers persistently refers to a book other than itself, specifically, sections of the book of Numbers. (But the selection of the sections chosen for treatment, specified on the table of contents, conforms to no clear pattern and so cannot find explanation by reference to some larger task or plan.) Still the fact that the authorship declares its dependence upon another authorship -- a fact deriving from entirely intrinsic traits, inductively discovered -- testifies to the canonical context in which our document comes into being. In point of fact, all we know about Sifré to Numbers is that it forms a document organized around another document, that is, in conventional language, it is a commentary to a text.

What does that mean? Simply this: were we to approach our document without the knowledge that the authors take as their point of departure -- organization and formal program of their book -- an already-available book written by someone else, we should understand very little in the book at hand. Sifré to Numbers read out of alignment with the book of Numbers presents unintelligible gibberish. To state matters affirmatively, we define the present book only when we can describe its relationship to the book that forms the trellice for its vine. But once we know that in hand is a commentary to a text, we still possess little more knowledge of the program and purpose of Sifré to

Numbers than we did prior to our observing that simple fact. For (to revert to the list of things we do not know) we still do not know who wrote the book, for what purpose, with the intent of advancing what ideas or program. We do not even know what made the author select as the organizing structure for his book the book of Numbers in particular, or whether some other book would have served his purpose just as well.

Nonetheless, when we have worked out the points our authorship wishes to make in the reading of the book of Numbers, we shall have come a long way toward defining the purpose and polemic of Sifré to Numbers. For all propositions must emerge, in a commentary to a text, out of the relationship between the commentary and the text. And since that relationship, by definition, proves fixed and consistent, we indeed can say what, over all, in form and in the implications of form, the authorship proposed to demonstrate: its main points. These, as we shall see, concern specific propositions, exemplified in the reading of the book of Numbers. But these same points can have been made, and in fact were made, through the systematic reading of at least one other pentateuchal book, the book of Leviticus. So it is not the book of Numbers that has dictated the program of Sifre to Numbers. It is a sustained program, defined and set forth by the authorship at hand, that has told that authorship what, in the book of Numbers, demands comment, and what comment must be made.

The upshot? The extrinsic traits of the document at hand tell us practically nothing about the book and do not permit us to define it. So we cannot say what Sifré to Numbers is and is not, who wrote it, to make what point, when, why, where, and on and on. And if we cannot answer these questions, we also cannot make sense of the document before us. We know what it says, but we do not know what it means. Lacking all context, Sifré to Numbers provides a set of merely formal observations. We simply do not know what the book is, even though we can say what is in the book (and even define the meanings of words and phrases in the interstices of discourse). But where shall we look to find a context for description? The answer is the internal traits. The sole fact in hand is the document itself. For even the context -- the canonical setting -- is imputed by others, by circumstance and sentiment beyond the pages of the book.

2. Sorting Out Internal Evidence: An Inductive Approach

Inductive evidence derives from the way in which the authorship at hand has organized and expressed its ideas. The document rests upon clearcut choices of formal and rhetorical preference, so it is, from the viewpoint of form and mode of expression, cogent. Formal choices prove uniform and paramount. How to discover the forms of discourse? To begin with I analyze one *pisqa*, to show its recurrent structures. These as a matter of hypothesis I describe and categorize. Then, I proceed to survey two more *pisqaot* to see whether or not a single cogent taxonomic structure provides a suitable system of classification for diverse units of discourse. We then proceed to survey the *pisqaot*, 1-115, presented in my part of the complete translation. If one taxonomy serves all and encompasses the bulk of the units of discourse at hand, I may fairly claim that Sifré to Numbers does constitute a cogent formal structure, based upon patterns of rhetoric uniform and characteristic throughout. The importance of that fact will lie on the very surface. For on that basis we can describe -- and we shall be able to -- the incremental message, the cumulative effect, of the formal traits of speech and thought revealed in the uniform rhetoric and syntax of the document. The framers or redactors followed a set of rules which we are able to discern. These rules lead us deep into the interiority of our authorship: people say things the way they mean to say them, and how they express their ideas imparts meaning to what they say.

3. Recurrent Literary Structures of Sifré to Numbers

We proceed to the definition of the forms of Sifré to Numbers. These forms I call literary structures. A literary structure is a set of rules that dictate those recurrent conventions of expression, organization, or proportion, that are *extrinsic* to the message of the author. The conventions at hand bear none of the particular burden of the author's message, so they are not idiosyncratic but systemic and public. A literary structure imposes upon the individual writer a limited set of choices about how he will convey whatever message he has in mind. Or the formal convention will limit an editor or redactor to an equally circumscribed set of alternatives about how to arrange received materials. These conventions then form a substrate of the literary culture that preserves and expresses the world view and way of life of the system at hand. When we can define the literary structures, we also can ask about the program of thought -- recurrent modes of analysis and exercises of conflict and resolution -- that dictate the content of the commentary. For how I think and what the syntax of my language and thought permits me to say dictates what I shall think and why I shall think it: this, not that.

How are we to recognize the presence of such structures? On the basis of forms that merely appear to be patterned or extrinsic to particular meaning and so entirely formal, we cannot allege that we have in hand a fixed, literary structure. Such a judgment would prove subjective. Nor shall we benefit from bringing to the text at hand recurrent syntactic or grammatical patterns shown in *other* texts, even of the same canon of literature, to define conventions for communicating ideas. Quite to the contrary, we find guidance in a simple principle:

A text has to define its own structures for us.

This its authors do by repeatedly resorting to a severely circumscribed set of linguistic patterns and literary conventions and to no others. These patterns, we shall soon see, dictate not only formal syntax and principles of composition but also logical analysis and the propositions of argument. On the basis of inductive evidence alone a document will testify that its authors adhere to a fixed canon of literary forms and that these forms guide the authors to the propositions for, or against, which they choose to argue: the program of the book, not only its plan. If demonstrably present, these forms present an author or editor with a few choices on how ideas are to be organized and expressed in intelligible -- again, therefore, public -- compositions. So internal evidence and that alone testifies to the literary structures of a given text.

The adjective "recurrent" constitutes a redundancy when joined to the noun "structure." For -- to state matters negatively -- we cannot know that we have a structure if the text under analysis does not repeatedly resort to the presentation of its message through that disciplined structure external to its message on any given point. And, it follows self-evidently, we do know that we have a structure when the text in hand repeatedly follows recurrent conventions of expression, organization, or proportion *extrinsic* to the message of the author. The literary structures or patterns find definition in entirely formal and objective facts: the placement of the key-verse subject to discussion in the composition at hand, the origin of that verse. No subjective or impressionistic judgment intervenes.

How shall we proceed to identify the structures of the document before us? It seems to me we had best move first to the analysis of a single *pisqa*. We seek, within that *pisqa*. to identify what holds the whole together. For this purpose I shall try to describe what I conceive to be the underlying and repeated structures of formulation or pattern. These I do one by one, simply experimenting with the possibility that a way of forming ideas will recur and so constitute a pattern. The description of course is inductive: I say what I see. The reader can check every step and form his or her own judgments. The second step then is to see whether what I have identified exemplifies formations beyond itself or forms a phenomenon that occurs in fact only once or at random. For the first exercise, we take up *Pisqa* Six, and for the second, *Pisqaot* Fifty-nine and One Hundred Seven, the former brief, the latter long. As we proceed, we examine all one hundred fifteen of the *pisqaot* of Sifré to Numbers covered in this part of the translation and sort out the results on analytical lists.

4. Literary Structures of Sifré to Numbers 6

VI:I.

1. A.   "...every man's holy thing shall be his; whatever any man gives to the priest shall be his" (Num. 5:10).

     B.   All manner of consecrated produce originally was covered by the general principle stated here: "...every man's holy thing shall be his; whatever any man gives to the priest shall be his."

     C.   Scripture thus drew all Holy Things and assigned them to the priest, among them omitting reference only to the thanksgiving-offering, peace-offering, Passover-offering, tithe of cattle, produce in the status of Second Tithe, and fruits of an orchard in the fourth year after its planting, all of which are to belong to the farmer [not to the priest].

The form consists of the citation of an opening verse, followed by an issue stated in terms extrinsic to the cited verse. That is to say, no word or phrase of the base verse (that is, the cited verse at the beginning) attracts comment. Rather a general rule of exegesis is invoked. C then introduces a broad range of items not at all subject to attention in the verse at hand. The formal traits: [1] citation of a base verse from Numbers, [2] a generalization ignoring clauses or words in the base verse, [3] a further observation without clear interest in the verse at hand. But the whole is linked to the theme of the base verse -- and to that alone. So an extrinsic exegetical program comes to bear. We shall provisionally call this the extrinsic exegetical form. In due course the extrinsic patterns will undergo their own differentiation, as will the corresponding internal ones.

VI:II

1. A. "...every man's holy thing shall be his; whatever any man gives to the priest shall be his" (Num. 5:10).

    B. On the basis of this statement you draw the following rule:

    C. **If a priest on his own account makes a sacrificial offering, even though it falls into the week [during which] another priestly watch than his own [is in charge of the actual cult, making the offerings and receiving the dues], lo, that priest owns the priestly portions of the offering, and the right of offering it up belongs to him [and not to the priest ordinarily on duty at that time, who otherwise would retain the rights to certain portions of the animal] [T. Men. 13:17].**

What we have is simply a citation of the verse plus a law in prior writing (Mishnah, Tosefta) which the verse is supposed to sustain. The formal traits require [1] citation of a verse, with or without comment, followed by [2] verbatim citation of a passage of the Mishnah or the Tosefta. What we have is a formal construction in which we simply juxtapose a verse, without or with intervening words of explanation, with a passage of the Mishnah or the Tosefta.

VI:III

1. A. "'...every man's holy thing shall be his; whatever any man gives to the priest shall be his' (Num. 5:10).

    B. "Why does Scripture make this statement?

    C. "Because, with reference to the fruit of an orchard in the fourth year after its planting, it is said, 'And in the fourth year all their fruit shall be holy, an offering of praise to the Lord' (Lev. 19:24), [I do not know whether the sense is that] it is holy for the farmer or holy for the priesthood. Accordingly, Scripture says, '...every man's holy thing shall be his; whatever any man gives to the priest shall be his,' Scripture thereby speaks of produce of an orchard in the fourth year after its planting, indicating that it should belong to the farmer," the words of R. Meir.

    D. R. Ishmael says, "It is holy to the farmer."

E.   "You maintain that it is holy for the farmer.. Or is it holy for the priesthood? Lo, this is how you may logically [rather than by reference to the exegesis, B-C, based on Scripture] deal with the problem:

F.   "Produce in the status of second tithe is called holy, and the fruit of an orchard in the fourth year after its planting is called holy. If I draw the analogy to produce in the status of second tithe, which belongs only to the farmer, then likewise produce of an orchard in the fourth year after its planting should belong only to the farmer."

G.   No, produce separated as heave-offering [for priestly use] proves to the contrary, for it too is called Holy, but it belongs only to the priest. And that furthermore demonstrates for produce of an orchard in the fourth year after its planting that even though it is called holy, it should belong only to the priesthood.

H.   "You may then offer [the following argument to the contrary, showing the correct analogy is to be drawn not to heave-offering but to produce in the status of second tithe, as follows:] the correct separation of produce in the status of second tithe involves bringing the produce to the holy place [of Jerusalem, where it is to be eaten], and, along these same lines, produce of an orchard in the fourth year after its planning likewise involves bringing that produce to the holy place. If, therefore, I draw the rule for produce in the status of second tithe, maintaining that it belongs to the owner, so produce of an orchard in the fourth year after its planting likewise should belong only to the owner."

I.   [No, that argument can be disproved from another variety of produce entirely:] lo, produce designated as first fruits will prove to the contrary, for such produce likewise has to be brought to the holy place, but it belongs only to the priest. So produce in that classification will prove for produce of an orchard in the fourth year after its planting, showing that even though it has to be brought to the holy place, it also should belong only to the priests. [So the labor of classification continues.]

J.   "You may compose [the following argument to reply to the foregoing:] The [result of the] separation of produce in the status of second tithe falls into the classification of holy and has to be brought to the holy place, but further is subject to redemption [in that one can redeem the actual fruit and replace it with ready cash, and one may then bring that cash to Jerusalem and buy for it produce to be eaten in Jerusalem under the rules governing second tithe]. Produce of an orchard in the fourth year after its planting likewise is called holy, has to be brought to the holy place, and is subject to the rules of redemption. But let the matter of heave offering not come into the picture, for even though it is called holy, it does not have to be brought to the holy place [but is eaten wherever it is located], and let the matter of first fruit likewise not enter the picture, for even though it is produce that has to be brought to the holy place, it is not called holy."

K.   Lo, there is the case of the firstling, which *is* called holy, and which has to be brought to the holy place, but which belongs only to the priesthood. [So we can now provide an appropriate analogy.] And that case will prove [the rule for other sorts of produce subject to the same traits, specifically] produce of an orchard in the fourth year after its planting, for, even though it is called holy, and even though it has to be brought to the holy place, it should belong only to the priesthood.

L. "You may invoke the consideration of separating [the produce into one of its several classifications]. Let me call to account three distinct considerations in a single exercise:

M. "[1] Food in the status of second tithe is called holy, requires delivery to the holy place, and is subject to the rules of redemption,

N. "[2] Produce of an orchard in the fourth year after its planting is called holy, requires delivery to the holy place, and is subject to the rules of redemption.

O. "[1] But let not food that has been designated as heave-offering enter into consideration. For even though it is called holy, it does not require delivery to the holy place,

P. "And [2] let not first fruits enter into consideration. For even though it requires delivery to the holy place, it is not called holy.

Q. "Nor should [3] the firstling enter into consideration. For even though it is called holy and requires delivery to the holy place, it is not subject to the rules of redemption.

R. "Let me then draw the appropriate analogy from the correct source, and let me then compose a logical argument on the basis of the correct traits of definition.

S. "I shall draw an analogy on the basis of three shared traits from one matter to another, but I shall not drawn an analogy from something which exhibits three traits to something which does not share these same traits, but only one or two of them.

T. "If then I draw an analogy to produce in the status of second tithe, which belongs only to the owner, so too in the case of produce of an orchard in the fourth year after its planting, it should belong only to the owner."

VI:IV

2. A. R. Joshua says, "What is called holy belongs to the owner.

B. "You maintain that what is called holy belongs to the owner. But perhaps it belongs only to the priesthood?

C. "Scripture states, 'But in the fifth year you may eat of their fruit that they may yield more richly for you' (Lev. 19:25). To whom does the increase go? To him to whom the produce already has been assigned [that is to say, the farmer, not the priesthood]."

We have a debate on whether reason unaided by Scripture can prevail. A-C prove essential to what is to follow, since Ishmael's purpose is not merely to make his point, D, but to demonstrate that logic, without Scripture, can sustain that same point, E-T. The form of argument is fairly standard through our document, with a series of arguments by analogy. We prove that the item at hand is like another item and therefore follows its rule, or is unlike that item and therefore follows the opposite of its rule. The argument is formalized to an extreme, and there are very few variations among exempla of this form, though one -- the matter of length -- should not be missed. The exegesis of the verse at hand plays no substantial role, beyond its initial introduction. What is critical is the issue of the reliability of logic. The base verse before us contributes virtually nothing and in no way serves as the foundation for the composition at hand, which is sustained and handsomely executed. The fundamental issue, of course, transcends the subject-matter: can we on the basis of unaided reason reach the correct conclusions (which, as a matter of fact, we already know)? Ishmael shows we can, Meir first, then Joshua offer a narrowly-exegetical proof for the same proposition.

VI:IV

1. A. "...every man's holy thing shall be his; whatever any man gives to the priest shall be his" (Num. 5:10).

   B. Why is this verse articulated? Because it is said, "All the holy offerings which the people of Israel present to the Lord I give to you [priests]" (Num. 18:19), might I infer that the priests may seize these gifts by force?

   C. Scripture says, "...every man's holy thing shall be his; whatever any man *gives* to the priest shall be his" (Num. 5:10).

   D. This indicates that the gratitude for the benefit of holy things belongs to the farmer [and the priest cannot seize the things by force but must accept them as gifts and give gratitude to the farmer for assigning those gifts to him in particular].

The verse itself is clarified in contrast with another verse that makes the same point. Now the focus is on the base verse and not a broader issue. We may call this an intrinsic exegetical form, in that the focus of exegesis is on the verse, which is cited and carefully spelled out.

VI:V

1. A. "...every man's holy thing shall be his; whatever any man gives to the priest shall be his" (Num. 5:10).

   B. Lo, if one has taken the measure of the produce on the ground, and further produce is added to them pile, is it possible that I may invoke in connection with the pile as a whole the verse, "...every man's holy thing shall be his" (Num. 5:10) [so that the farmer now owns all of the produce]?

   C. Scripture states, "...whatever any man gives to the priest shall be his." [The priest retains the right to the produce originally designated but cannot stake a claim on the priestly share of the additional produce.]

   D. Or is it possible that even if one has measured out the designated produce in a basket, and further produce is added to what has been designated, I may invoke in that regard, "...every man's holy thing shall be his"?

   E. Scripture states, "...whatever any man gives to the priest shall be his." [The priest retains the right to the produce originally designated.]

VI:V

2. A. R. Yose says, "Lo, if one has paid the priest the redemption money for his first born son within the thirty days after birth, but the infant has died, might I invoke in that case, '...whatever any man gives to the

priest shall be his [the priest's]? [Then the priest would not have to return the money.] [No, for] Scripture further states, '...every man's holy thing shall be his.' [The priest does have to return the money.]

B. "If the child dies after thirty days, the money may not be recovered from the priest's possession, and I recite in that connection, '...whatever any man gives to the priest shall be his [the priest's].'"

Once again the apparent contradiction between the two clauses of the verse is smoothed out, by assigning each statement to a different circumstance. The exegesis of the verse then forms the center of interest. Thus the classification is the intrinsic exegetical form. We may now define the formal conventions of Pisqa 6:

i. Extrinsic Exegetical Form:

The form consists of the citation of an opening verse, followed by an issue stated in terms extrinsic to the cited verse. That is to say, no word or phrase of the base verse (that is, the cited verse at the beginning) attracts comment. Rather a general rule of exegesis is invoked. C then introduces a broad range of items not at all subject to attention in the verse at hand. The formal traits: [1] citation of a base verse from Numbers, [2] a generalization ignoring clauses or words in the base verse, [3] a further observation without clear interest in the verse at hand. But the whole is linked to the theme of the base verse -- and to that alone. So an extrinsic exegetical program comes to bear. We shall call this the extrinsic exegetical form. But in our final catalogue, we shall find reason to differentiate among a number of extrinsic-exegetical forms.

ii. Intrinsic Exegetical Form:

The verse itself is clarified. In the first instance, the exegesis derives from the contrast with another verse that makes the same point. But the formal trait should not be missed. It is that the the focus is on the base verse and not on a broader issue. We may call this an intrinsic exegetical form, in that the focus of exegesis is on the verse, which is cited and carefully spelled out. We shall know that we have it when the base verse is cited, clause by clause or in other ways, and then given an ample dose of attention.

The distinction between extrinsic and intrinsic exegesis emerges from a simple formal trait: do verses other than the base verse, that is, the verse of the book of Numbers under discussion, play a considerable part? Are there many such verses besides the base one, or only a few? Do those many verses deal with the topic of the base verse or other topics? If the former, then they may serve to illuminate the verse under discussion, if the latter, then all the verses together, including the one chosen from the book of Numbers, may serve to demonstrate a given proposition external to all of the proof-texts. These questions find answers not in impressions but in simple facts: number of verses other than the base verse, origins of those other verses. No one can answer those questions merely on the basis of subjective impressions. But we have now to move quickly to the promised differentiation within the two gross categories, extrinsic and intrinsic.

iii. Dialectical Exegesis: Intrinsic

While this form does not occur above, it is so important that we should introduce it in our initial catalogue. It consists of a sequence of arguments about the meaning of a passage, in which the focus is upon the base verse, and a sequence of possibilities is introduced to spell out the meaning of that verse. At issue is not the power of logic but the meaning of the base verse, but that issue is pursued through an argument of many stages.

iv. Dialectical Exegesis: The Fallacy of Logic Uncorrected by Exegesis of Scripture

Whether or not this is an intrinsic or an extrinsic exegesis is beside the point, because the pattern at hand is not interested in the exegesis of a verse, though exegesis plays a role in the pattern. Rather, the focus is upon an issue that applies to all exegeses: is exegesis necessary at all, or can logic, independent of the evidence of scriptural verses, reach firm and reliable conclusions?

Formally, we deal with another moving, or dialectical, exegetical form, but while the basic trait is familiar -- a sequence of shifts and turns in the possibility of interpretation, all of them subjected to close logical scrutiny, the purpose is different. And the purpose comes to expression not in content, particular to diverse passages, but in form. The formal indicator is the presence of the question, in one of several versions: is it not a matter of logic? That is the never-failing formal indicator. From that clause we invariably move on to a set of arguments of a highly formalized character on taxonomic classification: what is like, or unlike? What is like follows a given rule, what is unlike follows the opposite rule, and it is for us to see whether the likenesses or unlikenesses prevail. The argument is formalized to an extreme, and there are very few variations among our document's exempla of this form, though one -- the matter of length -- should not be missed. The exegesis of the verse at hand plays no substantial role, beyond its initial introduction. What is critical is the issue of the reliability of logic. The base verse before us contributes virtually nothing and in no way serves as the foundation for the composition at hand. An important example is given at CVII:III.3, but we shall see many others. Let us quickly review a fine example of the form.

CVII:III

3. A. Issi b. Aqabia says, "'...to the Lord from the herd or from the flock...to make a pleasing odor to the Lord' means, from this species by itself or from that species by itself.

B. "You say that it means, from this species by itself or from that species by itself.

C. "But perhaps one may bring both simultaneously?

D. "For there is an argument *a fortiori* : Now if the lambs brought for the Pentecost offering, which are brought in pairs, are valid if they come from a single species, a burnt offering, which is not brought in a pair [but is brought all by itself], surely should be valid if it is of the same species as [the species of the other beast which accompanies it]!

E. "No, if you have stated that rule in the case of the two lambs brought for Pentecost, concerning which Scripture imposed fewer requirements in connection with bringing them, and so validated them even if they come from a single species, will you say the same of the burnt offering, in which case Scripture has imposed more requirements in connection with the offering. Therefore it should not be valid unless it [and the beast accompanying it] derive from two different species.

F. "Now the goats brought on the Day of Atonement and those brought on the New Month should prove the contrary. For Scripture has imposed on those offerings multiple requirements and yet they are valid if they all come of a single species. So they should provide a valid analogy for the burnt-offering, so that, even though it comes along with numerous requirements, it too should be valid if it [and the beasts accompanying it] come from a single species.

G. "No, if you have stated that rule concerning the goats brought on the Day of Atonement and those brought on the New Month, for even though Scripture has imposed on those offerings multiple requirements, they are not brought on every day of the year [but only on specified occasions], and therefore they all may derive from a single species. But will you say the same of the burnt-offering, for, even though it comes along with numerous requirements, it may be offered on every day of the year. Therefore it should be valid only if it is accompanied by beasts of other species.

H. "Lo, a sin-offering will prove to the contrary. For in its regard Scripture has imposed numerous requirements, and it may be offered on every day of the year, and it may come only if it is from a single species. So that should prove the rule for the burnt-offering, in which case, even though Scripture has imposed numerous requirements, and even though it is brought every day of the year, it should be valid only if it derives from a single species.

I. "No, if you have stated that rule concerning the sin-offering, on which Scripture has imposed limitations, since it may not be brought by reason of a vow or a freewill offering, and therefore it is valid only if it derives from a single species, will you say the same of the burnt-offering, which is available for a variety of purposes, since it may be brought in fulfilment of a vow or as a freewill offering? Therefore it should be valid only if it derives from a single species.

J. "Why then is it necessary for Scripture to specify, '...to the Lord from the herd or from the flock...to make a pleasing odor to the Lord,' meaning, from this species by itself or from that species by itself."

Issi's proof, No. 3, is that only Scripture can give reliable guidance as to the law. The issue again is whether the beasts for the specified offerings encompass both sheep and goats, or whether one may bring two sheep or two goats. The exercise presents the usual frustrations, since each analogy is shown to be inadequate. In consequence, argument by analogy by itself does not suffice, and only a clear exegesis of Scripture settles the question. As we see, there is no interest only in the explanation of the cited verses or even of their topic. The real issue -- the generative and precipitating intellectual program of the pericope -- lies elsewhere. It is whether or not logic alone suffices. That issue is extrinsic to the passage at hand. But it occurs throughout our document and forms one of its recurrent formal choices.

v.   Scriptural Basis for a Passage of the Mishnah

What we have is simply a citation of the verse plus a law in prior writing (Mishnah, Tosefta) which the verse is supposed to sustain. The formal traits require [1] citation of a verse, with or without comment, followed by [2] verbatim citation of a passage of the Mishnah or the Tosefta.

vi.   Miscellanies

We leave room for the possibility that we cannot classify a given composition within the available categories.

So far as I can see, then five large units of Pisqa 6 all fall within these formal compositions. Do these suffice? Are other formal patterns to be defined? To answer these questions we proceed to two further *pisqaot*, selected at random.

5. Literary Structures of Sifré to Numbers 59 and 107

Sifré to Numbers 59

LIX:I

1. A. "Now the Lord said to Moses, 'Say to Aaron and tell him, When you set up the lamps, [the seven lamps shall give light in front of the lampstand.' And Aaron did so. He set up its lamps to give light in front of the lampstand, as the Lord commanded Moses. And this was the workmanship of the lampstand, hammered work of gold; from its base to its flowers, it was hammered work; according to the pattern which the Lord had shown Moses, so he made the .lampstand]" (Num. 8:1-4):

    B. Why is this passage spelled out?

    C. Because Scripture says, "Make seven lamps for this and mount them to shed light over the space in front of it" (Ex. 25:37).

    D. On this basis should I infer that all of the lights should illumine the entire face of the candelabrum?

    E. Scripture says, "...shall give light in front of the lampstand."

    F. It is so that the lamps will converge on the candelabrum and the candelabrum on the lamps. How so? Three will go toward the east, three to the west, one in the middle, so that all of them converge on the middle one.

G. On this basis R. Nathan says, "The one in the middle is the most honored of them all."

Form II: Intrinsic-exegetical

XLIX:I

2. A. "...Say to Aaron:"
   B. Because the entire matter depends on the action of Aaron, Aaron is included in the statement to begin with.

Form II: Intrinsic-exegetical

XLIX:I

3. A. "... and tell him:"
   B. Lo, in this way Aaron is admonished.

Form II: Intrinsic-exegetical

XLIX:I

4. A. "...When you set up the lamps:"
   B. [Since the word for "set up" and the word for "steps" make use of the same root, the sense is:] make steps [for the candelabrum].

Form II: Intrinsic-exegetical

XLIX:I

5. A. "... in front of the lampstand:"
   B. Make for the candelabrum a front and an inner part.

Form II: Intrinsic-exegetical

XLIX:I

6. A. "...the seven lamps shall give light [in front of the lampstand]:"
   B. May I infer that they should give light at all times?
   C. Scripture says, "...from dusk to dawn before the Lord" (Lev. 24:3).
   D. May I infer that then the priest should put out the lamp?
   E. Scripture says, "...from dusk to dawn before the Lord continually" (Lev. 24:3).
   F. How so? The seven lamps will give light from evening to morning, "before the Lord continually."
   G. The sense is that the westernmost lamp should be kept burning continually, and from that the lamp is to be kindled at dusk.

Form II: Intrinsic-exegetical

XLIX:I

7. A. "...the seven lamps shall give light [in front of the lampstand]:"
   B. May I infer that they should give light at all times?

C. Scripture says, "...from dusk to dawn before the Lord" (Lev. 24:3).

D. May I infer that then the priest should put out the lamp?

Form II: Intrinsic-exegetical

Sifré to Numbers 107

CVII:I

1. A. "The Lord said to Moses, 'Say to the people of Israel, When you come into the land you are to inhabit']" (Num. 15:1-16):

B. R. Ishmael says, "Scripture's purpose is to indicate that the Israelites were obligated to bring drink-offerings [to accompany animal offerings] only after they had entered the land."

Form II: Intrinsic-exegetical

CVII:I

2. A. [Continuing the thesis of Ishmael:] Scripture addresses the period after the division and inheritance [settlement] of the Land.

B. You say that Scripture addresses the period after the division and settlement of the Land. But perhaps it speaks of the time immediately upon their entry into the Land [and before the division and settlement]?

C. Scripture says, "When you come into the land which the Lord your God is giving to you and have inherited it and settled in it" (Deut. 17:14).

D. Since the word "coming" is mentioned without further specification, and, further, Scripture has given you details of the meaning of the word in one of the cases in which it occurs, namely, that "coming" speaks only after actual inheritance and settlement, so here too, in all places in which the word "coming" occurs in the Torah, it speaks only of the case after the inheritance and settlement.

Form II: Intrinsic-exegetical

CVII:I

3. A. And the further fact is that every such passage refers to your dwelling *in* the land [and not outside of it].

B. Said to him R. Aqiba, "Since Scripture says, 'It is a Sabbath to the Lord in all your dwellings' (Lev. 23:3), may I draw the inference that that is both in the land and outside of the land?"

C. Said to him R. Ishmael, "It is not a necessary inference at all. Just as the most minor of religious duties pertain both outside of the land and in the land, the Sabbath, a principal religious duty, all the more so should apply in the land as well as outside of the land."

Form I: Extrinsic Exegetical
[No special interest in the terms of the cited verse at all (but this is continuous with the foregoing)]

CVII:I

4. A. Said one of the disciples of R. Ishmael, "The verse of Scripture comes to tell you that an individual was obligated to bring drink-offerings only after the entry into the land."

    B. R. Simeon b. Yohai says, "Scripture comes to tell you in regard to drink-offerings that they are to be offered on a high place [before the building of the Temple]."

    C. Abba Hanin says in the name of R. Eliezer, "Why is this statement made? It is because one might have reasoned thus: since we find that the number of garments used for the cult in the eternal house [the Temple in Jerusalem] is greater than the number of garments to be worn in the tent of meeting, so we should require more drink-offerings in the eternal house than the number of drink-offerings required in the tent of meeting.

    D. "Scripture therefore states, '...and you offer to the Lord from the herd or from the flock an offering by fire or a burnt offering or a sacrifice,' to indicate that even though the number of garments used for the cult in the eternal house [the Temple in Jerusalem] is greater than the number of garments to be worn in the tent of meeting, we not should require more drink-offerings in the eternal house than drink-offerings in the tent of meeting."

> **Form I: Extrinsic Exegetical**
> [No special interest in the terms of the cited verse at all]

CVII:II

1. A. "...and you offer to the Lord from the herd or from the flock an offering by fire [or a *burnt offering* or a *sacrifice*, to fulfil a vow or as a freewill offering, or at your appointed feasts]:"

    B. May I infer that whatever is offered as an offering by fire requires a drink offering?

    C. Scripture refers specifically to a burnt-offering.

    D. I know only that that is the case of a *burnt offering*.

    E. How do I know that the same rule applies to peace-offerings?

    F. Scripture alludes to a *sacrifice*.

    G. How about a thankoffering?

    H. Scripture refers to a sacrifice.

    I. Is the implication that one bring drink-offerings with these and likewise with a sin-offering or a guilt offering?

    J. Scripture states, "...to fulfil a vow or as a freewill offering:" I have therefore encompassed within the rule [that drink offerings are required] only Holy Things that are brought on account of a vow or a freewill offering.

    K. Then the inference is that I exclude these [a sin-offering or a guilt offering, which do not require drink offerings], but then I should further exclude a burnt-offering brought in fulfilment of an obligation on the pilgrim festivals [since that would be excluded by the rule that what is brought on one's own option requires the drink-offerings].

L. When Scripture makes explicit reference to "at your appointed feasts," Scripture encompasses the obligatory burnt-offering brought on festivals. [That sort of offering requires drink-offerings as well.]

M. Then the inference is that one encompasses in the requirement of bringing drink offerings a burnt offering brought as a matter of obligation on pilgrim festivals and likewise a sin-offering that also is brought as a matter of obligations on festivals.

N. Scripture says, "... you offer to the Lord from the herd or from the flock." An animal "from the herd" was encompassed by the general rule but singled out from the general rule to teach you a trait of the encompassing rule itself.

O. That is, specifically, just as an animal of the herd is brought on account of a vow or as a freewill offering and requires drink offerings, so whatever is brought on account of a vow or as a freewill offering requires drink-offerings.

P. Then a sin-offering and a guilt offering are excluded, for these do not come on account of keeping a vow or as a thank-thank-offering [but only when the obligation is imposed on account of an inadvertent violation of the law], and so these do not require drink-offerings.

Form III: Dialectical Exegesis: Intrinsic

This is a masterpiece of dialectical exegesis, in which a single line of thought is spun out through a variety of possibilities. The exegesis is moving, as it progresses from point to point, but remarkably cogent. I cannot imagine how a more uniform composition can have been written. At every point each issue is addressed to the base-verse, and every conceivable problem of analogical logic has been worked out. And the base verse is always in focus.

CVII:III

1. A. "'...from the herd or from the flock an offering by fire or a burnt offering or a sacrifice, to fulfil a vow or as a freewill offering, or at your appointed feasts, to make a pleasing odor to the Lord:'

B. "Why is this stated?

C. "Since it is said, '... and you offer to the Lord from the herd or from the flock an offering by fire or a burnt offering or a sacrifice,' I might infer that the same rule applies to a burnt-offering brought of fowl, namely, that drink-offerings should be required.

D. "Scripture specifies, '...from the herd or from the flock,' to indicate that burnt-offerings of fowl do not require drink offerings," the words of R. Josiah.

E. R. Jonathan says, "Such an argument is not required. For in any case it is said, '...or a sacrifice.' Just as a sacrifice always derives from a beast, so a burnt offering under discussion here involves a beast [and not fowl, so drink offerings are not required for fowl].

F. "Why then does Scripture say, "...from the herd or from the flock an offering by fire or a burnt offering or a sacrifice, to fulfil a vow or as a freewill offering, or at your appointed feasts, to make a pleasing odor to the Lord'?

G. "Because Scripture says, 'and you offer to the Lord from the herd or from the flock an offering by fire.'

H. "The point is, if someone has said, 'Lo, incumbent on me is a burnt offering and peace offerings,' should I infer that he should bring the two of them simultaneously [of the same species]?

I. "Scripture says, '...from the herd or from the flock,' to indicate that one brings a beast of this species by itself and one of that species by itself."

Form II: Intrinsic Exegetical

CVII:III

2. A. On the basis of the present passage, furthermore, you may derive the rule governing the animal to be designated as a Passover offering.

B. Since Scripture says, "Your lamb shall be without blemish, a male a year old; you shall take it from the sheep or from the goats" (Ex. 12:5), the meaning is, from this species by itself or from that species by itself.

C. You say that one should take a beast from this species by itself or from that species by itself.

D. Or perhaps one may bring from both species simultaneously?

E. Scripture says, "If his gift for a burnt offering is from the flock, from the sheep or goats, he shall offer a male without blemish" (Lev. 1:10).

F. Now that statement produces an argument *a fortiori*: if a burnt offering, which is a weighty matter, is suitable if it derives from a single species, a Passover, which is a lighter-weight offering, all the more so that it should be valid if it come from one species. Then why does Scripture say, "...you shall take it from the sheep or from the goats"? To indicate, from this species by itself or from that species by itself.

Form I: Extrinsic Exegetical

CVII:III

3. A. [Given above.]

Form IV: Dialectical Exegesis
Fallacy of Logic

No. 3, proves that only Scripture can give reliable guidance as to the law. Each analogy is shown to be inadequate. In consequence, argument by analogy by itself does not suffice, and only a clear exegesis of Scripture settles the question.

CVII:IV

1. A. "...then [the one who brings the offering] shall offer:" (Num. 15:1-16):

B. I know only that a man is subject to the rule. How do I know that the woman also is required [to bring drink offerings]?

C. Scripture says, "*The one who brings* the offering" -- encompassing all cases.

Form II: Intrinsic Exegetical

CVII:IV

2. A. "...then the one who brings the offering] shall offer:" (Num. 15:1-16):

    B. R. Nathan says, "This passage forms the generative analogy for all cases in which one voluntarily brings a meal-offering, that he should bring no less than a tenth ephah of fine flour and a log of oil."

Form II: Intrinsic Exegetical

CVII:IV

3. A. "...then he who brings his offering shall offer to the Lord a cereal offering of a tenth of an ephah of fine flour, mixed with a fourth of a hin of oil, and wine for the drink offering, a fourth of a hin:"

    B. The oil is for stirring and the wine for a drink offering.

Form II: Intrinsic Exegetical

CVII:V

1. A. "...[then he who brings his offering shall offer to the Lord a cereal offering of a tenth of an ephah of fine flour, mixed with a fourth of a hin of oil, and wine for the drink offering, a fourth of a hin,] you shall prepare with the burnt offering, or for the sacrifice, for each lamb:" (Num. 15:1-16):

    B. Why is the statement made, [that is, "...you shall prepare with the burnt offering, or for the sacrifice, for each lamb"]?

    C. Since Scripture says, "...you offer to the Lord from the herd or from the flock an offering by fire or a burnt offering or a sacrifice," if then someone has said, "Lo, incumbent on me is a burnt offering, lo, incumbent on me are peace-offerings," might I infer that one may bring a single drink-offering to cover both pledges?

    D. Scripture states, "...you shall prepare with the burnt offering, or for the sacrifice, for each lamb" so as to indicate that one brings drink offerings for this beast by itself and for that beast by itself. [The partitive language of Scripture is explicit that a burnt offering or a sacrifice requires individual drink offerings.]

Form II: Intrinsic Exegetical

    E. Abba Hanin says in the name of R. Eliezer, "The contrary rule might have appeared logical: if in a case in which the rites required for an offering are the same, namely, the rites for offering an ox as a burnt offering and the rites required for a lamb as a burnt offering [since both are subject to the same rule, that is, the rule governing the burnt offering], the two offerings are not equivalent as to the requirement of drink offerings, in a case in which the rites required for the one are *not* the same as the rites required for the other, namely, the rites of a lamb offered as a burnt offering as compared to the rites required of the lamb as peace-offerings [the burnt offering is wholly consumed by the altar fire, the peace offering yields meat for the priest and the *sacrifier* and his family], is it not reasonable to suppose that the rule regarding drink offerings should not be the same? [In fact, the rule *is* the same, so logic would have misled us.]

F.   "On that account Scripture says, '...you shall prepare with the burnt offering, or for the sacrifice,' to indicate that even though the rites required for the lamb offered as a burnt offerings are not the same as the rites required for a lamb when offered as peace offerings, nonetheless they are equivalent as to the requirement of drink offerings."

Form IV: Dialectical Exegesis
Fallacy of Logic

CVII:V

2. A.   R. Nathan says, "'...you shall prepare with the burnt offering,' refers to the burnt offering brought by the leper. '...for the sacrifice,' refers to the sin-offering brought by him. '...*or* for the sacrifice' then encompasses his guilt offering."

B.   R. Jonathan says, "'...for each lamb,' encompasses the burnt offering brought by a woman after childbirth, who has to bring drink offerings, a rule which we have not derived anywhere else in the entire Torah.

C.   "Or perhaps it speaks only of the ram?

D.   "When Scripture says, '... for a ram you shall prepare for a cereal offering two tenths of an ephah of fine flour mixed with a third of a hin of oil; *and for the drink offering* you shall offer a third of a hin of wine,' lo, reference is made to the ram. So how shall I interpret the statement, "...for each lamb'? It is to encompass the burnt offering brought by a woman after childbirth, who has to bring drink offerings, a rule which we have not derived anywhere else in the entire Torah."

E.   Another matter: "...for each lamb" encompasses the eleventh lamb produced in the tithing of the flock.

Form II: Intrinsic Exegetical

CVII:VI

1. A.   "...for a ram you shall prepare for a cereal offering:"

B.   The purpose of Scripture is to distinguish the drink offerings of a lamb from the drink offerings of a ram. [There is a different rule for each classification of animal.]

C.   For one might have reasoned to the contrary: an animal taken from the herd requires drink offerings, and an animal taken from the flock requires drink offerings. If therefore I draw an analogy to the animal taken from the herd, in which case the Torah has not distinguished the drink offerings brought for a calf from those brought for a full-grown ox, so the law should not distinguish the drink offerings brought for a lamb from the drink offerings brought for a ram. [They should be the same in all cases.]

D. So Scripture states, "...for a ram you shall prepare for a cereal offering:"

E. The purpose of Scripture is to distinguish the drink offerings of a lamb from the drink offerings of a ram. [Even though such a distinction does not cover the calf and the ox, it does cover the lamb and the ram.]

Form IV: Dialectical Exegesis
Fallacy of Logic

CVII:VI

2. A. Abba Hanin says in the name of R. Eliezer, "Why is this statement made? It is because reason would have led me to a different conclusion.

B. "Specifically: if in a case in which Scripture required many drink offerings, Scripture did not distinguish among the drink offerings required for a calf from those required for an ox, in a case in which Scripture did not demand many drink offerings, is it not reasonable that we should not require more for a ram than a lamb?

C. "Scripture says, '....for a ram you shall prepare for a cereal offering.' Scripture thus makes the point that even though Scripture has diminished the number of drink offerings that are required, it has made an increase whether for a lamb or for a ram."

D. Another matter: "....for a ram you shall prepare for a cereal offering:" Scripture thereby encompasses a ram brought as a burnt offering, etc. [*sic!*].

Form IV: Dialectical Exegesis
Fallacy of Logic

CVII:VII

1. A. "...[for a ram] you shall prepare for a cereal offering two tenths of an ephah of fine flour [mixed with a third of a hin of oil; and for the drink offering you shall offer a third of a hin of wine, a pleasing odor to the Lord]:

B. Why is this statement made?

C. Since logic would have led to the contrary conclusion: since the lamb brought with the sheaf of first grain requires two tenths of fine flour, and the ram that is brought as a burnt offering requires two tenths of fine flour, if I draw an analogy to the lamb that is brought with the sheaf of first grain, in which case even though the number of tenths is doubled, the number of drink offerings is not doubled, so in the case of the ram brought as a burnt offering, even though the law has required double the number of tenths, we should not double the number of drink offerings.

D. Scripture thus says, "...for a ram you shall prepare for a cereal offering two tenths of an ephah of fine flour mixed with a third of a hin of oil; and for the drink offering you shall offer a third of a hin of wine," so informing us that just as the Torah has doubled the number of tenths to be brought with it, so it has doubled the volume of drink offerings.

Form IV: Dialectical Exegesis
Fallacy of Logic

CVII:VII

2. A. "...and for the drink offering you shall offer a third of a hin of wine:"
   B. Oil for mixing with the flour, wine for mixing a drink-offering.

Form II: Intrinsic Exegesis

CVII:VII

3. A. "...a pleasing odor to the Lord:"
   B. "It is a source of pleasure for me, for I have spoken and my will has been done."

Form II: Intrinsic Exegesis

CVII:VII

4. A. "And when you prepare a bull for a burnt offering [or for a sacrifice, to fulfil a vow or for peace offerings to the Lord, then one shall offer with the bull a cereal offering of three tenths of an ephah of fine flour, mixed with half a hin of oil, and you shall offer for the drink offering half a hin of wine, as an offering by fire, a pleasing odor to the Lord]:"
   B. The bull as a burnt offering was covered by the foregoing general statements. Why then has it been singled out? It is to teach a rule governing the encompassing law, specifically:
   C. just as a bull may be brought in fulfillment of a vow or as a freewill offering and requires drink offerings, so whatever is brought in fulfillment of a vow or as a freewill offering requires drink offerings.
   D. Excluded are the sin-offering and the guilt-offering, which are not brought merely in fulfillment of a vow or as a freewill offering and which do not require drink offerings.

Form II: Intrinsic Exegesis

CVII:VIII

1. A. "[And when you prepare a bull] for a burnt offering or for a sacrifice [to fulfil a vow or for peace offerings to the Lord, then one shall offer with the bull a cereal offering of three tenths of an ephah of fine flour, mixed with half a hin of oil, and you shall offer for the drink offering half a hin of wine, as an offering by fire, a pleasing odor to the Lord]:"
   B. Why is this statement made?
   C. Because it is said, " as an offering by fire," if one has said, "Lo, incumbent on me is a burnt offering, lo, incumbent on me are burnt offerings as peace offerings," I might infer that he may bring a single drink offering for both of them.
   D. Scripture says, "...for a burnt offering or for a sacrifice," so indicating that one brings drink offerings for this one by itself and for that one by itself.
   E. Might one then maintain that even if one has said, "Lo, incumbent on me are five oxen for a burnt offering, five oxen for peace-offerings," that he may bring a single drink offering for all of them?

F. Scripture says, "for a burnt offering or for a sacrifice," so indicating that one brings drink offerings for each one by itself.

Form II: Intrinsic Exegesis

CVII:VIII

2. A. Abba Hanin in the name of R. Eliezer says, "Why is this statement made?

    B. "For reason might have produced an error, namely:

    C. "if in a case in which the rites of a lamb brought as a burnt offering are the same as the rites of an ox brought as peace offerings, is it not reasonable that the drink offerings should not be the same?

    D. "Scripture therefore says, '...for a burnt offering or for a sacrifice,' indicating that even though the rites of an ox brought as a burnt offering are not the same as the rites of an ox brought as peace offerings, they are the same as to drink offerings."

Form IV: Dialectical Exegesis
Fallacy of Logic

CVII:IX

1. A. "[And when you prepare a bull for a burnt offering or for a sacrifice, to fulfil a vow or for peace offerings to the Lord,] then one shall offer with the bull a cereal offering of three tenths of an ephah of fine flour, mixed with half a hin of oil, and you shall offer for the drink offering half a hin of wine, as an offering by fire, a pleasing odor to the Lord:"

    B. The oil is for mixing with the flour, and the wine for a mixing drink offering.

Form II: Intrinsic Exegesis

CVII:IX

2. A. "...as an offering by fire, a pleasing odor to the Lord:"

    B. It is offered on grills.

    C. You say that the offering by fire is placed on grills. But perhaps it is placed directly on the flames?

    D. If you make that rule, you will turn out to put the bonfire out, while the Torah has said, "A perpetual fire will be lit on the altar, it shall not go out" (Lev. 6:6).

    E. Lo, how shall I interpret the statement of the Torah, "...as an offering by fire, a pleasing odor to the Lord"?

    F. It is to be placed on grills.

Form II: Dialectical Exegesis, Intrinsic

CVII:IX

3. A. "...as an offering by fire, a pleasing odor to the Lord:"

B.   "It is a pleasure to me that I spoke and my will was carried out."

Form II: Intrinsic Exegesis

CVII:X

1. A.   "Thus it shall be done for *each* bull or ram or for *each* of the male lambs or the kids, according to the number that you prepare, so shall you do with every one according to their number:"

   B.   Scripture thus stresses that there is no difference between the drink offerings brought for a calf and the drink offerings brought for an ox.

   C.   For one might have reasoned wrongly, as follows: the animal drawn from the flock requires drink offerings, and so does one drawn from the herd. If I draw an analogy, in that the Torah has made a distinction between the drink offerings required of a lamb and those required of a ram, so I should draw a distinction between the drink offerings required for a calf and those required for an ox.

   D.   So the Torah specifies to the contrary: "Thus it shall be done for each bull [or ram or for each of the male lambs or the kids]," indicating that the Torah has made no distinction between the drink offerings brought for a calf and those brought for an ox.

Form II: Intrinsic Exegesis

CVII:X

2. A.   Abba Hanin in the name of R. Eliezer says, "Why is this statement made? Because logic would have made us err, specifically, in a case in which the law has diminished the number of drink offerings, it has demanded more for a ram than a lamb, in a case in which the law has demanded many drink offerings, is it not reasonable that the law should require more for an ox than a calf?

   B.   "So the Torah specifies to the contrary: 'Thus it shall be done for each bull [or ram or for each of the male lambs or the kids],' indicating that the Torah has made not demanded more drink offerings for an ox than those to be brought for a calf."

Form IV: Dialectical Exegesis
Fallacy of Logic

CVII:XI

1. A.   "[Thus it shall be done for] each bull or ram [or for each of the male lambs or the kids, according to the number that you prepare, so shall you do with every one according to their number. All who are native shall do these things in this way, in offering an offering by fire, a pleasing odor to the Lord]:"

   B.   Why is this point stressed?

   C.   It is because logic would have suggested otherwise: since we find that the Torah has made a distinction between the drink offerings required of a one year old beast and those to be brought for a two year old beast, so the Torah should distinguish the drink offerings brought for a two year old beast from those brought for a three year old.

D. Scripture says, "...or for each ram," indicating that even though the Torah has distinguished the drink offerings brought for a one year old beast from those for a two year old, the Torah does not distinguish those brought for a two year old from those brought for a three year old.

Form IV: Dialectical Exegesis
Fallacy of Logic

CVII:XI

2. A. "...or for each of the male lambs or the kids:"

B. Why is this stated?

C. It is because logic would have suggested otherwise: since we find that the Torah has made a distinction between the drink offerings required of lamb from those required of a ram, so the Torah should distinguish between the drink offerings brought for a female lamb from those brought for a sheep.

D. So Scripture states, ""...or for each of the male lambs or the kids."

Form IV: Dialectical Exegesis
Fallacy of Logic

CVII:XII

1. A. "...according to the number that you prepare, so shall you do with every one according to their number:"

B. I know only that the law covers those listed. How do I know that the law covers beasts that are declared to be substitutes for the beasts at hand?

C. Scripture says, "...according to the number that you prepare."

Form II: Intrinsic Exegesis

CVII:XII

2. A. "'...according to the number that you prepare:'

B. "This means that one may not give less.

C. "But is it the law that if one wants to give more, he may do so?

D. "Scripture says, '...so shall you do with every one according to their number,'" the words of R. Josiah.

E. R. Jonathan says, "Such a proof is not required. For lo, in any event it is said, 'All who are native shall do these things in this way.'"

Form II: Intrinsic Exegesis

CVII:XII

3. A. "All who are native shall do these things:"

B. This means that one may not give less.

C. But is it the law that if one wants to give more, he may do so?

D. Scripture says, "according to their number."

E. Or if one wants to give double, may he give double?

F. Scripture says, "so shall you do with every one" -- in accord with the number applying to each of them.

G. On this basis sages have ruled:

H. **The priests may mix together [and offer as one] the drink offerings brought with oxen with those brought with other oxen, the ones brought with rams with those brought with other rams, those brought with lambs with those brought with other lambs, those brought with brought by an individual and those brought with an animal offered by the community, those brought on a given day with those brought on the preceding day. But they may not mix the drink offerings brought with lambs and those brought with oxen or those brought with rams [M. Men. 9:4].**

I. They have further ruled:

K. **He who says, "Lo, incumbent on me is a gift of wine," a log of wine he may not bring, two he may not bring, three he may bring. If he said four, five he may not bring, six he may bring. From that point, he may bring [any volume]. Just as the community brings wine as a matter of obligation, so an individual is permitted to make a voluntary gift of wine. [M. Men. 12:4J: They do not volunteer as a freewill offering a single log of wine, two or five. But they volunteer as a freewill offering three, four, or six, and any number more than six.].**

L. "...so shall you do with every one:" this serves to encompass the eleventh [beast designated as tithe of the flock].

A-F = Form II: Intrinsic Exegesis

G-L = Form V: Scriptural Basis for a Passage of the Mishnah

CVII:XIII

1. A. "All who are native shall do these things in this way:"

    B. Why is this said?

    C. Since it is said, "If its testicles have been crushed or bruised, torn or cut, you shall not present it to the Lord...You shall not procure any such creature from a foreigner and present it is food for your God. [Their deformity is inherent in them, a permanent defect, and they will not be acceptable on your behalf]" (Lev. 22:25),

    D. [one might have argued:] *these* you shall not acquire from them, but you may acquire from them unblemished beasts.

    E. Now that I have learned that a gentile may offer a burnt-offering, I have grounds to propose a logical argument as at the outset:

    F. An Israelite brings a burnt-offering, and a gentile brings a burnt-offering. Then just as an Israelite brings drink offerings, so does a gentile bring drink offerings?

    G. Scripture says, "All who are native shall do these things in this way," meaning, "These things does an Israelite do, bringing drink offerings, but a gentile does not bring drink offerings."

H.   Might one maintain then that his burnt offering should not require drink offerings at all?

I.   Scripture says, "In this way," meaning, as sages have ruled: If a gentile sent a burnt offering from overseas and did not send the cost of drink offerings with it, the drink offerings are to derive from community funds.

Form III: Dialectical Exegesis, Intrinsic

Our survey of the two *pisqaot* has produced no forms that fall outside of our original classification system, except as specified at the outset. We may now proceed to our broader survey.

We may rapidly observe that no fixed order seems to govern the use of the several forms. While it is common to commence, "Why has this statement been made," with the answer a broad-based inquiry into the relationship among a number of passages that deal with the same topic, no rule emerges. So if the document before us is cogent, the cogency must derive wholly from the resort to a fixed and limited number of formal compositions, and not from the fixed and disciplined arrangement of types of those formal compositions. I see no counterpart to the fixed rule, in Leviticus Rabbah, and Genesis Rabbah, that one type of form nearly always comes first, another type nearly always comes last. By way of compensation, as we shall see shortly, the forms of Sifré to Numbers bear a clear statement of their own, while the forms of Leviticus Rabbah and Genesis Rabbah do not speak, through their arrangement of words, a specific message.

6. The Forms of Sifré to Numbers 1-115

We have found that five forms encompass all of the literary structures of the three *pisqaot* we have reviewed. Now that we have clarified the formal repertoire of a sample of our document, let us proceed to test our hypothesis that the framers resort to a limited repertoire of exegetical forms. Our task is to review all 115 *pisqaot* translated in these two volumes and to classify them as to their formal traits. We shall differentiate somewhat within the five classifications of forms, for reasons that become obvious. Our classifications should not homogenize essentially distinct formal traits, and, so far as I can, I highlight the diverse species of a given formal genus.

The catalogues begin with an example of the form at hand and proceed to list all exempla.

I.   Extrinsic Exegetical Form

The form consists of the citation of an opening verse, followed by an issue stated in terms extrinsic to the cited verse. That is to say, no word or phrase of the base verse (that is, the cited verse at the beginning) attracts comment. Rather a general rule of exegesis is invoked. C then introduces a broad range of items not at all subject to attention in the verse at hand. The formal traits: [1] citation of a base verse from Numbers, [2] a generalization ignoring clauses or words in the base verse, [3] a further observation without clear interest in the verse at hand. But the whole is linked to the theme of the base verse -- and to that alone. So an extrinsic exegetical program comes to bear. We shall call this the extrinsic exegetical form. The types of this form are specified as the exercise unfolds.

Form C: Syllogistic argument on the meaning of words or phrases, in which the base verse of Numbers occurs as one among a set of diverse items.

I.III

1. A. R. Judah b. Beterah says, "The effect of a commandment stated in any context serves only [1] to lend encouragement.

   B. "For it is said, 'But command Joshua and encourage and strengthen him' (Deut. 3:28).

   C. "Accordingly, we derive the lesson that strength is granted only to the strong, and encouragement only to the stout of heart."

   D. R. Simeon b. Yohai says, "The purpose of a commandment in any context is only [2] to deal with the expenditure of money, as it is said, 'Command the children of Israel to bring you pure oil from beaten olives for the lamp, that a light may be kept burning continually outside the veil of the testimony in the tent of meeting, Aaron shall keep it in order from evening to morning before the Lord continually; it shall be a statute for ever throughout your generations' (Lev. 24:2). 'Command the people of Israel that they put out of the camp every leper and every one having a discharge, and every one that is unclean through contact with the dead' (Num. 5:1-2). 'Command the children of Israel that they give to the Levites from the inheritance of their possession cities to dwell in, and you shall give to the Levites pasture lands round about the cities' (Num. 35:2). 'Command the people of Israel and say to them, "My offering, my food for my offerings by fire, my pleasing odor you shall take heed to offer to me in its due season"' (Num. 28:2). Lo, we see in all these cases that the purpose of a commandment is solely to bring about the expenditure of money.

   E. "There is one exception, and what is that? It is this verse: 'Command the people of Israel and say to them, "When you enter the land of Canaan, this is the land that shall fall to you for an inheritance, the land of Canaan in its full extent"' (Num. 34:2).

   F. "You must give encouragement to them in the matter of the correct division of the land."

   G. And Rabbi [Judah the Patriarch] says, "The use of the word, 'commandment' in all passages serves only for the purpose of [3] imparting an admonition [not to do a given action], along the lines of the following: 'And the Lord God commanded the man, saying, "You may freely eat of every tree of the garden, but of the tree of the knowledge of good and evil you shall not eat"' (Gen. 2:16)."

I:III.1	I:X.1-3	II:I.2	II:IV.1	VII:V.1
VIII:VIII.1	XVII:III.1	XVIII:I.1	XVIII:II.1	XXIII:II.1-2
XXIII:III.1	XXXII:1.3	XXXIX:1.1	XXXIX:II.1	XLII:I.1
XLII:II.1-9	XLII:II.1-3	XLIV:I.2	XLVI:II.1	LVIII:I.2
LXI:I.1	LXVII:I.1	LXIX:IV.1	LXXIII:II.1-3	LXXVII:I.1
LXXXIII:I.1	LXXXIV:IV.1	LXXXV:I.1	LXXXV:III.1	LXXXVI.III.1
LXXXVIII:II.1	XCII:II.1	XCII:IV.1	XCIV:I.1	XCIX:I.1-2
XCIX:III.2	CII:III.1	CV:V.2	CVII:I.3	CXII:IV.1-6

II. Intrinsic Exegetical Form

The verse itself is clarified. In the first instance, the exegesis derives from the contrast with another verse that makes the same point. But the formal trait should not be missed. It is that the the focus is on the base verse and not on a broader issue. We may call this an intrinsic exegetical form, in that the focus of exegesis is on the verse, which is cited and carefully spelled out. We shall know that we have it when the base verse is cited, clause by clause or in other ways, and then given an ample dose of attention. Since the present category presents numerous variations, we shall subdivide as we go along. The key-words of the species of the genus at hand will supply the basis for differentiation, as will be clear throughout.

Simple Examples

[Verse plus a simple declarative sentence that states the meaning]

I:XI.1-2	III:III.1	IV:I.1	IV:I.2	IV:III.1
V:I.3	I:I.1	VII:II.1	VII:IV.1	VII:V.2
VII:VII.1	VII:VIII.1	VII:XIII.1	VIII:III.1	VIII:VII.1
X:I.1	X:II.2	X:V.1	XI:I.1	XI:II.1
XI:II.2	XI:IV.1	XI:IV.2	XII:III.1	XIII:I.1-2
XIV:11.2	·XVI:1.1	XVI:III.2	XVIII:I.3	XVII:V.1
XVII:VI.1	XIX:II.1-2	XIX:III.2-3	XX:I.1	XXI:II.1
XXI:III.1	XXII:VI.1	XXIII:III.2	XXV:V.1-4	XXVI.I.1
XXVI:III.2.3	XXVIII:VI.1	XXX:II.1	XXXII:I.1-2	XXXII:I.1
XXXV:I.4-5	XXXVI:I.1-4	XXXVII:I.1-3	XXXVII:II.1	XXXVIII:I.1
XXXVIII:II.1	XXXIX:VI.1-2	XL:I.1-10	XLI.I.1-2	XLI:II.1-5
XLIII:II.2-3	XLIV:I.1	XLIV:II.1-3	LXV:I.1-2	XLV:II.1-4
XLVI:I.1-2	XLVI:II.2	LXVII:I.1	XLVII:2.1	XLVII:I.1-2
L:I.1	LI:I.1-2	LI:II.1-3	LI:III.1	LII:1-2

LIII:I.2-3	LV:I.1-2	LVI:I.2	LVIII:I.2-3	LVIII:II.1-2
LIX:I.2-6	LX:I.1-2	LXI:I.2-3	LXI:I.5	LXII:I.2
LXIII:I.1	LXIII:II.1	LXV:II.2	LXVII:II.1	LXVIII:I.1
LXVIII:II.1	LXVIII:III.1	LXVIII:IV.1	LXVIII:V.1-3	LXIX:I.1
LXIX:II.1	LXIX:IV.2	LXIX:V.1	LXX:I.1-4	LXX:II.2
LXX:III.1	LXXI:I.1	LXXI:II.1	LXXII:II.1-2	LXXII:III.1-4
LXXV:III.2	LXXVI:I.1	LXXVI:II.2-4	LXXVIII:I.1-3	LXXVII:IV.2
LXXVIII:I.2	LXVIII:II.1	LXXVIII:III.1	LXXVIII:IV.1	LXXVIII:V.1
LXXIX:I.1	LXXX:I.1	LXXX:I.1	LXXX:I.2	LXXX:II.1-3
LXXXI:I.1	LXXXII.I.1	LXXXII:II.1-2	LXXXII:II.1	LXXXIV:II.1
LXXXIV:III.1	LXXXIV:IV.2	LXXXIV:V.1-2	LXXXV:II.1	LXXXV:IV.1
LXXXV:V.1-2	LXXXVI:I.1	LXXXVI:II.1	LXXXVI:IV.1	LXXXVI:V.1
LXXXVI:VI.1	LXXXVII:I.1	LXXXVII:II.1	LXXXVIII:I.1	LXXXIX:I.1
LXXXIV:I.2	LXXXIX:II.1	LXXXIX:III.1	LXXXIX:IV.1-2	LXXXIX:V.1
LXXXIX:V:2	XC:I.1	XC:II.1	XC:III.1	XC:III.1
XC:IV.1	XCI:I.1	XCI:II.1	XCI:III.1	XCII:III.1-2
XCII:v.1-2	XCII:VI.1	SCII:VII.1	XCII:VIII.1	XCIII:I.1-3
XCIV:II.1-2	XCIV:III.1	SCV:I.1-2	XCV:II.1-2	XCVI:I.1
XCVI:II.1	XCVI:III.1	XCVI:IV.1	XCVII:I.1-3	XCVII:II.1
XCVIII:I.1	XCVIII:II.1-2	XCVIII:III.1	XCVIII:IV.1	XCVIII:V.1
XCIX:II.1-2	XCIX:III.1	C:I.1-2	CI:I.2	CII:I.1-2
CIII:I.1	CIII:II.1	CIII:III.1-2	CIII:VI.1	CIV:I.1
CV:I.1-3	CV:III.1	CV:III.1	CV:III.2-3	CV:IV:1
CV:V.1	CV:VI.1	CVI:I.1	CVI:II.3	CVI:III.2
CVII:IV.1-3	CVII:V.2	CVII:VII.2-4	CVII:IX.I.3	CVII:XI.2
CVII:XII.1	CVIII:I.1	CIX:I.1-2	CIX:I.5	CX:I.1
CXI.II.1	CXI:II.3	CXI:III.1-2	CXI:IV.2	CXI:V.1-2
CXII.I.3-5,8	CXII:II.4	CXII:III.1-5	CXIII:I.1	CXIII:I.3-4
CXIII:1.6	CXIV:I.1-4,6	CXV:I.1	CXV:II.2	CXV:II.4-8
CXV:III.2	CXV:IV.1-5	CXV:V.1	CXV:V.3,4	CXV:V.6

Form A: Explaining the Purpose of a Passage

Citation of base verse plus "For what purpose is this passage presented?"

I:I

1. A. "The Lord said to Moses, 'Command the people of Israel that they put out of the camp [every leper and every one having a discharge, and every one that is unclean through contact with the dead]'" (Num. 5:1-2).

    B. For what purpose is this passage presented?

    C. Because it is said, "But the man who is unclean and does not cleanse himself, [that person shall be cut off from the midst of the assembly, since he has defiled the sanctuary of the Lord, because the water for impurity has not been thrown upon him, he is unclean]" (Num. 19:20).

    D. Consequently, we are informed of the penalty [for contaminating the sanctuary]. But where are we informed of the admonition not to do so?

    E. Scripture accordingly states, "Command the people of Israel that they put out of the camp every leper and every one having a discharge, and every one that is unclean through contact with the dead" (Num. 5:1-2).

    F. Lo, here is an admonition that unclean persons not come into the sanctuary ["out of the camp"] in a state of uncleanness. [Consequently, the entire transaction -- admonition, then penalty -- is laid forth.]

I:XI.1-2	III:III.1	IV:I.1	IV:I.2	IV:III.1
V:I.3	CI:I.1	VII:II.1	VII:IV.1	VII:V.2
VII:VII.1	VII:VIII.1	VII:XIII.1	VIII:III.1	VIII:VII.1
XXIV:II.1	XXI:I.1	XXII:I.1	XXIII:I.2	XXIII:V.1
XXIII:VI.1	XXIV:V.1	XXV:IV.1	XXV:V.1	XXV:VI.1
XXV:VII.1	XXV:IX.1	XXVII:I.1	XLII:I.1	XLIII:II.1
LII:I.1	LIV:I.1	LVI:I.	LVII:I.1	[LVIII:I.1]
LIX:I.1	LXI:I.4	LXV:I.1	LXV:II.1	LXVI:I.1-2
LXXII:I.1	LXXIV:I.1	LXXV:I.1	LXXV:III.1	LXXVII:III.1
LXXVII:III.1	LXXVII:IV.1	LXXXII.III.1	XCIII:I.1	XCIII:I.4
XCIX:IV.1	CIII:IV.2	XVII:I.1	CVII:I.4	CVII:III.1
CVII:III.3	CVII:V.1	CVII:VIII.1	CVII:XI.1-2	[CVII:XIII.1]
CVIII:I.3	CIX:I.3-4	CX:IV.1	CX:IV.3	CX:VIII.1
CXI:II.2	CXI:II.4	CXII:II.1-2	CXIII:I.5	CXV:II.1,3
CXV:V.5				

Form B: The Passage Means X, but How about Possibility Y?

Here we have the citation of a word or clause in the base verse, followed by a declarative sentence explaining the purpose and meaning of the cited passage. Then we ask, "You say this, but perhaps it means that." Then we proceed to justify the original statement. This is a fine example of the dialectical exegesis of an intrinsic character.

I:II

1. A. "Command" (Num. 5:2):

    B. The commandment at hand is meant both to be put into effect immediately and also to apply for generations to come.

    C. You maintain that the commandment at hand is meant both to be put into effect immediately and also to apply for generations to come.

    D. But perhaps the commandment is meant to apply only after a time [but not right away, at the moment at which it was given].

    E. [We shall now prove that the formulation encompasses both generations to come and also the generation to whom the commandment is entrusted.] Scripture states, "The Lord said to Moses, 'Command the people of Israel that they put out [of the camp every leper and every one having a discharge, and every one that is unclean through contact with the dead. You shall put out both male and female, putting them outside the camp, that they may not defile their camp, in the midst of which I dwell.'] And the people of Israel did so and drove them outside the camp, as the Lord said to Moses, *so the people of Israel did*" (Gen. 5:1-4). [The verse itself makes explicit the fact that the requirement applied forthwith, not only later on.]

    F. Lo, we have learned that the commandment at hand is meant to be put into effect immediately.

    G. How then do we derive from Scripture the fact that it applies also for generations to come? [We shall now show that the same word used here, *command*, pertains to generations to come and not only to the generation at hand.]

    H. Scripture states, "Command the children of Israel to bring you pure oil from beaten olives [for the .lamp, that a light may be kept burning continually outside the veil of the testimony in the tent of meeting, Aaron shall keep it in order from evening to morning before the Lord continually; it shall be a statute for ever throughout your generations]" (Lev. 24:2).

    I. Lo, we here derive evidence that the commandment at hand is meant both to be put into effect immediately and also to apply for generations to come, [based on the framing of the present commandment].

    J. How, then, do we drive evidence that all of the commandments that are contained in the Torah [apply in the same way]? [We wish now to prove that the language, *command*, always bears the meaning imputed to it here.]

    K. R. Ishmael maintained, "Since the bulk of the commandments stated in the Torah are presented without further amplification, while in the case of one of them [namely, the one at hand], Scripture has given explicit details, that commandment [that has been singled out] is meant both to be put into effect immediately and also to apply for generations to come. Accordingly, I apply to all of the other commandments in the Torah the same detail, so that in all cases the commandment is meant both to be put into effect immediately and also to apply for generations to come."

I:II.1	I:VI.1-2	I:VII.1-2	II:VI.1	IV:I.3
IV:II.1	IV:IV.1	VII:IX.1	VII:XI.1	XV:I.1
XXII:IV.1	XXII:V.1	XXII:VI.1	XXIII:VII.1	XXV:III.1
XXVII.II.1	XXVIII:V.1	XXXV:I.1-3	XXXIX:III.1	XXXIX:IV.1
XXXIX:V.1	XXXIX:VII.1	LIII:I.1	LXIX:V.2	LXX:II.1
LXXVI:II.1	LXXVII:II.1	CI:I.1	CIII:IV.1	CIII:V.1
CVII:I.2	CVII:III.2	CVIII:IX.2	CVII:XII.2-3	CVIII:I.2
CX:IV.2	CXI:I.2	CXII:I.2	CXIII:I.2	CXIV:I.5
CXV:III.1	CXV:V.2			

III. Dialectical Exegesis: Intrinsic

While this form does not occur above, it is so important that we should introduce it in our initial catalogue. It consists of a sequence of arguments about the meaning of a passage, in which the focus is upon the base verse, and a sequence of possibilities is introduced to spell out the meaning of that verse. At issue is not the power of logic but the meaning of the base verse, but that issue is pursued through an argument of many stages. Here is the first example of our document:

I:IV

1.   A.   "[The Lord said to Moses, 'Command the people of Israel that] they put out of the camp [every leper and every one having a discharge, and every one that is unclean through contact with the dead']" (Num. 5:1-2).

   B.   Is it from the [innermost] camp, of the Presence of God, or should I infer that it is only from the camp of the Levites?

   C.   Scripture states, "...they put out them of the camp." [The sense is that they are to be put outside of the camp of the Presence.]

   D.   Now even if Scripture had not made the matter explicit, I could have proposed the same proposition on the basis of reasoning [that they should be put outside of the camp of the Presence]:

   E.   If unclean people are driven out of the camp that contains the ark, which is of lesser sanctity, all the more so should they be driven out of the camp of the Presence of God, which is of greater sanctuary.

   F.   But if you had proposed reasoning on that basis, you would have found yourself in the position of imposing a penalty merely on the basis of reason [and not on the basis of an explicit statement of Scripture, and one does not impose a penalty merely on the basis of reason].

   G.   Then is why it is stated: "...they put out of the camp."

   H.   Making that matter explicit in Scripture serves to teach you that penalties are not to be imposed merely on the basis of logic [but require explicit specification in Scripture]. [That is, Scripture made a point that reason could have reached, but Scripture made the matter explicit so as to articulate a penalty applicable for violating the rule.]

I.   [Rejecting that principle,] Rabbi says, "It is not necessary for Scripture to make the matter explicit, since it is a matter of an argument *a fortiori*:

J.   "If the unclean people are driven out of the camp that contains the ark, which is of lesser sanctity, all the more so should they be driven out of the camp of the Presence of God, which is of greater sanctity.

K.   "Then is why it is stated: '...they put out of the camp every leper and every one having a discharge, and every one that is unclean through contact with the dead'?

L.   "[By specifying that all three are put out of the camp,] Scripture thereby served to assign to them levels or gradations [of uncleanness, with diverse rules affecting those levels, as will now be spelled out. Since we know that that rule applies to the ostracism of the leper, the specification that the others also are to be put out of the camp indicates that a singular rule applies to each of the category. If one rule applied in common, then the specification with respect to the leper alone would have sufficed to indicate the rule for all others.]"

M.   [We review the distinctions among several gradations of uncleanness affecting human beings, inclusive of the three at hand: the leper, the one having a discharge, and the one unclean through contact with the dead.] "The Lord said to Moses, 'Command the people of Israel that they put out of the camp every leper and every one having a discharge, and every one that is unclean through contact with the dead'" (Num. 5:1-2).

N.   Shall I then draw the conclusion that all three of those listed [the leper, the one affected by a discharge, the one unclean with corpse-uncleanness] are to remain in the same locale [in relationship to the Temple]?

O.   With respect to the leper, Scripture states explicit, "He shall dwell by himself; outside of the camp shall be his dwelling" (Lev. 13:46).

P.   Now the leper fell into the same category as the others, and he has been singled out from the general category, thereby serving to impose a single rule on the category from which he has been singled out.

Q.   [And this is the rule applicable to the leper and hence to the others from among whom he has been singled out:] Just as in the case of the leper, who is subject to a most severe form of uncleanness, and who also is subjected to a more severe rule governing ostracism than that applying to his fellow, so all who are subject to a more severe form of uncleanness likewise are subject to a more severe rule of ostracism than that applying to his fellow.

R.   On this basis sages listed distinctions that apply to those that are unclean [since a different rule applies to each of them, in descending order of severity, as is now spelled out]:

S.   To any object that one affected by a flux imparts uncleanness, a leper imparts uncleanness. A leper is subject to a more severe rule, however, in that a leper imparts uncleanness through an act of sexual relations.

T.   To any object that one unclean with corpse-uncleanness imparts uncleanness, one affected by a flux imparts uncleanness. But a more severe rule affects one affected by a flux, in that he imparts uncleanness to an object located far beneath a rock in the deep [imparting uncleanness to that deeply-buried object merely by the application of the pressure of his weight, while one unclean with corpse-uncleanness does not impart uncleanness merely by pressure of his weight alone].

U. To any object that one unclean by reason of waiting for sunset after immersion imparts uncleanness one unclean by corpse-uncleanness imparts uncleanness. A more severe rule applies to one unclean by corpse-uncleanness, for he imparts uncleanness to a human being [which is not the case of one who is unclean by reason of waiting for sunset after his immersion].

V. What is made unfit by one who has not yet completed his rites of atonement following uncleanness and purification is made unfit by one who awaits for sunset to complete his process of purification. A more strict rule applies to one awaiting sunset for the completion of his rite of purification, for he imparts unfitness to food designated for priestly rations [while the one who has completed his rites of purification but not yet offered the atonement-sacrifice on account of his uncleanness does not impart unfitness to priestly rations that he may touch].

I:IV.1	I:VI.3	I:VII.3-4	XIX:I.1	XXIV:II.1
XXVI:III.1	XXXVIII:III.1	XXXIX:VIII.1	XLIX:I.1	XLIX:II.1
LXIV:I.1	LXXXIII:II.2	CII:IV.1	CVII:II.1	CX:III.1
CXI:I.3	CXV:I:3-5			

IV. Dialectical Exegesis: The Fallacy of Logic Uncorrected by Exegesis of Scripture

This is another moving, or dialectical, exegetical form, but while the basic trait is familiar -- a sequence of shifts and turns in the possibility of interpretation, all of them subjected to close logical scrutiny, the purpose is different. And the purpose comes to expression not in content, particular to diverse passages, but in form. The formal indicator is the presence of the question, in one of several versions: is it not a matter of logic? That is the never-failing formal indicator. From that clause we invariably move on to a set of arguments of a highly formalized character on taxonomic classification: what is like, or unlike? What is like follows a given rule, what is unlike follows the opposite rule, and it is for us to see whether the likenesses or unlikenesses prevail. The argument is formalized to an extreme, and there are very few variations among our document's exempla of this form, though one -- the matter of length -- should not be missed. The exegesis of the verse at hand plays no substantial role, beyond its initial introduction. What is critical is the issue of the reliability of logic. The base verse before us contributes virtually nothing and in no way serves as the foundation for the composition at hand.

I:VI.3	VII:VI.1	VII:XII.1	VII:XIV.1	VIII:VI.1
[VII:IX.1-2]	X:II.1	XII:I.1	XII:II.1	XVI:II.1

XXII:II.1	XXII:III.1	XXIII:I.1,3	XXIII:IV.1	XXIV:I.1
XXIV:IV.1	XXIV:VI.1	XXV:VIII.1	XXVI:II.1-5	XXVIII:I.1
XXVIII:II.1-2	XXVIII:III.1	XXVIII:IV.1	XXIX:I.1	XXX:I.1
XXXI:III.1-2	XXXI:IV.1	XXXIV:I.1	XXXIV:II.1	XXXVII:II.2
LVIII:I.1	LX:II.1	LXII:I.1	LXXIII:I.1-2	CVII:VII.1
CVII:VIII.2	CVII:X.1-2	CVII:XIII.1	CX:II.1	CX:V.1
CX:VI.1	CX:IX.1	CXI:V.3	CXII:I.6-7	CXII:II.3

V. Scriptural Basis for a Passage of the Mishnah

What we have is simply a citation of the verse plus a law in prior writing (Mishnah, Tosefta) which the verse is supposed to sustain. The formal traits require [1] citation of a verse, with or without comment, followed by [2] verbatim citation of a passage of the Mishnah or the Tosefta.

Form E: Citation of a verse of Scripture and verbatim citation of a passage of the Mishnah or the Tosefta

I:IX

1. A. "[You shall put out both male and female, putting them outside the camp,] that they may not defile their camp, [in the midst of which I dwell]:"

    B. On the basis of this verse, the rule has been formulated:

    C. There are three camps, the camp of Israel, the camp of the Levitical priests, and the camp of the Presence of God. From the gate of Jerusalem to the Temple mount is the camp of Israel, from the gate of the Temple mount to the Temple courtyard is the camp of the Levitical priesthood, and from the gate of the courtyard and inward is the camp of the Presence of God [T. Kelim 1:12].

I:IX.1	VI:II.1	VII:III.1	VII:X.1	XII:XIV.2
VIII:I.1	VIII:IX.1-2	IX:I.1	IX:II.1	IX:III.1
XI:II.3	XI:III.1	XIII:I.3	[XV:I.1]	XV:II.1
XVI:III.1	XVII:I.1-2	XVII:II.1	XVII:IV.1	XIX:III.1
XX:II.1	XXIV:III.1	XXV:II.1	XXVIII:VII.1	[XXXI:III.2]
XXXVIII:III.2	LX:1.3	LXI:I.4	LXIX:III.1	CVI:II.2
CVII:XII.3	CVIII:I.2	CX:I.21CX:II.1	CX:IV.1	CX:VIII.1
CXIV:I.7,8	CXV			

Form F: Linking a law stated in apodictic form to a verse of Scripture

This is a somewhat less well framed entry. Here we have a statement of a rule, in which the Mishnah or Tosefta is not cited verbatim. That is the undefined side. But the rule that is presented is not intrinsic to the verse at hand, in that the verse does not refer in any way to the case or possibility framed as the issue. In that case we do not have a clearcut exegesis of the verse in its own terms. But we also do not have an example of the linking of Scripture to the Mishnah. An example of this type follows. I give in underlining the part of the passage I deem apodictic, not exegetical:

III:I

1. A.   "[And the Lord said to Moses, 'Say to the people of Israel, When a man or woman commits any of the sins that men commit by breaking faith with the Lord, and that person is guilty,] he shall confess his sin which he has committed, [and he shall make full restitution for his wrong, adding a fifth to it, and giving it to him to whom he did the wrong.']" (Num. 5:5-10).

    B.   But [in stressing, "his sin," Scripture makes it clear that he does not have to make confession] for what his father did.

    C.   For if one said to him, "Give me the bailment that I left with your father," and he says, "You left no bailment," [and the other says,] "I impose an oath on you," and the first says, "Amen,"

    D.   [and if] after a while the [son] remembers [that a bailment indeed had been left and must be handed over] --

    E.   should I conclude that the son is liable [to make confession, not merely to hand over the bailment]?

    F.   Scripture says, " he shall confess his sin which *he* has committed," but he does not make confession for what his father did.

The proof-text serves for a proposition given in apodictic form. The point is that the son does not confess the father's sin, though he has to make up for it. Scripture then yields the stated law by its stress. We shall now derive laws from the verses at hand to cover further such situations.

III:I.1	IV:V.I	IV:VI.1	V:I.1	V:I.2
VI:V.1	VI:V.2	VIII:I.2	X:III.1	X:IV.1
XIV:I.1	XV:II.2	XX:III.1	XXII:III.2	XXII:V.3
XXIX:II.1	XXIX:III.1	XXX:III.1	XXXI:I.1	XXXI:II.1
XXXIX:V.2	LXXV:II.1	LXXXIV:I.1	CV:III.1	CV:VII.1
CX:IZ.1	CXI:I.1	CXI:IV.1	CXII:I.1	CXV:I.2

VI. Miscellanies

There are a few items that in form do not pretend to provide an exegesis of Scripture at all.

XXII:VI.2   Simeon the Righteous and the Nazirite

CV:VI.2   Eliezer and Disciples

CXV:V.7   Story of Disciple of Hiyya

We observe one more fact. In the formative processes undertaken by the rabbinic movement in the Land of Israel (as well as in Babylonia) people did make up and preserve stories about sages. But in the redactional processes by which available materials were selected and arranged in large-scale documents, such as the one at hand, no provision whatsoever was made to accommodate these stories. While used, they found for themselves no formal-redactional setting, in which they defined the purpose of the document at hand. To state matters simply, sages did not compile stories and so create gospels or even sustained narratives of the lives of holy men. Since lives of holy men provided a major mode of redacting materials among other groups of the same time and place, the decision not to make books ("documents") out of materials of this sort takes on meaning.

These stories fall entirely outside of the formal range of our document. They present stunning proof that our document's authorship proposed an exegetical program, defined very narrowly. There is no form in the pages of Sifré Numbers that serves an other-than-exegetical task -- not one. The document contains only exegetical materials; these exceptions prove the rule. When comparison and contrast to Genesis Rabbah and Leviticus Rabbah go forward, that fact will take on meaning. For the moment the focus of our document becomes still more clear, and we see the precision of definition that governed the work of our authorship: this, not that. They knew not only what they wanted, but also what they did not want. That fact forms part of their implicit message, the one that form-analysis helps us to discern.

7. What Is at Stake in Defining Sifré to Numbers

Having framed the question I wish to take up, let me restate what I hope now to make explicit out of the form-analysis just completed. I repeat what I said above: my purpose is to describe the incremental message, the cumulative effect, of the formal traits of speech and thought revealed in the uniform rhetoric and syntax of the document. So I ask this question: What do the formal structures of our document emphasize, and what(as in the case of stories about sages) do they ignore? Let us rapidly review them, highlighting their main traits.

I. Extrinsic Exegetical Form The form consists of the citation of an opening verse, followed by an issue stated in terms extrinsic to the cited verse. The formal traits: [1] citation of a base verse from Numbers, [2] a generalization ignoring clauses or words in the base verse, [3] a further observation without clear interest in the verse at hand. The form yields a syllogism proved by a list of facts beyond all doubt.

II. Intrinsic Exegetical Form: The verse itself is clarified. The focus is on the base verse and not on a broader issue. There are diverse versions of this exercise, some consisting only of a verse or a clause and a statement articulating the sense of the matter, others rather elaborate. But the upshot is always the same.

III. Dialectical Exegesis: Intrinsic: A sequence of arguments about the meaning of a passage, in which the focus is upon the base verse focuses upon the meaning of the base verse. This is the internal-exegetical counterpart to the on-going argument on whether logic works. Now logic pursues the sense of a verse, but the results of logic are tested, forthwith and one by one, against the language at hand, e.g., why is this stated? or: you say it means X but why not Y? Or, if X, then what about Y? if Y, then what about Z? All of these rather nicely articulated exegetical programs imposes a scriptural test upon the proposals of logic.

IV. Dialectical Exegesis: Extrinsic. The Fallacy of Logic Uncorrected by Exegesis of Scripture: The formal indicator is the presence of the question, in one of several versions: is it not a matter of logic? The exegesis of the verse at hand plays no substantial role.

V. Scriptural Basis for a Passage of the Mishnah: What we have is simply a citation of the verse plus a law in a prior writing (Mishnah, Tosefta) which the verse is supposed to sustain. The Mishnah's or the Tosefta's rule then cannot stand as originally set forth, that is, absent any exegetical foundation. On the contrary, the rule, verbatim, rests on a verse of Scripture, given with slight secondary articulation: verse, then Mishnah-sentence. That suffices, the point is made.

VI. Miscellanies: All three formally miscellaneous items turn out to have a single characteristic. They involve stories about sages.

Let us now characterize the formal traits of Sifré to Numbers as a commentary. These we have reduced to two classifications, based on the point of origin of the verses that are catalogued or subjected to exegesis: exegesis of a verse in the book of Numbers in terms of the theme or problems of that verse, hence, intrinsic exegesis; exegesis of a verse in Numbers in terms of a theme or polemic not particular to that verse, hence, extrinsic exegesis.

The forms of extrinsic exegesis: The implicit message of the external category proves simple to define, since the several extrinsic classifications turn out to form a cogent polemic. Let me state the recurrent polemic of external exegesis.

[1] **The Syllogistic Composition:** Scripture supplies hard facts, which, properly classified, generate syllogisms. By collecting and classifying facts of Scripture, therefore, we may produce firm laws of history, society, and Israel's everyday life. The diverse compositions in which verses from various books of the Scriptures are compiled in a list of evidence for a given proposition -- whatever the character or purpose of that proposition -- make that one point. And given their power and cogency, they make the point stick.

[2] **The Fallibility of Reason Unguided by Scriptural Exegesis:** Scripture alone supplies reliable basis for speculation. Laws cannot be generated by reason or logic unguided by Scripture. Efforts at classification and contrastive-analogical exegesis, in which Scripture does not supply the solution to all problems, prove few and far between (and always in Ishmael's name, for whatever that is worth). This polemic forms the obverse of the point above.

So when extrinsic issues intervene in the exegetical process, they coalesce to make a single point. Let me state that point with appropriate emphasis the recurrent and implicit message of the forms of external exegesis:

Scripture stands paramount, logic, reason, analytical processes of classification and differentiation, secondary. Reason not built on scriptural foundations yields uncertain results. The Mishnah itself demands scriptural bases.

The forms of intrinsic exegesis: What about the polemic present in the intrinsic exegetical exercises? This clearly does not allow for ready characterization. As we saw, at least three intrinsic exegetical exercises focus on the use of logic, specifically, the logic of classification, comparison and contrast of species of a genus, in the explanation of the meaning of verses of the book of Numbers. The internal dialectical mode, moving from point to point as logic dictates, underlines the main point already stated: logic produces possibilities, Scripture chooses among them. Again, the question, why is this passage stated? commonly produces an answer generated by further verses of Scripture, e.g., this matter is stated here to clarify what otherwise would be confusion left in the wake of other verses. So Scripture produces problems of confusion and duplication, and Scripture -- and not logic, not differentiation, not classification — solves those problems.

To state matters simply: Scripture is complete, harmonious, perfect. Logic not only does not generate truth beyond the limits of Scripture but also plays no important role in the harmonization of difficulties yielded by what appear to be duplications or disharmonies. These forms of internal exegesis then make the same point that the extrinsic ones do.

In so stating, of course, we cover all but the single most profuse category of exegesis, which we have treated as simple and undifferentiated: [1] verse of Scripture or a clause, followed by [2] a brief statement of the meaning at hand. Here I see no unifying polemic in favor of, or against, a given proposition. The most common form also proves the least pointed: X bears this meaning, Y bears that meaning, or, as we have seen, citation of verse X, followed by, [what this means is].... Whether simple or elaborate, the upshot is the same.

What can be at issue when no polemic expressed in the formal traits of syntax and logic finds its way to the surface? What do I do when I merely clarify a phrase? Or, to frame the question more logically: what premises must validate my *intervention*, that is, my willingness to undertake to explain the meaning of a verse of Scripture? These seem to me propositions that must serve to justify the labor of intrinsic exegesis as we have seen its results here:

[1] My independent judgment bears weight and produces meaning. I -- that is, my mind -- therefore may join in the process.

[2] God's revelation to Moses at Sinai requires my intervention. I have the role, and the right, to say what that revelation means.

[3] What validates my entry into the process of revelation is the correspondence between the logic of my mind and the logic of the document.

Why do I think so? Only if I think in accord with the logic of the revealed Torah can my thought-processes join issue in clarifying what is at hand: the unfolding of God's will in the Torah. To state matters more accessibly: if the Torah does not make statements in accord with a syntax and a grammar that I know, I cannot so understand the Torah as to explain its meaning. But if I can join in the discourse of the Torah, it is because I speak the same language of thought: syntax and grammar at the deepest levels of my intellect.

[4] Then to state matters affirmatively and finally: Since a shared logic of syntax and grammar joins my mind to the mind of God as revealed in the Torah, I can say what a sentence of the Torah means. So I too can amplify, clarify, expand, revise, rework: that is to say, create a commentary.

It follows that the intrinsic exegetical forms stand for a single proposition:

While Scripture stands paramount, logic, reason, analytical processes of classification and differentiation, secondary, nonetheless, man's mind joins God's mind when man receives and sets forth the Torah.

The Purpose of the Authorship of Sifré to Numbers: Can we then state in a few words and in simple language what the formal rules of the document tell us about the purpose of Sifré to Numbers? Beyond all concrete propositions, the document as a whole through its fixed and recurrent formal preferences or literary structures makes two complementary points.

[1] Reason unaided by Scripture produces uncertain propositions.

[2] Reason operating within the limits of Scripture produces truth.

To whom do these moderate and balanced propositions matter? Sages in particular, I think. The polemic addresses arguments internal to their circles. How do we know, and how may we be certain? If we contrast the polemic of our document about the balance between revelation and reason, Torah and logic, with the polemic of another canonical document about some other topic altogether, the contrast will tell. Then and only then shall we see the choices people faced. In that way we shall appreciate the particular choice the authorship at hand has made. With the perspective provided by an exercise of comparison, we shall see how truly remarkable a document we have in Sifré to Numbers. By itself the book supplies facts. Seen in context, the book makes points. So we require a context of comparison.

Having characterized the position, based on the formal rhetoric, of Sifré to Numbers, I turn to the description of another document of the same general venue, that is, a canonical document produced by sages some time before the closure of the Talmud of Babylonia, in ca. A.D. 600, but after the formation of the Mishnah, in ca. A.D. 200, that is, a document emerging around ca. A.D. 400, in the time of the Talmud of the Land of Israel and perhaps of Sifré to Numbers. For that purpose, I choose Genesis Rabbah. If we may guess that our document reached closure sometime before 400, and we may guess that Genesis Rabbah reached redaction at about that same time, we then are comparing to pieces of writing of pretty much the same period (give or take a hundred years). So let me repeat what I offer elsewhere as an overall characterization of Genesis Rabbah.

The authorship of Genesis Rabbah focuses its discourse on the proposition that the book of Genesis speaks to the life and historical condition of Israel, the Jewish people. The entire narrative of Genesis is so formed as to point toward the sacred history of Israel, the Jewish people: its slavery and redemption; its coming Temple in Jerusalem; its exile and salvation at the end of time. The powerful message of Genesis in the pages of Genesis Rabbah proclaims that the world's creation commenced a single, straight line of events, leading in the end to the salvation of Israel and through Israel all humanity. Therefore a given story will bear a deeper message about what it means to be Israel, on the one side, and what in the end of days will happen to Israel, on the other.

If I had to point to the single most important proposition of Genesis Rabbah, it is that, in the story of the beginnings of creation, humanity, and Israel, we find the message of the meaning and end of the life of the Jewish people. The deeds of the founders supply signals for the children about what is going to come in the future. So the biography of Abraham, Isaac, and Jacob also constitutes the history of Israel later on. If the sages could announce a single syllogism and argue it systematically, that is the proposition on which they would insist. The sages understood that stories about the progenitors, presented in the book of Genesis, define the human condition and proper conduct for their children, Israel in time to come. Accordingly, they systematically asked Scripture to tell them how they were supposed to conduct themselves at the critical turnings of life. In a few words let me restate the conviction of the framers of Genesis Rabbah about the message and meaning of the book of Genesis:

"We now know what will be in the future. How do we know it? Just as Jacob had told his sons what would happen in time to come, just as Moses told the tribes their future, so we may understand the laws of history if we study the Torah. And in the Torah, we turn to beginnings: the rules as they were laid out at the very start of human history. These we find in the book of Genesis, the story of the origins of the world and of Israel.

"The Torah tells us not only what happened but why. The Torah permits us to discover the laws of history. Once we know those laws, we may also peer into the future and come to an assessment of what is going to happen to us -- and, especially, of how we shall be saved from our present existence. Because everything exists under the aspect of a timeless will, God's will, and all things express one thing, God's program and plan, in the Torah we uncover the workings of God's will. Our task as Israel is to accept, endure, submit, and celebrate."

We now ask ourselves a simple question: is the message of Sifré to Numbers the same as that of Genesis Rabbah? The answer is obvious. No, these are different books. They make different points in answering different questions. In plan and in program they yield more contrasts than comparisons. Why does that fact matter ito my argument? Since these *are* different books, which *do* use different forms to deliver different messages, it must follow that there is nothing routine or given or to be predicted about the point that the authorship of Sifré tio Numbers wishes to make. Why not? Because it is not a point that is simply "there to be made." It is a striking and original point. How, again, do we know it? The reason is that, when the sages who produced Genesis Rabbah read Genesis, they made a different point from the one at hand. So contrasting the one composition with the other shows us that each composition bears its own distinctive traits -- traits of mind, traits of plan, traits of program. (My comparison of Genesis Rabbah and Leviticus Rabbah, in *Comparative Midrash: The Plan and Program of Genesis Rabbah and Leviticus Rabbah* [Atlanta, 1986: Scholars Press for Brown Judaic Studies] underscores this result.) The upshot is simple. Once we characterize the persistent polemic of Sifré to Numbers and then compare that polemic to the characteristic point of argument of Genesis Rabbah (and, as it happens, Leviticus Rabbah as well), we see that our document has chosen forms to advance its own distinctive, substantive argument. Its exegetical program points, explicitly in extrinsic exegesis, implicitly in intrinsic exegesis, to a single point, and that point is made on every page.

Let me conclude by answering two broad questions. [1] Does the document at hand deliver a particular message and viewpoint or does it merely serve as a repository for diverse, received materials? [2] Does the authorship deliver its message, its choices as to form and meaning, or merely transmit someone else's? To broaden the question: do we have a cogent statement or a mere scrapbook?

Let me spell out the meaning of the issue I propose to settle. The choices are clear. A document may serve solely as a convenient repository of prior sayings and stories, available materials that will have served equally well (or poorly) wherever they took up their final location. A composition may exhibit a viewpoint, a purpose of authorship distinctive to its framers or collectors and arrangers. Such a characteristic literary purpose would be so powerfully particular to one authorship that nearly everything at hand can be shown to have been (re)shaped for the ultimate purpose of the authorship at hand. These then are collectors and arrangers who demand the title of authors. Context and circumstance then form the prior condition of inquiry, the result, in exegetical terms, the contingent one. I believe that the second of the two propositions finds ample support in the pages of this chapter.

If we ask about the textuality of a document -- is it a composition or a scrap book? -- we wish to know whether the materials unique to a document also cohere, or whether they prove merely miscellaneous. In form and in polemic, in plan and in program, the materials assembled in Sifré to Numbers do cohere. Not only so, but the program -- the framing of a position on the role of logic and reason in the mind of sages -- and the plan -- the defining of recurrent rhetorical forms and patterns -- join into a single statement. And since they do cohere, we may conclude that the framers of the document indeed have followed a single plan and a program. That justifies my claim that the framers of Sifré to Numbers have carried out a labor not only of conglomeration, arrangement and selection, but also of genuine authorship or composition in the narrow and strict sense of the word. Sifré to Numbers emerges from authors, not merely arrangers and compositors.

It remains to observe that just as Genesis Rabbah bears formal and substantive affinity to Leviticus Rabbah; the plan and program of both documents present an essential congruity, so too in plan and in program Sifra and Sifré to Numbers form a community. The forms and polemic of Sifra and Sifré to Numbers cohere, with the forms so designed as to implicitly state and so to reenforce the substantive argument of both books. And, I am inclined to think, further study will suggest the same for the forms of Genesis Rabbah and Leviticus Rabbah. If, then, I may end with a point worth further study: we may then classify Sifra (serving Leviticus) and Sifré to Numbers as inner-directed, facing within, toward issues of the interior life of the community vis a vis revelation and the sanctification of the life of the nation, and, intellectually, as centered on issues urgent to sages themselves. For to whom are the debates about the relationship between Torah and logic, reason and revelation, going to make a difference, if not to the intellectuals of the textual community at hand? Within the same classification-scheme, Genesis Rabbah and Leviticus Rabbah appear outer-directed, addressing issues of history and salvation, taking up critical concerns of the public life of the nation vis a vis history and the world beyond. Sifra and Sifré to Numbers address sanctification, Genesis Rabbah and Leviticus Rabbah, salvation.

The four documents respectively do not merely assemble this and that, forming a hodgepodge of things people happen to have said. In the case of each document we can answer the question: Why this, not that? The four are not compilations but compositions; seen as a group, therefore, (to state matters negatively) they are not essentially the same, lacking all viewpoint, serving a single undifferentiated task of collecting and arranging whatever was at hand.

Quite to the contrary, these documents of the Oral Torah's exegesis of the written Torah emerge as rich in differences from one another and sharply defined each through its distinctive viewpoints and particular polemics, on the one side, and formal and aesthetic qualities, on the other. We deal with a canon, yes, but with a canon made up of highly individual documents. But that, after all, is what a canon is: a mode of classification that takes a library and turns it into a cogent if composite statement. A canon comprises separate books that all together make a single statement. In terms of the Judaism of the dual Torah, the canon is what takes scriptures of various kinds and diverse points of origin and turns scriptures into Torah, and commentaries on those scriptures into Torah as well, making them all into the one whole Torah -- of Moses, our rabbi.

Chapter Five

Analysis of a Text in the Context of its Time
Genesis Rabbah in the Setting of the Fourth Century

In the book of Genesis, as the sages who composed Genesis Rabbah see things, God set forth to Moses the entire scope and meaning of Israel's history among the nations and salvation at the end of days. Genesis drew their attention more than any other book of the Pentateuch -- the five books of Moses, and, as a matter of fact, the opening synagogue lection, or *parashah*, *Bereshit*, received nearly as much comment as the other eleven weekly synagogue lections of the book of Genesis put together. Sages, who flourished in the third and fourth centuries in the Land of Israel, read Genesis not as a set of individual verses, one by one, but as a single and coherent statement, whole and complete. So in a few words let me restate the conviction of the framers of Genesis Rabbah about the message and meaning of the book of Genesis:

> "We now know what will be in the future. How do we know it? Just as Jacob had told his sons what would happen in time to come, just as Moses told the tribes their future, so we may understand the laws of history if we study the Torah. And in the Torah, we turn to beginnings: the rules as they were laid out at the very start of human history. These we find in the book of Genesis, the story of the origins of the world and of Israel.
>
> "The Torah tells us not only what happened but why. The Torah permits us to discover the laws of history. Once we know those laws, we may also peer into the future and come to an assessment of what is going to happen to us -- and, especially, of how we shall be saved from our present existence. Because everything exists under the aspect of a timeless will, God's will, and all things express one thing, God's program and plan, in the Torah we uncover the workings of God's will. Our task as Israel is to accept, endure, submit, and celebrate."

In general people read the book of Genesis as the story of how Israel saw the past, not the future: the beginning of the world and of Israel, humanity from Adam to Noah, then from Noah to Abraham, and the story of the three patriarchs and four matriarchs of Israel, -- Abraham, Isaac, Jacob, Sarah, Rebecca, Leah and Rachel, -- and finally, Joseph and his brothers -- from creation to the descent into Egypt. But to the rabbis who created Genesis Rabbah, the book of Genesis tells the story of Israel, the Jewish people, in the here and now. The principle? What happened to the patriarchs and matriarchs signals what will happen to their descendants: the model of the ancestors sends a message for the children. So the importance of Genesis, as the sages of Genesis Rabbah read the book, derives not from its lessons about the past but its message for Israel's present -- and, especially, future.

Their conviction is that what Abraham, Isaac, and Jacob did shaped the future history of Israel. If, therefore, we want to know the meaning of events now and tomorrow, we look back at yesterday to find out. But the interest is not merely in history as a source of lessons. It is history as the treasury of truths about the here and now and especially about tomorrow: the same rules apply. What the patriarchs did supplies the model, the message, the meaning for what Israel should do. Why did the sages come to Genesis with the questions of their own day? Because, they maintained, the world reveals not chaos but order, and God's will works itself out not once but again and again. If we can find out how things got going, we also can find meaning in today and method in where we are heading. So did our sages believe. And that is why they looked to a reliable account of the past and searched out the meaning of their own days. Bringing to the stories of Genesis that conviction that the book of Genesis told not only the story of yesterday but also the tale of tomorrow, the sages whose words are before us in this anthology transformed a picture of the past into a prophesy for a near tomorrow.

What made Israel's sages look longingly at the beginnings of the world and of Israel? Because in their own day they entertained deep forebodings about Israel's prospects. To understand why, we have to ask where and when our book, Genesis Rabbah, this enlarged or greater view of the book of Genesis, reached its conclusion. We want also to know who stands behind the work, its authorship and -- in particular -- how the authorship expressed itself.

Let us begin with the simplest fact in our hands: the literary character of our book. It is a composite of paragraphs, not a sustained essay. Each paragraph takes up a verse of the book of Genesis in sequence. So the whole book is organized around the order of another book, that is, Genesis Rabbah (as its name tells us), follows the sequence of verses of the book of Genesis. Then who speaks through the book before us? I hear two different voices, [1] the voice of the author of the paragraph, [2] the voice of the one who selected the paragraph and put it in the document, so speaking *through* choosing and including the paragraph, but not through writing it. We hear both voices, the ones who formed the stories and sayings, the ones who selected and arranged them. The former -- the narrators -- are named throughout. They are mostly later third and fourth century sages. The organizers and editors are not named, but they do not have to be: we hear from them above all.

What sort of voice is this? It is the voice of the compiler, editor, arranger. As the editor of a newspaper speaks through the selection and arrangement of stories, so the framers of Genesis Rabbah talk to us through what they have chosen and how they have laid things out. It is the picture created by a great arrangement of flowers, the tableau deep with meaning created in choreography. It is as if you determined to write a book by selecting paragraphs from letters you have received. Your book would have two voices, the voice of your correspondents, and, as the one who selected and arranged their messages, your voice too. It is like the place of the artist in creating a collage. The artist does not create the materials, but the artists sees and conveys the message. So Genesis Rabbah speaks through selection and arrangement, and also through what is chosen. That is why, for our part, when we want to know from whom we hear in this book, we turn first of all to the people who made the choices and arranged the book's materials as we now have them. We do not know who wrote the paragraphs before us, where, when, or why someone composed them as we have them. But we do have the document itself, and the document as a matter of fact accurately represents the selection and arrangement of the writings -- therefore the mind and imagination of the people who made the selections and accomplished their arrangement.

This digression into literary questions matters, because it tells us the answer to the question just now raised: *from whom do we hear in this book* ? When we know the answer to that question, we also can say why the message proved urgent and immediate, why, in other words, the sages before us turned to Genesis with the questions they found compelling, rather than with other questions. Since, in our own day, the book of Genesis forms the battlefield among theologians, some of whom wish to read it in a very literal way, as a work in geology, and others of whom do not, we have to assess what brings people to this holy book, before we try to understand what they find in it.

Now, all scholars agree, Genesis Rabbah came to closure around the year 400, give or take a half a century either way, that is, some time between 350 at the earliest and 450 at the latest. Taking as fact the conclusions of people who have worked hard on the problem, we can place the document in one location -- time, country -- and not some other. Once we know where and when the document reached its conclusion, we also can see more clearly to whom its message made a difference. And, the answer of the question of where and when, is simple: [1] in the Land of Israel, [2] toward the end of the fourth century of the Common Era.

What made that particular time crucial in the life of Israel, the Jewish people, in the Land of Israel, is an event that also shaped the entire history of Western civilization. For in the fourth century the roman Empire became Christian, and the history of the West as Christian commenced. Judaism in the West from that time to nearly the present had to address a world in which the truths of Christianity were found self-evident, those of Judaism not.

We may, in fact, locate the sages' rereading of the Torah's account of the beginnings, the beginnings of the world and of Israel, that is, the book of Genesis, at exactly that moment at which Western civilization also came to its genesis. That is, the fourth century marked the beginning of the West as it reached its continuing and enduring definition. So here, in a way our sages cannot have known, the West really did find its genesis, and the choice of the book of Genesis bore an aptness our sages did not then discern.

What made all the difference, and what happened in that turning point in time? It was, first, the conversion of Constantine, the emperor of Rome, to Christianity and the legalization of Christianity, then its designation as the state's favored religion, and finally, by the end of the century, the establishment of Christianity as the religion of Rome. To the Christians, it was an age of vindication and validation. Some of the church's leading figures had met persecution and imprisonment in the decades just prior to Constantine's conversion, and then ended their lives as high officials of the Roman empire at his court.

If the great German rabbi, Leo Baeck, had been taken out of the concentration camp where he was located in 1945 and, by the end of 1947, had become prime minister of Germany under the successor of Adolph Hitler, we could begin to imagine the power of events as Christians experienced them. The triumph of Christianity changed the history of the West, because, from that point onward, the principal institutions of politics, culture, and social organization in Western civilization found definition and meaning in the Christian religion -- pure and simple. Since Rome encompassed the greater part of then-known civilization in the West, the fourth century therefore encompassed the redefinition of the West. What happened may be summarized very simply: Rome became Christian, and a formerly despised and illicit religious group took power.

But that event, by itself, need not greatly have confounded Israel and its sages. A second event, at the same critical time, did matter. To understand it, we have to recall that Israel, the Jewish people, had hoped, from the destruction of the Temple in 70, to witness the rebuilding, together with the restoration of Israel's government in its land and the advent of Israel's righteous and correct ruler, the Messiah. Reason for that hope derived from the destruction of the first Temple, in 586 B.C.E., about a thousand years earlier, when, after the passage of a few generation, Israel returned to its land, the Levites to their platform, and the priests to the altar of God. So hope persisted that the same pattern would final renewal, and the prophets' promises of redemption -- which the Christians claimed had already been kept in the restoration after 586 -- would once more be kept. Then Israel's faith as the ancient prophets had formed it would find that vindication that, Christianity (from Israel's viewpoint, momentarily) had now enjoyed.

As the years passed, from Constantine's conversion in 312 onward, Israel's thinkers may well have pondered the meaning of events. We know that the counterparts in the Christian world found they had to revise and rewrite the entire history of the world, from creation onward, to provide an explanation of the new age in the continuity of time. It would be speculative to claim that Israel, the Jewish people, as a whole expected the Messiah just now, as the claim so long rejected that Jesus had been Christ and that Christ now triumphed made its way. For Christians claimed, quite plausibly for many, that the conversion of the hated Rome to Christianity validated and vindicated their original conviction about Jesus as the Christ.

Whether or not Israel in its land worried over that matter we do not know. But we do know one stunning fact., In 360, a generation beyond Constantine's conversion, an emperor came to the throne who threw off Christianity and reaffirmed paganism. Julian, whom Christians from then to now have called "the apostate," reestablished the overthrown idols, reopened the philosophical schools of pagan tradition, and presented paganism in its elegant and cultured form, to a startled empire. At the same time Julian undertook to embarass and humiliate the Christians.   Since the Christians had by no means gained a majority of the population when Julian revealed this stunning turn in world history, the Christian dream seemed to turn into a nightmare. For the worst thing that can happen, beyond remission, is a new growth of cancer, and, for those who recalled the miracle of Constantine's conversion and the consequent upward move of Christianity, the moment foreboded a miserable end.

Why all this affected Israel is simple. As part of his program to embarass Christianity and disprove its claims, Julian announced that the Jews might go back to Jerusalem and rebuild their Temple. The Gospels represent Jesus as predicting that no stone on stone would remain, for the Temple would be destroyed and never rebuilt. Well, no stone did remain on another. But now, it appeared, Jesus' prediction would be shown a lie. Then what would come of the rest of his other claims, as these circulated in the New Testament and in the church? And how would the Christians now disprove the Jews' insistence that the prophets' promises of old would yet be kept? Since the Christians had long pointed to the destruction of the Temple and the loss of Jerusalem as mark of Israel's punishment for rejecting Jesus' claim to be the messiah, that is, the Christ, Julian's action certainly pointed toward a malicious intent. Here, in Julian's mind, people could find yet another cause to reject Christianity and all its claims. For the Jews, of course, Julian's move stood for something quite the opposite: the vindication of Israel's patience, endurance, and hope. Julian seemed to some God's agent, as much as Nebuchadnezzar had been -- but for a different reason. Now it all seemed to come true, -- and that on the eve of the three hundredth anniversary of the destruction. By the Jews' reckoning, the Temple had been destroyed in the year 68, so if it took a few years, from 360 onward, by the year 368, Israel would regain the sacred city and its holy altar, God the sacrifices so long suspended, and -- by Israel's hopeful reckoning -- the world would conclude the sorry history and celebrate the coming of the Messiah.

But it was not to be. Within the year, Julian died on a battlefield in far-off Iran, near the waters of Babylon where so large a portion of Israel then lived.

Christians reported that on his lips, as he breathed his last, were the words, "Galilean, thou hast triumphed." Whatever he said -- if anything -- hardly matters. How people understood the event does matter, and Christians now claimed that the anti-Christ was dead and Christ's rule would endure for millenia, as indeed, from their persepctive, the Christian empire did endure. So the Christian world concluded that Jesus now was finally vindicated as the Christ. Julian's death in his campaign against the Iranian empire under its most brilliant ruler, Shapur II, of the dynasty known as the Sasanian (hence, in the history books, Sasanian Iran), for all time wiped out the last hope of pagan renaissance in Rome. For Israel in its land, the disappointment proved only the least problem.

For ahead, over the next generation, lay a trial the Jewish people in the Roman empire had never before known. Judaism in Rome from the beginnings of Roman rule in the Middle East before the time of the Maccabees had enjoyed the status of a protected, completely licit religion. Jews enjoyed freedom to practice their religion. They could not, for example, be forced to violate the Sabbath. Buildings built for Judaic worship enjoyed the protection of the state. Constantine had done little to limit the Jews' rights, either as citizens or as believers in their faith. But now that freedom for the first time faced abridgement -- and worse. What was happening was simple. After Julian, the initial policy of tolerance of both paganism and Judaism shifted. The once-more-Christian Roman government determined to make certain that the Christian grasp on power never again would weaken. So laws against paganism in all its forms went forth from Coinstantinople to the entire empire, placing severe restraints on all forms of pagan worship and imposing heavy penalties on those who fostered paganism.

When Christian zealots attacked pagan temples, they went after synagogues and Jews as well, just as, in times past, pagan zealots had harassed and murdered Christians. For in the counterattack on paganism, the net that was cast caught Israel too. Before Constantine, of course, Christianity had no politics, therefore, by the way, no policy for Israel, the Jewish people, either. Afterward in a matter of a few generations Christianity had to develop a politics, a view of history, and a policy of a political character governing Israel, the Jewish people. As a matter of theology, there had been a Christian policy of toleration for Israel, meant to await the second coming and the last judgment as witness to the truth of Christianity. That, in general, yielded a political policy that Jews were not to be exterminated, as pagans in time to come would be exterminated, and Judaism was not to be extirpated, as, in the future, paganism would be destroyed. But that was to be the general policy for the long haul. What in particular happened now -- toward the end of the fourth century, from Julian's death after 360 to the turn of the fifth century? A policy, drawn from the program against paganism, limited Israel's right to that security and freedom that the nation had enjoyed, in its land, with only a few (if bitter) periods, from the coming of Roman governance and rule in the first century B.C.E. Specifically, synagogues were destroyed, Jews lost the right to convert slaves whom they purchased, and in various other ways Jews' former privileges and rights were abridged or revoked; Jews who became Christians enjoyed the protection of the state. By the turn of the fifth century, around 410, the Jews' institution of self-government in the land of Israel, the rule by their patriarch, came to an end. In all, it was a very difficult time, not because of trouble alone, not even because of the unprecedented character of the new laws and outrages, but because of the disappointment and despair that followed the high hopes kindled by Julian's abortive scheme.

To revert to our sad analogy, if in 1937 Hitler had given way to a democratic government, which restored Jewish rights, and in 1939, a new Nazi government had come back to power and annulled those rights again, we might have a relevant analogy to the awful dread that affected despairing Israel. What now? And what of the brief hope of yesterday? In consequence of the restoration of Christian rule and the disappointment attached to the failure of Julian's scheme to rebuild the Temple, Israel's hope for the restoration of the holy Temple and the near-coming of the Messiah turned into disaster. Not only would the Temple not be rebuilt, but the Christian claim that Israel's hope was lost, its land beyond its grasp, its future in doubt enjoyed renewed self-evidence for those who believed it, and they were now many. Historians tell us that by the end of the fourth century the Land of Israel, now the Holy Land, possessed a Christian, not a Jewish majority. Whether or not that is so I cannot say, but it does suggest what happened.

So the fourth century in fact presented the West, including Israel, with its first Christian century. While the Jewish people had managed on the whole to ignore the Christians' slow but steady rise to power, they no longer could pretend that Christianity constituted a temporary setback in the journey to the end of time. It was not temporary, it was far more than a setback, and it had to be dealt with. So Genesis Rabbah came to closure, all scholars generally concur, toward the end of the fourth century. And that fact matters for one reason: the Land of Israel now found itself in the domain of Christianity, an enormous and historical shift in the status of the Land and of the Jewish people - - therefore also of the Torah. In Genesis Rabbah every word is to be read against the background of the world-historical change that had taken place in the time of the formation of the document. The people who compiled the materials we shall now see made a statement through what they selected and arranged. This then is their collage, their creation. Genesis Rabbah in its final form emerges from that momentous first century in the history of the West as Christian, the century in which the Rome empire passed from pagan to Christian rule, and, in which, in the aftermath of the Emperor Julian's abortive reversion to paganism in 360, Christianity adopted that policy of repression of paganism that rapidly engulfed Judaism as well.

That is the power of Genesis Rabbah, why, if we listen to its messages, we hear something remarkable. It is how Israel's sages reopened the book of Genesis and reconsidered its story of beginnings. Why? Because in that story they hoped to find, and they did find, the counterpart, namely, the story of the day at hand, which, they anticipated, would indeed form the counterpart and conclusion to the story of beginnings. From creation to conclusion, from the beginnings of salvation in the patriarchs and matriarchs to the ending of salvation and its fulfilment in their own day: this is what our sages sought to discover. And in the book of Genesis, in the doings of the founders, they found models for deeds of the descendants. That, in a few words, tells us the setting of Genesis Rabbah. Brought into being in the age of crisis, the work, which presents comments on successive verses in the book of Genesis, told Israel the meaning of its day and of many days to come. For Genesis Rabbah, the first statement of Judaism on the meaning of the book of Genesis to be written down, formed the source for centuries to follow.

When for the coming, difficult centuries Israel would turn to Genesis, the Jewish people would encounter that book through the eyes of the sages who originally assembled the passages before us. And when Israel faced disappointment in its messianic hope, when Israel wondered where things were heading, when Jews asked why they should go on and what their duties were, they found answers to their questions in the book of Genesis. That was because the sages of Genesis Rabbah had turned that book into a message for Israel's living history. No longer about long-dead ancestors, the genealogy and family history of the book of Genesis, imposed on the house of and destiny of Israel, explained not a distant past but an immediate moment: today, tomorrow, the near-coming of redemption.

Before proceeding, let me give one concrete example of how sages responded. Their doctrine of Rome must prove critical. Rome now claims to be Israel, that is, Christian and heir to the testament of the founders. How do the sages of Genesis Rabbah deal with this new definition of who is Rome? They do not deny it, they affirm it: Rome is Esau, or Moab, or Ishmael. And we? We are Israel. Identifying Rome as Esau is a fresh idea. In the Mishnah, two hundred years earlier, Rome appears as a place, not as a symbol. But in Genesis Rabbah Rome is symbolized by Esau. Why Esau in particular? Because Esau is sibling: relations, competitor, enemy, brother. In choosing Rome as the counterpart to Israel, sages simply opened Genesis and found there Israel, that is Jacob, and his brother, his enemey, in Esau. So why not understand the obvious: Esau stands for Rome, Jacob for Israel, and their relationship represents then what Israel and rome would work out even now, in the fourth century, the first century of Christian rule. So Esau rules now, but Jacob possesses the birthright. Esau/Rome is the last of the four great empires (Persia, Media, Greece, Rome). On the other side of Rome? Israel's age of glory. And why is Rome now brother? Because, after all, the Christians do claim a common patrimony in the Hebrew Scriptures and do claim to form part of Israel. That claim was not ignored, it was answered: yes, part of Israel, the rejected part. Jacob bears the blessing and transmits the blessing to humanity, Esau does not. Such a message bore meaning only in the present context. So in a concrete way Genesis talks the here and now, about "us," Israel, and about *our sibling,* Rome. That concession -- Rome is a sibling, a close relative of Israel -- represents an implicit recognition of Christianity's claim to share the patrimony of Judaism, to be descended from Abraham and Isaac. So how are we to deal with the glory and the power of our brother, Esau? And what are we to say about the claim of Esau to enthrone Christ? And how are we to assess today the future history of Israel, the salvation of God's first, best love? It is not by denying Rome's claim but by evaluating it, not by turning a back to the critical events of the hour but by confronting those events forcefully and authoritatively.

Genesis then told about beginnings so as to point to happy endings, and in reading the book of Genesis, Israel could find reason to hope for its future in the certain facts of a long-ago past. That, in a single sentence, states the power of Genesis Rabbah, the astonishing achievement of the sages who brought together the paragraphs they chose and formed them into the message at hand. So, to conclude, Genesis Rabbah forms part of the great labor of presenting the one whole Torah of Moses, our rabbi, revealed by God to Israel at Mount Sinai. Genesis Rabbah forms an important component of the complete Torah worked out by the rabbis of ancient times, from the publication of the Mishnah at ca. 200 to the completion of the Babylonian Talmud at ca. 600. At ca. 400 C.E., Genesis Rabbah comes midway in the unfolding of the Torah -- the one whole Torah of Moses, our rabbi. Sages' reading of Genesis transcends the age in which they did their work. For how the great Judaic sages of that time taught the interpretation of the stories of Genesis would guide later Judaic exegetes of the same biblical book. So when we follow the work before us, we gain entry into the way in which Judaism in its normative and classical form, from that day to this, would understand the stories of the creation of the world.

Part Three

CONTEXT AND INTERPRETATION

Chapter Six

Interpretation in the Context of Accepted Opinion

The Other in General, Rome in Particular
Correcting a Major Error of Interpreetation

I

The Methodological Issue

Judaism and Christianity in late antiquity present histories that mirror one another. When Christianity began, Judaism was the dominant tradition in the Holy Land and framed its ideas within a political framework until the early fifth century. Christianity there was subordinate and had to work out against the background of a politically definitive Judaism. (Elsewhere, of course, Christianity had to work out of its subordinate position as well.) From the time of Constantine onward, matters reversed themselves. Now Christianity predominated, expressing its ideas in political and institutional terms. Judaism, by contrast, had lost its political foundations and faced the task of working out its self-understanding in terms of a world defined by Christianity, now everywhere triumphant and in charge of politics. The important shift came in the early fourth century. When I speak of the West's first century, therefore, I mean the fourth. That was when the West began in the union of Christian religion and Roman rule. Let me now turn to the issue of method to be illustrated in the topic at hand.

The relationships between Rome and Israel in late antiquity, from the destruction of the Temple in A.D. 70 to the Muslim conquest of the Land of Israel in the mid-seventh century, have attracted attention over the years.[1] What is at issue has not always come to the fore. What scholars have done, when approaching the rabbinic writings of the age, is to collect and organize all the sayings on Rome and to treat the resulting composite as "the Talmudic," or "the rabbinic" view of Rome. In doing so they have followed the established way in which to investigate the thought of classical Judaism on any given subject. It

---

[1] See, for the first systematic work, Shmuel Krauss, *Persia and Rome in Talmud and Midrash* (Jerusalem, 1947, in Hebrew), and, most recently, Mireille Hadas-Lebel,"La fiscalité romaine dans la littérature rabbinique," *Revue des études juives* 1984, 143:5-29.

is to collect pertinent sayings among the diverse documents and to assemble the all these sayings into a composite, a portrait, for example, "*the* rabbinic view of Rome." The composite will divide up the sayings in accord with the logic of the topic at hand. If, for example, we want to know the thought of classical Judaism about God, we collect everything and then divide up the result among such rubrics as God's attributes, God's love, or Providence, or reward and punishment, and the like. Differentiation therefore affects not the documents but the topic. That is to say, whatever we find, without regard to the document in which the saying or story occurs, joins together with whatever else we find, to form an undifferentiated aggregate, thus to illuminate a given aspect of our topic, thus God's love or Providence, as these topics are treated in a diversity of documents. How then do we organize our data? It is by allowing the topic we study to tell us its divisions, that is to say, the logic of differentiation derives from the topic, not the sources from which we draw sayings about the topic at hand.

My research for a number of years has led me to differentiate among documents and to ask each document to deliver its particular viewpoint to me. When, therefore I wish to trace the history of an idea, it produces the representations of that idea as yielded by documents, read singly and one by one, then in the sequence of their closure.[2] I do not join together everything I find, without regard to its point of origin in a given compilation of rabbinic sayings. Rather I keep things apart, so that I record what I find in document A, then in document B, and onward through the alphabet. What this yields is a history of the idea at hand as the document, laid out in their sequence, tell me that history.

Now how shall we test whether the approach just now outlined proves superior to the established one? The answer is to ask what we discover if we do not differentiate among documents, as against what we find when we do. Let me spell this out, and then proceed to an examination of the issue at hand: a particular topic, sources for which are laid forth one way, then investigated and interpreted in two different ways. In the present context, I may not have to plead guilty of excessive criticism of colleagues' scholarship, since both approaches to the description and interpretation of the relationship of Rome and Israel derive from my own work, that is, the one that failed to differentiate among sources, then the one that does effect what I maintain is the required differentiation. In setting forth the positions of Neusner *versus* Neusner, I shall explain where and how I erred and why I think my revision is correct.

---

[2]For reasons I spell out in my *Religious Study of Judaism. Description, Analysis, Interpretation. First Series* (Lanham, 1986: University Press of America), I call this "the canonical history of ideas." The matter does not require attention here.

II

Testing the Worth of Differentiation among Documents

Let me begin by asking, how shall we know which approach is better, or even right? The answer to the question derives from a test of falsification: how can we show, therefore how do we know, whether we are right or wrong. One way of testing the viability of a method is to ask whether it facilitates or impedes the accurate description and analysis of data. Let me spell out this criterion.

My test of the proposed approach of differentiating among documents consists in trying one approach and then its opposite to see the result: a perfectly simple experiment. Our criterion for evaluating results is simple: if we do things in two different ways, in the results of which of the two ways do we see the evidence with greater, in which lesser, perspicacity? That criterion will rapidly prove its entirely objective value. So these are the questions to be raised. If we do not differentiate among documents, then we ask what happens if we do differentiate. If we do differentiate, we ask what happens if we do not. These are simple research experiments, which anyone can replicate.

To spell them out also poses no great difficulty. If differentiating yields results we should have missed had we not read the documents one by one, then our category has obscured important points of difference. If *not* differentiating yields a unity that differentiating has obscured, so that the parts appear, seen all together, to cohere, then the category that has required differentiation has obscured important points in common. How shall we know one way or the other? Do we not invoke a subjective opinion when we conclude that there is, or is not, a unity that differentiation has obscured? I think not. In fact the operative criterion is a matter of fact and does not require subjective judgment. How so? Let me state the objective criterion with emphasis:

[1] *If we find that each one of the documents says on its own essentially what all of the documents say together, so that the parts do turn out to be interchangeable, then imposing distinctions suggests differences where there is none. The parts not only add up to the sum of the whole, as in the case of a homogenizing category. Each of the parts replicates the fundamental structure of the whole. In that case, differentiation proves misleading.*

[2] *If, by contrast, when viewed one by one, our documents in fact do not say the same thing by themselves that all of them say when read together, our category, failing to recognize differences, suggests a unity and a cogency where there is none. The parts may well add up to the sum of the whole, but each of the parts appears to stand by itself and does not replicate the statement to which, as part of a larger whole, it contributes. In that case, not effecting a considerable labor of description of the documents one by one will obscure the very center and heart of matters: that the documents, components of the whole, are themselves*

autonomous, though connected (if that can be shown) and also continuous (if that can be shown).

Accordingly, the results of an experiment of differentiation where, up to now, everything has been read as a single harmonious statement, will prove suggestive -- an interesting indicator of the effect and usefulness of the category at hand. At the end we shall return to these questions and answer them.

Since, in the case of "the Talmudic view of Rome," we treat all writings produced by all Jews as essentially homologous testimonies to a single encompassing Judaism, we shall now engage in a hitherto-neglected exercise of differentiation. We ask what each source produced by Jews in late antiquity, read by itself, has to say about the subject at hand. How shall we differentiate among the available writings? The simplest route is to follow the lines of distinction imposed by the writings themselves, that is, simply, to read one book at a time, and in the order in which the several books are generally held to have reached closure.

III

The Canonical Principle in Category-Formation

The limns of documents then generate, form, and define our initial system of categories. That is, the document to begin with is what demands description, then analysis by comparison and contrast to other documents, then interpretation as part of the whole canon of which it forms a part.[3] In the case at hand, what we have to do is simply ask the principal documents, one by one, to tell us their picture of the topic at hand, hence, Rome and Israel's relationship to Rome. Each document, it is clear, demands description, analysis, and interpretation, all by itself. Each must be viewed as autonomous of all others. At a later stage, each document also is to be examined for its relationships with other documents that fall into the same classification (whether that classification is simply "Jewish" or still more narrowly and hence usefully defined). Then, at the end, each document is to be allowed to take its place as part of the undifferentiated aggregation of documents that, all together, constitute the evidence of a Judaism, in the case of the rabbinic kind, the canon of the Torah.

Let me spell this out. If a document reaches us within its own framework as a complete book with a beginning, a middle, and an end, we do not commit an error in simple logic by reading that document as it has reached us, that is, as a book by itself. If further a document contains materials shared verbatim or in substantial content with other documents of its classification, or if a document explicitly refers to some other writings and their contents, then we have to ask the question of connection. We have to seek the facts of connectedness and ask

---

[3] I hasten to add, I do not take the canon to be a timeless category, as my analysis of the Mishnah and its associates indicates. Quite to the contrary, the canon itself takes shape in stages, and these form interesting categories for study.

for the meaning of those connections. In the description of a Judaism, we have to take as our further task the description of the whole out of the undifferentiated testimony of all of its parts. For a Judaism does put together a set of once discrete documents and treat them as its canon. So in our setting we do want to know how a number of writings fit together into a single continuous and harmonious statement. In the present setting, only the part of the work is required.

IV

The Outsider in General, Rome in Particular

We come to the topic at hand: Rome and Israel. To begin with we approach the matter from its most abstract angle: Rome as representative of the outsider. The outsider in general represented a danger that took many forms, for the outsider found definition in a variety of ways. He could be an Israelite holding views other than those of sages. A perfectly loyal man, for example, who did not accept the rabbis' remarkable claims in behalf of the sanctity of what they knew, or all of their rules, posed a threat. An outsider could be a woman, simply because, in sages' view, men were normal, women abnormal. It could be a Samaritan, sharing Scripture but reading it differently. It could be a Christian, with the old Scripture and a new one, claimed to complete the old. It could be some sort of pagan, wholly outside of the frame of Israelite tradition. It could be a Roman, alien and powerful. It could be an Iranian, from the other side of the frontier, or someone still more different than that. So, in all, we may invent a hierarchy of difference, from nearest to farthest away, and we may further postulate not only degrees of difference but also differentiation among the different, and that on a polythetic basis.

Let us now proceed to review four important sources as autonomous components of a larger canon and to ask each of them to speak for itself, all by itself, on the topic at hand. These fall into two groups: the Mishnah (inclusive of tractate Abot) and a document of Mishnah-exegesis, the Tosefta, and two documents of Scripture exegesis, Genesis Rabbah and Leviticus Rabbah. The former testify to the minds of compositors who flourished in the late second and third centuries (before Christianity became the state religion of the Roman empire), the later, the late fourth and fifth centuries (after the establishment of Christianity as imperial cult and faith). We shall parse the ideas at hand as they unfold in these four compilations.[4] Then we shall trace the result, which is the canonical history of the topic at hand. Finally, we shall review the original results and show where and how they erred -- and, above all, explain the reason why. In that way we shall carry out an exercise in the testing of a method. That is to say, we ask what happens when we do, and when we do not, differentiate.

V

Differentiating among Documents

1. Rome (Esau, Edom) in the Mishnah and Tractate Abot

If we ask the Mishnah, ca. A.D. 200, its principal view of the world beyond, it answers with a simple principle: the framers of the document insist that the world beyond was essentially undifferentiated. Rome to them proved no more, and no less, important than any other place in that undifferentiated world, and, so far as the epochs of human history were concerned, these emerged solely from within Israel, and, in particular, the history of Israel's cult, as M. Zeb. 14:4-9 lays matters out in terms of the cult's location, and M. R.H. 4:1-4 in terms of the before and after of the destruction.[5] The undifferentiation of the outside world may be conveyed in a simple fact. The entire earth outside of the Land of Israel in the Mishnah's law was held to suffer from contamination by corpses. Hence it was unclean with a severe mode of uncleanness, inaccessible to the holy and life-sustaining processes of the cult. If an Israelite artist were asked to paint a wall-portrait of the world beyond the Land, he would paint the entire wall white, the color of death. The outside world, in the imagination of the Mishnah's law, was the realm of death. Among corpses, how are we to make distinctions? We turn then to how the Mishnah and tractate Abot treat Rome, both directly and in the symbolic form of Esau and Edom. Since the system at hand treats all gentiles as essentially the same, Rome, for its part, will not present a theme of special interest. So if my description of the Mishnah's basic mode of differentiation among outsiders proves sound, then Rome should not vastly differ from other outsiders.

---

[4]Since we cannot demonstrate that what is attributed to authorities within the pages of thee documents really was said by them, we also cannot impute to a generation prior to that of redaction anh of the ideas expressed in the several documents: what we cannot show, we do not know. And, to the contrary, what we can show, which is that the documents demonstrably speak for the authorship of the final redaction, we do know: the opinions of the ultimate, sometimes also the penultimate, redactors. That is all we know at this time. So whether or not the Mishnah or Leviticus Rabbah contains ideas held prior to the generation of redaction is not at issue. I claim here to say what the authorship at the end wished to state, in the time and circumstance of redaction. What else these documents contain, to what other ages and authorships they testify, -- these are separate questions, to be taken upon in their own terms. I have done so for the Mishnah and Tosefta in various works of literary and historical study, listed at the end of this document.

[5]In my *Messiah in Context, Israel's History and Destiny in Formative Judaism*(*Foundations of Judaism*,. Vol. II. *Teleology*) (Philadelphia, 1983: Fortress) I dealt at some length with the larger question of later the reimagining of Israel's history. But that is not at issue here.

As a matter of fact, if we turn to H. Y. Kasovsky, *Thesaurus Mishnae* (Jerusalem, 1956) I, II, IV, and look for Edom, Esau, Ishmael, and Rome, we come away disappointed. "Edom" in the sense of Rome does not occur. The word stands for the Edomites of biblical times (M. Yeb. 8:3) and the territory of Edom (M. Ket. 5:8). Ishmael, who like Edo later stands for Rome, supplies a name of a sage, nothing more. As to Rome itself, the picture is not terribly different. There is a "Roman hyssop," (M. Par. 11:7, M. Neg. 14:6), and Rome occurs as a place-name (M. A.Z. 4:7). Otherwise I see not a single passage indicated by Kosovsky in which Rome serves as a topic of interest, and, it goes without saying, in no place does "Rome" stand for an age in human history, let alone the counterpart to and opposite of Israel. Rome is part of the undifferentiated other, the outside world of death beyond. That fact takes on considerable meaning when we turn to the later fourth and fifth century compilations of scriptural exegeses. But first, we turn to the Mishnah's closest companion, the Tosefta.

VI

Differentiating among Documents

2. Rome in the Tosefta

When we come to the Tosefta, a document containing systematic and extensive supplements to the sayings of the Mishnah, we find ourselves entirely within the Mishnah's circle of meanings and values. When, therefore, we ask how the Tosefta's authors incorporate and treat apocalyptic verses of Scripture, as they do, we find that they reduce to astonishingly trivial and local dimensions materials bearing for others world-historical meaning -- including symbols later invoked by sages themselves to express the movement and meaning of history. No nation, including Rome, plays a role in the Tosefta's interpretation of biblical passages presenting historical apocalypse, as we now see in the the Tosefta's treatment of the apocalyptic vision of Daniel. There we find that history happens in what takes place in the sages' debates -- there alone!

T. Miqvaot 7:11

A. A cow which drank purification-water, and which one slaughtered within twenty-four hours --

B. This was a case, and R. Yose the Galilean did declare it clean, and R. Aqiba did declare it unclean.

C. R. Tarfon supported R. Yose the Galilean. R. Simeon ben Nanos supported R. Aqiba.

D. R. Simeon b. Nanos dismissed [the arguments of] R. Tarfon. R. Yose the Galilean dismissed [the arguments of] R. Simeon b. Nanos.

E. R. Aqiba dismissed [the arguments of] R. Yose the Galilean.

F. After a time, he [Yose] found an answer for him [Aqiba].

G. He said to him, "Am I able to reverse myself?"

H. He said to him, "Not anyone [may reverse himself], but you [may do so], for you are Yose the Galilean."

I. [He said to him,] "I shall say to you: Lo, Scripture states, And they shall be kept for the congregation of the people of Israel for the water for impurity (Num. 19:9).

J. "Just so long as they are kept, lo, they are water for impurity -- but not after a cow has drunk them."

K. This was a case, and thirty-two elders voted in Lud and declared it clean.

L. At that time R. Tarfon recited this verse:

M. "I saw the ram goring westward and northward and southward, and all the animals were unable to stand against it, and none afforded protection from its power, and it did just as it liked and grew great (Dan. 8:4) --

N. "[This is] R. Aqiba.

O. "'As I was considering, behold, a he-goat came from the west across the face of the whole earth, without touching the ground; and the goat had a conspicuous horn between his eyes.

P. "'He came to the ram with the two horns, which I had seen standing on the bank of the river, and he ran at him in his mighty wrath. I saw him come close to the ram, and he was enraged against him and struck the ram and broke his two horns' -- this is R. Aqiba and R. Simeon b. Nanos.

Q. "'And the ram had no power to stand before him' -- this is R. Aqiba.

R. "'But he cast him down to the ground and trampled upon him' -- this is R. Yose the Galilean.

S. "'And there was no one who could rescue the ram from his power' -- these are the thirty-two elders who voted in Lud and declared it clean.'"

I cite the passage here only to underline the contrast between the usage at hand and the one we shall find in the late fourth or early fifth century composition.

Since, in a moment, we shall take up writings universally assigned to the later fourth or early fifth century, when Rome had turned definitively Christian, we do well to ask the Tosefta to tell us how it chooses to speak of Christianity. Here too the topic (if it is present at all) turns out to produce a trivial and not a world-historical comment, a fact that in a moment will strike us as significant. To the first-century authority, Tarfon is attributed the angry observation that there were people around who knew the truth of the Torah but rejected it:

Tosefta Shabbat 13:55

The books of the Evangelists and the books of the minim they do not save from a fire [on the Sabbath]. They are allowed to burn up where they are, they and [even] the references to the Divine Name that are in them...

Said R. Tarfon, "May I bury my sons if such things come into my hands and I do not burn them, and even the references to the Divine Name which are in them. And if someone was running after me, I should escape into a temple of idolatry, but I should not go into their houses of worship. For idolators do not recognize the Divinity in denying him, but these recognize the Divinity and deny him.   About them Scripture states, 'Behind the door and the doorpost you have set your symbol for deserting me, you have uncovered your bed' (Is. 57:8)."

This statement has long persuaded scholars that the rabbinic authority recognized the difference between pagans and those minim under discussion, reasonably assumed to be Christian.   I see no reason to differ from the established consensus.   The upshot is simple: when Christians came under discussion, they appear as a source of exasperation, not asIsrael's counterpart and opposite, lete alone as ruler of the world and precurser to Israel's final triumph in history.   We stand a considerable distance from deep thought about Israel and Rome, Jacob and Esau, this age and the coming one.   What we witness is a trivial dispute within the community at hand: heretics who should, but do not, know better.   And when we hear that mode of thought, we shall look back with genuine disappointment upon the materials at hand.   They in no way consider the world-historical issues that would face Israel, and the reason, I maintain, is that, at the point at which the document in which the passage occurs was brought to closure, no one imagined what would ultimately take place: the conversion of the empire to Christianity, the triumph of Christianity on the stage of history.

We turn, finally, to the usage of the words Esau, Edom, Ishmael, and Rome, which in just a moment will come to center stage.   Relying on H. Y. Kosovsky [here: Chaim Josua Kasowski], *Thesaurus Thosephthae* (Jerusalem, I: 1932; III: 1942; VI, 1961), we find pretty much the same sort of usages, in the same proportions, as the Mishnah has already shown us.   Specifically, Edom is a biblical people, T. Yeb. 8:1, Niddah 6:1, Qid. 5:4.   Ishmael is a proper name for several sages.   More important, Ishmael never stands for Rome.   And Rome itself?   We have Todor of Rome (T. Bes. 2:15), Rome as a place where people live, e. g., "I saw it in Rome" (T. Yoma 3:8), "I taught this law in Rome" (T. Nid. 7:1, T. Miq. 4:7).   And that is all.

If we were to propose a thesis on "Rome" and "Christianity" in the Talmud and Midrash" based on the evidence at hand, it would not produce many propositions.   Rome is a place, and no biblical figures or places prefigure the place of Rome in the history of Israel.   That is so even though the authors of the Mishnah and the Tosefta knew full well who had destroyed the Temple and closed of Jerusalem and what these events had meant.   Christianity plays no role of consequence; no one takes the matter very seriously.   Christians are people who know the truth but deny it: crazies.   To state the negative: Rome does not stand for Israel's nemesis and counterpart, Rome did not mark an epoch in the history of the world, Israel did not encompass Rome in Israel's history of humanity, and Rome did not represent one of the four monarchies -- the last, the worst, prior to Israel's rule.   To invoke a modern category, Rome stood for a perfectly secular matter: a place, where things happened.   Rome in no way symbolized anything beyond itself. And Israel's sages did not find they had to take seriously the presence or claims of Christianity.[6]

VII

Differentiating among Documents
3. Rome in Genesis Rabbah

So much for books brought to closure, in ase of the Mishnah, at ca. A.D. 200, and, in the case of the Tosefta, about a hundred years later (no one knows). We come now to the year 400 or so, t up documents produced in the century after "such momentous events as, first the conversion of Constantinte to Christianity, second, the catastrophe of Julian's failure in allowing the Temple to be rebuilt, the repression of paganism and its affect on Judaism, the Christianization of the Holy Land, and, it appears, the conversion of sizable numbers of Jews in the Land of Israel to Christianity and the consequent Christianitzation of Palestine (no longer, in context, the Land of Israel at all). We turn first to Genesis Rabbah, generally assigned to the year 400. What do we find there?

In Genesis Rabbah sages read the book of Genesis as if it portrayed the history of Israel and Rome -- and Rome in particular. Now Rome plays a role in the biblical narrative, with special reference to the counterpart and opposite of the patriarchs, first Ishmael, then Esau, and, always, Edom. For that is the single obsession binding sages of the document at hand to common discourse with the text before them. Why Rome in the form it takes in Genesis Rabbah? And how come the obsessive character of sages disposition of the theme of Rome? Were their picture merely of Rome as tyrant and destroyer of the Temple, we should have no reason to link the text to the problems of the age of redaction and closure. But now it is Rome as Israel's brother, counterpart, and nemesis, Rome as the one thing standing in the way of Israel's, and the world's, ultimate salvation. So the stakes are different, and much higher.

Let us begin with a simple example of how ubiquitous is the shadow of Ishmael/Esau/Edom/Rome. Wherever sages reflect on future history, their minds turn to their own day. They found the hour difficult, because Rome, now Christian, claimed that very birthright and blessing that they understood to be theirs alone. Christian Rome posed a threat without precedent. Now another dominion, besides Israel's, claimed the rights and blessings that sustained.israel. Wherever in Scripture they turned, sages found comfort in the iteration that the birthright, the blessing, the Torah, and the hope -- all belonged to them and to none other. Here is a striking statement of that constant proposition.

---

[6]The dogma that Christianity never made a difference to Judaism confused me too, as I shall point out presently.

LIII:XII.

1. A. "[So she said to Abraham, 'Cast out this slave woman with her son, for the son of this slave woman shall not be heir with my son Isaac.'] And the thing was very displeasing to Abraham on account of his son" (Gen. 21:11):

   B. That is in line with this verse: "And shuts his eyes from looking upon evil" (Is. 33:15). [Freedman, p. 471, n. 1: He shut his eyes from Ishmael's evil ways and was reluctant to send him away.]

2. A. "But God said to Abraham, 'Be not displeased because of the lad and because of your slave woman; whatever Sarah says to you, do as she tells you, for through Isaac shall your descendants be named'" (Gen. 21:12):

   B. Said R. Yudan bar Shillum, "What is written is not 'Isaac' but 'through Isaac.' [The matter is limited, not through all of Isaac's descendants but only through some of them, thus excluding Esau.]"

3. A. R. Azariah in the name of Bar Hutah: "The use of the B, which stands for two, indicates that he who affirms that there are two worlds will inherit both worlds [this age and the age to come]."

   B. Said R. Yudan bar Shillum, "It is written, 'Remember his marvelous works that he has done, his signs and the judgments of his mouth' (Ps. 105:5). I have given a sign , namely, it is one who gives the appropriate evidence through what he says. Specifically, he who affirms that there are two worlds will be called 'your seed.'

   C. "And he who does not affirm that there are two worlds will not be called 'your seed.'"

No. 1 makes "the matter" refer to Ishmael's misbehavior, not Sarah's proposal, so removing the possibility of disagreement between Abraham and Sarah. Nos. 2, 3 interpret the limiting particle, "in," that is, *among* the descendants of Isaac will be found Abraham's heirs, but not all the descendants of Isaac will be heirs of Abraham. No. 2 explicitly excludes Esau, that is Rome, and No. 3 makes the matter doctrinal in the context of Israel's inner life. As the several antagonists of Israel stand for Rome in particular, so the traits of Rome, as sages perceived them, characterized the biblical heroes. Esau provided a favorite target. From the womb Israel and Rome contended.

LXIII:VI.

1. A. "And the children struggled together [within her, and she said, 'If it is thus, why do I live?' So she went to inquire of the Lord. And the Lord said to her, 'Two nations are in your womb, and two peoples, born of you, shall be divided; the one shall be stronger than the other, and the elder shall serve the younger'] " (Gen. 25:22-23):

   B. R. Yohanan and R. Simeon b. Laqish:

   C. R. Yohanan said, "[Because the word, 'struggle,' contains the letters for the word, 'run,'] this one was running to kill that one and that one was running to kill this one."

   D. R. Simeon b. Laqish: "This one releases the laws given by that one, and that one releases the laws given by this one."

2. A. R. Berekhiah in the name of R. Levi said, "It is so that you should not say that it was only after he left his mother's womb that [Esau] contended against [Jacob].

    B. "But even while he was yet in his mother's womb, his fist was stretched forth against him: 'The wicked stretch out their fists [so Freedman] from the womb' (Ps. 58:4)."

3. A. "And the children struggled together within her:"

    B. [Once more referring to the letters of the word "struggled," with special attention to the ones that mean, "run,"] they wanted to run within her.

    C. When she went by houses of idolatry, Esau would kick, trying to get out: "The wicked are estranged from the womb" (Ps. 58:4).

    D. When she went by synagogues and study-houses, Jacob would kick, trying to get out: "Before I formed you in the womb, I knew you" (Jer. 1:5)."

4. A. "...and she said, 'If it is thus, why do I live?'"

    B. R. Haggai in the name of R. Isaac: "This teaches that our mother, Rebecca, went around to the doors of women and said to them, 'Did you ever have this kind of pain in your life?'"

    C. "[She said to them,] '"If thus:" If this is the pain of having children, would that I had not gotten pregnant.'"

    D. Said R. Huna, "If I am going to produce twelve tribes only through this kind of suffering, would that I had not gotten pregnant."

5. A. It was taught on Tannaite authority in the name of R. Nehemiah, "Rebecca was worthy of having the twelve tribes come forth from her. That is in line with this verse:

    B. "Two nations are in your womb, and two peoples, born of you, shall be divided; the one shall be stronger than the other, and the elder shall serve the younger.' When her days to be delivered were fulfilled, behold, there were twins in her womb. The first came forth red, all his body like a hairy mantle, so they called his name Esau. Afterward his brother came forth...' (Gen. 25:23-24).

    C. "Two nations are in your womb:' thus two.

    D. "'and two peoples:'thus two more, hence four.

    E. "'...the one shall be stronger than the other:' two more, so six.

    F. "'...and the elder shall serve the younger:' two more, so eight.

    G. "When her days to be delivered were fulfilled, behold, there were twins in her womb:' two more, so ten.

    H. "The first came forth red:' now eleven.

    J. "'Afterward his brother came forth:' now twelve."

    K. There are those who say, "Proof derives from this verse: 'If it is thus, why do I live?' Focusing on the word for 'thus,' we note that the two letters of that word bear the numerical value of seven and five respectively, hence, twelve in all."

6. A. "So she went to inquire of the Lord:"

    B. Now were there synagogues and houses of study in those days [that she could go to inquire of the Lord]?

C. But is it not the fact that she went only to the study of Eber?

D. This serves to teach you that whoever receives an elder is as if he receives the Presence of God.

Nos. 1-3 take for granted that Esau represents Rome, and Jacob, Israel. Consequently the verse underlines the point that there is natural enmity between Israel and Rome. Esau hated Israel even while he was still in the womb. Jacob, for his part, revealed from the womb those virtues that would characterize him later on, eager to serve God as Esau was eager to worship idols. The text invites just this sort of reading. No. 4 and No. 5 relate Rebecca's suffering to the birth of the twelve tribes. No. 6 makes its own point, independent of the rest and tacked on. In the next passage Rome appears as a pig, an important choice for symbolization, as we shall see in Leviticus Rabbah as well:

LXV:I.

1. A. "When Esau was forty years old, he took to wife Judith, the daughter of Beeri, the Hittite, and Basemath the daughter of Elon the Hittite; and they made life bitter for Isaac and Rebecca" (Gen. 26:34-35):

    B. "The swine out of the wood ravages it, that which moves in the field feeds on it" (Ps. 80:14).

    C. R. Phineas and R. Hilqiah in the name of R. Simon: "Among all of the prophets, only two of them spelled out in public [the true character of Rome, represented by the swine], Asaf and Moses.

    D. "Asaf: 'The swine out of the wood ravages it.'

    E. "Moses: 'And the swine, because he parts the hoof' (Deut. 14:8).

    F. "Why does Moses compare Rome to the swine? Just as the swine, when it crouches, puts forth its hoofs as if to say, 'I am clean,' so the wicked kingdom steals and grabs, while pretending to be setting up courts of justice.

    G. "So Esau, for all forty years, hunted married women, ravished them, and when he reached the age of forty, he presented himself to his father, saying, 'Just as father got married at the age of forty, so I shall marry a wife at the age of forty.'

    H. "'When Esau was forty years old, he took to wife Judith, the daughter of Beeri, the Hittite, and Basemath the daughter of Elon the Hittite.'"

How long would Rome rule, when would Isarael succeed? The important point is that Rome was next to last, Israel last. Rome's triumph brought assurance that Israel would be next -- and last:

LXXV:IV.

2. A. "And Jacob sent messengers before him:"

    B. To this one [Esau] whose time to take hold of sovereignty would come before him [namely, before Jacob, since Esau would rule, then Jacob would govern].

    C.   R. Joshua b. Levi said, "Jacob took off the purple robe and threw it before Esau, as if to say to him, 'Two flocks of starlings are not going to sleep on a single branch' [so we cannot rule at the same time].'"

3.   A.   "...to Esau his brother:"

    B.   Even though he was Esau, he was still his brother.

Esau remains Jacob's brother, and that Esau rules before Jacob will. The application to contemporary affairs cannot be missed, both in the recognition of the true character of Esau -- a brother! -- and in the interpretation of the future of history.

To conclude: Genesis Rabbah reached closure, people generally agree, toward the end of the fourth century. That century marks the beginning of the West as we have known it. Why so? Because in the fourth century, from the conversion of Constantine and over the next hundred years, the Roman empire became Christian -- and with it, the West. So the fourth century marks the first century of the history of the West in that form in which the West would flourish for the rest of time, to our own day. Accordingly, we should not find surprising sages' recurrent references, in the reading of Genesis, to the struggle of two equal powers, Rome and Israel, Esau and Jacob, Ishmael and Isaac. The world-historical change, marking the confirmation in politics and power of the Christians' claim that Christ was king over all humanity, demanded from sages an appropriate, and, to Israel, persuasive. response.

VIII

Differentiating among Documents

4. Rome in Leviticus Rabbah

What we see in Leviticus Rabbah is consistent with what we have already observed in Genesis Rabbah: how sages absorb events into their system of classification. So it is sages that make history through the thoughts they think and the rules they lay down. In such a context, we find no interest either in the outsiders and their powers, or in the history of the empires of the world, or, all the more so, in redemption and the messianic fulfillment of time. What is the alternative to the use of the sort of symbols just now examined? Let us turn immediately to the relevant passages of Leviticus Rabbah:

XIII:V

1.   A.   Said R. Ishmael b. R. Nehemiah, "All the prophets foresaw what the pagan kingdoms would do [to Israel].

    B.   "The first man foresaw what the pagan kingdoms would do [to Israel].

    C.   "That is in line with the following verse of Scripture: 'A river flowed out of Eden [to water the garden, and there it divided and became four rivers]' (Gen. 2:10). [The four rivers stand for the four kingdoms, Babylonia, Media, Greece, and Rome]."

2.   A.   R. Tanhuma said it, [and] R. Menahema [in the name of] R. Joshua b. Levi: "The Holy One, blessed be he, will give the cup of reeling to the nations of the world to drink in the world to come.

       B.   "That is in line with the following verse of Scripture: 'A river flowed out of Eden' (Gen 2:10), the place from which justice [DYN] goes forth."

3.   A.   "[There it divided] and became four rivers" (Gen 2:10) -- this refers to the four kingdoms.

       B.   "The name of the first is Pishon (PSWN); [it is the one which flows around the whole land of Havilah, where there is gold; and the gold of that land is good; bdellium and onyx stone are there]" (Gen. 2:11-12).

       C.   This refers to Babylonia, on account [of the reference to Babylonia in the following verse:] "And their [the Babylonians'] horsemen spread themselves (PSW)" (Hab. 1:8).

       D.   [It is further] on account of [Nebuchadnezzar's being] a dwarf, shorter than ordinary men by a handbreadth.

       E.   "[It is the one which flows around the whole land of Havilah" (Gen. 2:11).

       F.   "This [reference to the river's flowing around the whole land] speaks of Nebuchadnezzar, the wicked man, who came up and surrounded the entire Land of Israel, which places its hope in the Holy One, blessed be he.

       G.   That is in line with the following verse of Scripture: "Hope in God, for I shall again praise him" (Ps. 42:5).

       H.   "Where there is gold" (Gen. 2:11) -- this refers to the words of Torah, "which are more to be desired than gold, more than much fine gold" (Ps. 19:11).

       I.   "And the gold of that land is good" (Gen. 2:12).

       J.   This teaches that there is no Torah like the Torah that is taught in the Land of Israel, and there is no wisdom like the wisdom that is taught in the Land of Israel.

       K.   Bdellium and onyx stone are there" (Gen. 2:12) -- Scripture, Mishnah, Talmud, and lore.

4.   A.   "The name of the second river is Gihon; [it is the one which flows around the whole land of Cush]" (Gen. 2:13).

       B.   This refers to Media, which produced Haman, that wicked man, who spit out venom like a serpent.

       C.   It is on account of the verse: "On your belly will you go" (Gen. 3:14).

       D.   "It is the one which flows around the whole land of Cush" (Gen. 2:13).

       E.   [We know that this refers to Media, because it is said:] "Who rules from India to Cush" (Est. 1:1).

5.   A.   "And the name of the third river is Tigris (HDQL), [which flows east of Assyria] (Gen. 2:14).

       B.   This refers to Greece [Syria], which was sharp (HD) and speedy (QL) in making its decrees, saying to Israel, "Write on the horn of an ox that you have no portion in the God of Israel."

       C.   "Which flows east (QDMT) of Assyria" (Gen. 2:14).

D. Said R. Huna, "In three aspects the kingdom of Greece was in advance (QDMH) of the present evil kingdom [Rome]: in respect to ship-building, the arrangement of camp vigils, and language."

E. Said R. Huna, "Any and every kingdom may be called 'Assyria' (ashur), on account of all of their making themselves powerful at Israel's expense."

F. Said R. Yose b. R. Hanina, "Any and every kingdom may be called Nineveh (NNWH), on account of their adorning (NWY) themselves at Israel's expense."

G. Said R. Yose b. R. Hanina, "Any and every kingdom may be called Egypt (MSRYM), on account of their oppressing (MSYRYM) Israel."

6. A. "And the fourth river is the Euphrates (PRT)" (Gen. 2:14).

B. This refers to Edom [Rome], since it was fruitful (PRT), and multiplied through the prayer of the elder [Isaac at Gen. 27:39].

C. Another interpretation: "It was because it was fruitful and multiplied, and so cramped his world.

D. Another explanation: Because it was fruitful and multiplied and cramped his son.

E. Another explanation: Because it was fruitful and multiplied and cramped his house.

F. Another explanation: "Parat" -- because in the end, "I am going to exact a penalty from it."

G. That is in line with the following verse of Scripture: "I have trodden (PWRH) the winepress alone" (Is. 63:3).

7. A. [Gen. R. 42:2:] Abraham foresaw what the evil kingdoms would do [to Israel].

B. "[As the sun was going down,] a deep sleep fell on Abraham; and lo, a dread and great darkness fell upon him]" (Gen. 15:12).

C. "Dread" ('YMH) refers to Babylonia, on account of the statement, "Then Nebuchadnezzer was full of fury (HMH)" (Dan. 3:19).

D. "Darkness" refers to Media, which brought darkness to Israel through its decrees: "to destroy, to slay, and to wipe out all the Jews" (Est. 7:4).

E. "Great" refers to Greece.

F. Said R. Judah b. R. Simon, "The verse teaches that the kingdom of Greece set up one hundred twenty-seven governors, one hundred and twenty-seven hyparchs and one hundred twenty-seven commanders."

G. And rabbis say, "They were sixty in each category."

H. R. Berekhiah and R. Hanan in support of this position taken by rabbis: "'Who led you through the great terrible wilderness, with its fiery serpents and scorpions and thirsty ground where there was no water]' (Deut. 8:15).

I. "Just as the scorpion produces eggs by sixties, so the kingdom of Greece would set up its administration in groups of sixty."

J. "Fell on him" (Gen. 15:12).

K. This refers to Edom, on account of the following verse: "The earth quakes at the noise of their [Edom's] fall" (Jer. 49:21).

L.   There are those who reverse matters.

M.   "Fear" refers to Edom, on account of the following verse: "And this I saw, a fourth beast, fearful, and terrible" (Dan. 7:7).

M.   "Darkness" refers to Greece, which brought gloom through its decrees. For they said to Israel, "Write on the horn of an ox that you have no portion in the God of Israel."

O.   "Great" refers to Media, on account of the verse: "King Ahasuerus made Haman [the Median] great" (Est. 3:1).

P.   "Fell on him" refers to Babylonia, on account of the following verse: "Fallen, fallen is Babylonia" (Is. 21:9).

8.   A.   Daniel foresaw what the evil kingdoms would do [to Israel].

B.   "Daniel said, I saw in my vision by night, and behold, the four winds of heaven were stirring up the great sea. And four great beasts came up out of the sea, [different from one another. The first was like a lion and had eagles' wings. Then as I looked, its wings were plucked off... And behold, another beast, a second one, like a bear... After this I looked, and lo, another, like a leopard... After this I saw in the night visions, and behold, a fourth beast, terrible and dreadful and exceedingly strong; and it had great iron teeth]" (Dan. 7:3-7).

C.   If you enjoy sufficient merit, it will emerge from the sea, but if not, it will come out of the forest.

D.   The animal that comes up from the sea is not violent, but the one that comes up out of the forest is violent.

E.   Along these same lines: "The boar out of the wood ravages it" (Ps. 80:14).

F.   If you enjoy sufficient merit, it will come from the river, and if not, from the forest.

G.   The animal that comes up from the river is not violent, but the one that comes up out of the forest is violent.

H.   "Different from one another" (Dan. 7:3).

I.   Differing from [hating] one another.

J.   This teaches that every nation that rules in the world hates Israel and reduces them to slavery.

K.   "The first was like a lion [and had eagles' wings]" (Dan. 7:4).

L.   This refers to Babylonia.

M.   Jeremiah saw [Babylonia] as a lion. Then he went and saw it as an eagle.

N.   He saw it as a lion: "A lion has come up from his thicket" (Jer. 4:7).

O.   And [as an eagle:] "Behold, he shall come up and swoop down as the eagle" (Jer. 49:22).

P.   People said to Daniel, "What do you see?"

Q.   He said to them, "I see the face like that of a lion and wings like those of an eagle: 'The first was like a lion and had eagles' wings. Then, as I looked, its wings were plucked off, and it was lifted up from the ground [and made to stand upon two feet like a man and the heart of a man was given to it]' (Dan. 7:4).

R.   R. Eleazar and R. Ishmael b. R. Nehemiah:

S.   R. Eleazar said, "While the entire lion was smitten, its heart was not smitten.

T.   "That is in line with the following statement: 'And the heart of a man was given to it' (Dan. 7:4)."

U.   And R. Ishmael b. R. Nehemiah said, "Even its heart was smitten, for it is written, 'Let his heart be changed from a man's' (Dan. 4:17).

X.   "And behold, another beast, a second one, like a bear. [It was raised up one side; it had three ribs in its mouth between its teeth, and it was told, Arise, devour much flesh]" (Dan. 7:5).

Y.   This refers to Media.

Z.   Said R. Yohanan, "It is like a bear."

AA.   It is written, "similar to a wolf" (DB); thus, "And a wolf was there."

BB.   That is in accord with the view of R. Yohanan, for R.Yohanan said, "Therefore a lion out of the forest [slays them]' (Jer. 5:6) -- this refers to Babylonia.

CC.   "'A wolf of the deserts spoils them' (Jer. 5:6) refers to Media.

DD.   "'A leopard watches over their cities' (Jer. 5:6) refers to Greece.

EE.   "'Whoever goes out from them will be savaged' (Jer. 5:6) refers to Edom.

FF.   "Why so? 'Because their transgressions are many, and their backslidings still more' (Jer. 5:6)."

GG.   "After this, I looked, and lo, another, like a leopard [with four wings of a bird on its back; and the beast had four heads; and dominion was given to it]" (Dan. 7:6).

HH.   This [leopard] refers to Greece, which persisted impudently in making harsh decrees, saying to Israel, "Write on the horn of an ox that you have no share in the God of Israel."

II.   "After this I saw in the night visions, and behold, a fourth beast, terrible and dreadful and exceedingly strong; [and it had great iron teeth; it devoured and broke in pieces and stamped the residue with its feet. It was different from all the beasts that were before it; and it had ten horns]" (Dan. 7:7).

JJ.   This refers to Edom [Rome].

KK.   Daniel saw the first three visions on one night, and this one he saw on another night. Now why was that the case?

LL.   R. Yohanan and R. Simeon b. Laqish:

MM.   R. Yohanan said, "It is because the fourth beast weighed as much as the first three."

NN.   And R. Simeon b. Laqish said, "It outweighed them."

OO.   R. Yohanan objected to R. Simeon b. Laqish, "'Prophesy, therefore, son of man, clap your hands [and let the sword come down twice; yea, thrice. The sword for those to be slain; it is the sword for the great slaughter, which encompasses them]' (Ez. 21:14-15). [So the single sword of Rome weighs against the three others]."

PP.   And R. Simeon b. Laqish, how does he interpret the same passage? He notes that [the threefold sword] is doubled (Ez. 21:14), [thus outweighs the three swords, equally twice their strength].

9.   A.   Moses foresaw what the evil kingdoms would do [to Israel].

B.   "The camel, rock badger, and hare" (Deut. 14:7).   [Compare: "Nevertheless, among those that chew the cud or part the hoof, you shall not eat these: the camel, because it chews the cud but does not part the hoof, is unclean to you. The rock badger, because it chews the cud but does not part the hoof, is unclean to you. And the hare, because it chews the cud but does not part the hoof, is unclean to you, and the pig, because it parts the hoof and is cloven-footed, but does not chew the cud, is unclean to you" (Lev. 11:4-8).]

C.   The camel (GML) refers to Babylonia, [in line with the following verse of Scripture: "O daughter of Babylonia, you who are to be devastated!] Happy will be he who requites (GML) you, with what you have done to us" (Ps. 147:8).

D.   "The rock badger" (Deut. 14:7) -- this refers to Media.

E.   Rabbis and R. Judah b. R. Simon.

F.   Rabbis say, "Just as the rock badger exhibits traits of uncleanness and traits of cleanness, so the kingdom of Media produced both a righteous man and a wicked one."

G.   Said R. Judah b. R. Simon, "The last Darius was Esther's son. He was clean on his mother's side and unclean on his father's side."

H.   "The hare" (Deut 14:7) -- this refers to Greece. The mother of King Ptolemy was named "Hare" [in Greek: lagos].

I.   "The pig" (Deut. 14:7) -- this refers to Edom [Rome].

J.   Moses made mention of the first three in a single verse and the final one in a verse by itself [(Deut. 14:7, 8)]. Why so?

K.   R. Yohanan and R. Simeon b. Laqish.

L.   R. Yohanan said, "It is because [the pig] is equivalent to the other three."

M.   And R. Simeon b. Laqish said, "It is because it outweighs them."

N.   R. Yohanan objected to R. Simeon b. Laqish, "'Prophesy, therefore, son of man, clap your hands [and let the sword come down twice, yea thrice]' (Ez. 21:14)."

O.   And how does R. Simeon b. Laqish interpret the same passage? He notes that [the threefold sword] is doubled (Ez. 21:14).

10. A.   [Gen. R. 65:1:] R. Phineas and R. Hilqiah in the name of R. Simon: "Among all the prophets, only two of them revealed [the true evil of Rome], Assaf and Moses.

B.   "Assaf said, 'The pig out of the wood ravages it' (Ps. 80:14).

C.   "Moses said, 'And the pig, [because it parts the hoof and is cloven-footed but does not chew the cud]' (Lev. 11:7).

D.   "Why is [Rome] compared to a pig?

E.   "It is to teach you the following: Just as, when a pig crouches and produces its hooves, it is as if to say, 'See how I am clean [since I have a cloven hoof],' so this evil kingdom takes pride, seizes by violence, and steals, and then gives the appearance of establishing a tribunal for justice."

F. There was the case of a ruler in Caesarea, who put thieves, adulterers, and sorcerers to death, while at the same time telling his counsellor, "That same man [I] did all these three things on a single night."

11. A. Another interpretation: "The camel" (Lev. 11:4).

B. This refers to Babylonia.

C. "Because it chews the cud [but does not part the hoof]" (Lev. 11:4).

D. For it brings forth praises [with its throat] of the Holy One, blessed be he. [The Hebrew words for "chew the cud" -- bring up cud -- are now understood to mean "give praise." GRH is connected with GRWN, throat, hence, "bring forth [sounds of praise through] the throat."

E. R. Berekhiah and R. Helbo in the name of R. Ishmael b. R. Nahman: "Whatever [praise of God] David [in writing a psalm] treated singly [item by item], that wicked man [Nebuchadnezzar] lumped together in a single verse.

F. "'Now I, Nebuchadnezzar, praise and extol and honor the King of heaven, for all his works are right and his ways are just, and those who walk in pride he is able to abase' (Dan. 4:37).

G. "'Praise' -- 'O Jerusalem, praise the Lord' (Ps. 147:12).

H. "'Extol' -- 'I shall extol you, O Lord, for you have brought me low' (Ps. 30:2).

I. "'Honor the king of heaven' -- 'The Lord reigns, let the peoples tremble! He sits enthroned upon the cherubim, let the earth quake' (Ps. 99:1).

J. "'For all his works are right' -- 'For the sake of thy steadfast love and thy faithfulness' (Ps. 115:1).

K. "'And his ways are just' -- 'He will judge the peoples with equity' (Ps. 96:10).

L. "'And those who walk in pride' -- 'The Lord reigns, he is robed in majesty, the Lord is robed, he is girded with strength' (Ps. 93:1).

M. "'He is able to abase' -- 'All the horns of the wicked he will cut off' (Ps. 75:11)."

N. "The rock badger" (Lev. 11:5) -- this refers to Media.

O. "For it chews the cud" -- for it gives praise to the Holy One, blessed be he: "Thus says Cyrus, king of Persia, 'All the kingdoms of the earth has the Lord, the God of the heaven, given me" (Ezra 1:2).

P. "The hare" -- this refers to Greece.

Q. "For it chews the cud" -- for it gives praise to the Holy One, blessed be he.

R. Alexander the Macedonian, when he saw Simeon the Righteous, said, "Blessed be the God of Simeon the Righteous."

S. "The pig" (Lev. 11:7) -- this refers to Edom.

T. "For it does not chew the cud" -- for it does not give praise to the Holy One, blessed be he.

U. And it is not enough that it does not give praise, but it blasphemes and swears violently, saying, "Whom do I have in heaven, and with you I want nothing on earth" (Ps. 73:25).

12. A. Another interpretation [of GRH, cud, now with reference to GR, stranger:]

B. "The camel" (Lev. 11:4) -- this refers to Babylonia.

C. "For it chews the cud" [now: brings up the stranger] -- for it exalts righteous men: "And Daniel was in the gate of the king" (Dan. 2:49).

D. "The rock badger" (Lev. 11:5) -- this refers to Media.

E. "For it brings up the stranger" -- for it exalts righteous men: "Mordecai sat at the gate of the king" (Est. 2:19).

F. "The hare" (Lev. 11:6) -- this refers to Greece.

G. "For it brings up the stranger" -- for it exalts the righteous.

H. When Alexander of Macedonia saw Simeon the Righteous, he would rise up on his feet. They said to him, "Can't you see the Jew, that you stand up before this Jew?"

I. He said to them, "When I go forth to battle, I see something like this man's visage, and I conquer."

J. "The pig" (Lev. 11:7) -- this refers to Rome.

K. "But it does not bring up the stranger" -- for it does not exalt the righteous.

L. And it is not enough that it does not exalt them, but it kills them.

M. That is in line with the following verse of Scripture: "I was angry with my people, I profaned my heritage; I gave them into your hand, you showed them no mercy; on the aged you made your yoke exceedingly heavy" (Is. 47:6).

N. This refers to R. Aqiba and his colleagues.

13. A. Another interpretation [now treating "bring up the cud" (GR) as "bring along in its train" (GRR)]:

B. "The camel" (Lev. 11:4) -- this refers to Babylonia.

C. "Which brings along in its train" -- for it brought along another kingdom after it.

D. "The rock badger" (Lev. 11:5) -- this refers to Media.

E. "Which brings along in its train" -- for it brought along another kingdom after it.

F. "The hare" (Lev. 11:6) -- this refers to Greece.

G. "Which brings along in its train" -- for it brought along another kingdom after it.

H. "The pig" (Lev. 11:7) -- this refers to Rome.

I. "Which does not bring along in its train" -- for it did not bring along another kingdom after it.

J. And why is it then called "pig" (HZYR)? For it restores (MHZRT) the crown to the one who truly should have it [namely, Israel, whose dominion will begin when the rule of Rome ends].

K.   That is in line with the following verse of Scripture: "And saviors will come up on Mount Zion to judge the Mountain of Esau [Rome], and the kingdom will then belong to the Lord" (Ob. 1:21).

To stand back and consider this vast apocalyptic vision of Israel's history, we first review the message of the construction as a whole. This comes in two parts, first, the explicit, then the implicit. As to the former, the first claim is that God had told the prophets what would happen to Israel at the hands of the pagan kingdoms, Babylonia, Media, Greece, Rome. These are further represented by Nebuchadnezzar, Haman, Alexander for Greece, Edom or Esau, interchangeably, for Rome. The same vision came from Adam, Abraham, Daniel and Moses. The same policy toward Israel -- oppression, destruction, enslavement, alienation from the true God -- emerged from all four.

How does Rome stand out? First, it was made fruitful through the prayer of Isaac in behalf of Esau. Second, Edom is represented by the fourth and final beast. Rome is related through Esau, as Babylonia, Media, and Greece are not. The fourth beast was seen in a vision separate from the first three. It was worst of all and outweighed the rest. In the apocalypticizing of the animals of Lev. 11:4-8/Deut. 14:7, the camel, rock badger, hare, and pig, the pig, standing for Rome, again emerges as different from the others and more threatening than the rest. Just as the pig pretends to be a clean beast by showing the cloven hoof, but in fact is an unclean one, so Rome pretends to be just but in fact governs by thuggery. Edom does not pretend to praise God but only blasphemes. It does not exalt the righteous but kills them. These symbols concede nothing to Christian monotheism and biblicism. Of greatest importance, while all the other beasts bring further ones in their wake, the pig does not: "It does not bring another kingdom after it." It will restore the crown to the one who will truly deserve it, Israel. Esau will be judged by Zion, so Obadiah 1:21. Now how has the symbolization delivered an implicit message? It is in the treatment of Rome as distinct, but essentially equivalent to the former kingdoms. This seems to me a stunning way of saying that the now-Christian empire in no way requires differentiation from its pagan predecessors. Nothing has changed, except matters have gotten worse. Beyond Rome, standing in a straight line with the others, lies the true shift in history, the rule of Israel and the cessation of the dominion of the (pagan) nations.

To conclude, Leviticus Rabbah came to closure, it is generally agreed, around A.D. 400, that is, approximately a century after the Roman Empire in the east had begun to become Christian, and half a century after the last attempt to rebuild the Temple in Jerusalem had failed -- a tumultuous age indeed. Accordingly, we have had the chance to see how distinctive and striking are the ways in which, in the text at hand, the symbols of animals that stand for the four successive empires of humanity and point towards the messianic time, serve for the framers' message.

IX
The Result of Differentiating:
Issues of Symbolization among Documents

When the sages of the Mishnah and the Tosefta spoke of Edom and Edomites, they meant biblical Edom, a people in the vicinity of the land of Israel. By Rome they meant the city -- that alone. That fact bears meaning when we turn to documents produced two centuries later, and one hundred years beyond the triumph of Christianity. When the sages of Genesis Rabbah spoke of Rome, it was not a political Rome but a messianic Rome that is at issue: Rome as surrogate for Israel, Rome as obstacle to Israel. Why? It is because Rome now confronts Israel with a crisis, and, I argue, Genesis Rabbah constitutes a response to that crisis. Rome in the fourth century became Christian. Sages responded by facing that fact quite squarely and saying, "Indeed, it is as you say, a kind of Israel, an heir of Abraham as your texts explicitly claim. But we remain the sole legitimate Israel, the bearer of the birthright -- we and not you. So you are our brother: Esau, Ishmael, Edom." And the rest follows.

By rereading the story of the beginnings, sages discovered the answer and the secret of the end. Rome claimed to be Israel, and, indeed, sages conceded, Rome shared the patrimony of Israel. That claim took the form of the Christians' appropriation of the Torah as "the Old Testament," so sages acknowledged a simple fact in acceding to the notion that, in some way, Rome too formed part of Israel. But it was the rejected part, the Ishmael, the Esau, not the Isaac, not the Jacob. The advent of Christian Rome precipitated the sustained, polemical, and, I think, rigorous and well-argued rereading of beginnings in light of the end. Rome then marked the conclusion of human history as Israel had known it. Beyond? The coming of the true Messiah, the redemption of Israel, the salvation of the world, the end of time. So the issues were not inconsiderable, and when the sages spoke of Esau/Rome, as they did so often, they confronted the life-or-death decision of the day.

When we come to Leviticus Rabbah, we find ourselves several steps down the path explored by the compilers of Genesis Rabbah. The polemic represented in Leviticus Rabbah by the symbolization of Christian Rome, therefore, makes the simple point that, first, Christians are no different from, and no better than, pagans; they are essentially the same. Second, just as Israel had survived Babylonia, Media, Greece, so would they endure to see the end of Rome (whether pagan, whether Christian). But of course the symbolic polemic rested on false assumptions, hence conveyed a message that misled Jews by misrepresenting their new enemy. The new Rome really did differ from the old. Christianity was not merely part of a succession of undifferentiated modes of paganism. True, the symbols assigned to Rome attributed worse, more dangerous traits than those assigned to the earlier empires. The pig pretends to be clean, just as the Christians give the signs of adherence to the God of Abraham, Isaac, and Jacob.

That much the passage concedes. But it is not enough. For out of symbols should emerge a useful public policy, and the mode of thought represented by symbols in the end should yield an accurate confrontation with that for which the symbol stands.

This survey of four documents read one by one, then in pairs, yields a simple result. A striking shift in the treatment of Rome does appear to take place in the formative century represented by work on Genesis Rabbah and Leviticus Rabbah. In earlier times Rome symbolized little beyond itself, and Edom, Esau (absent in the Mishnah, a singleton in Tosefta), and Ishmael were concrete figures. In later times these figures bore traits congruent to the fact of Christian rule. The correspondence between the modes of symbolization -- the pig, the sibling -- and the facts of the Christian challenge to Judaism -- the same Scripture, read a new way, the same messianic hope, interpreted differently -- turns out to be remarkable and significant when we compare what the earlier compilers of canonical writings, behind the Mishnah and the Tosefta, produced to the writings of the later ones, behind the two Rabbah-compilations. When we differentiate one document from the next, the details of each document turn out to cohere to the systemic traits of the document as a whole. And, furthermore, what a document says about the common topic turns out to bear its own messages and meanings. That, in a single sentence, justifies the route of canonical differentiation I advocated at the outset.

X

The Result of Not Differentiating:
Missing a Distinction that Makes a Difference

When I originally worked on this problem, I took the view that the rabbinic canon, from beginning to end, fails to effect differentiation when it treats the outsider.[7] I maintained that the recognition of the outsider depends upon traits that, so far as the framers of the writings at hand are concerned, remain not only constant but uninteresting. The outsider is just that -- not worthy of further sorting out. And, as a result of that premise, in the unfolding of canonical doctrine on the outsider, I did not discern substantial change from one document to the next. So, I concluded, people put out of mind that with which they cannot cope, and the outsider stood for the critical fact of Israelite life, the nation's weak condition and vanquished status. So for the same fundamental cause that accounts for the persistence among the founders of the Mishnah's system of the priestly conception of Israelite life, so too a single tight abstraction masked the detailed and concrete features of the other. All

---

[7]I refer to "Stable Symbols in a Shifting Society: The Delusion of the Monolithic Gentile in Documents of Late Fourth-Century Judaism," *History of Religions* 1985, 25: 163-175. cf. also Jacob Neusner and Ernest S. Frerichs, eds., *"To See Ourselves as Others See us:" Christians, Jews, "Others" in Late Antiquity* (Atlanta, 1985: Scholars Press Studies in the Humanities, pp. 373-396.

"others" looked alike -- and posed a threat. The less response to that threat, the more comforting the illusion of inner control over an outer world wholly beyond one's power. Ignoring what could not be sorted out and focusing upon what could, the sages' Israelite kept at a distance a hostile world and retained command of a universe of rule and order. But I believe that in approaching matters as I did, I failed to see the traits stressed by the two Rabbah-collections, traits specific to Rome as Christian and irrelevant to all other outsiders. I missed the message because I failed to compare what the Mishnah and the Tosefta say about Rome/Esau/Ishmael/Edom with what the two Rabbah-compilations say about the same matter. And the reason was that it never entered my mind that Christianty would make much difference to Judaism -- a point to which I shall come back at the end.

Now to return to the methodological question. I can display the repertoire of results attained by a labor of harmonization simply by citing my own uncomprehending words. By seeing things without distinguishing among sources, what conclusions did I draw? Here, alas, are my ipsissima verba:

> What demands attention is the failure of people to reimagine a symbol that no longer corresponds to, or conveys, perceived reality. When, to be specific, people continue to speak in the same language about something that has in fact produced drastic change, we must ask why. For reason suggests symbols serve to construct an imaginary world that, for the structure to serve, must in some way correspond to the world out there. When, therefore, a critical area of social experience undergoes vast transformation, the symbols also should undergo metamorphosis. The one thing that should change is the character of the symbols through which people portray in their minds what is going on in that world that their minds and imaginations propose to mediate and to interpret.
>
> ...I point out that the mode of symbolization of the outsider, perceived as a nation and great power equivalent to Israel, remained stable during that period that marked Israel's complete transformation from one thing to something else.

As we have seen, this is simply not true. The opposite is the case. The movement from the Mishnah and its companion to the two Rabbah-compilations suggest no failure to reimagine a symbol, but a careful reconsideration of Scripture to find and appropriate a useful symbol to make sense of perceived reality. Scripture supplied the rules of history as much as the laws of society, and in Genesis sages found those rules, hence, Jacob and Esau told them the historical laws governing the relationship of Israel and Rome. In consequence, we see not a failure but an enormously imaginative and successful intellectual initiative.

> At the outset of the period at hand, before A.D. 70, Israel in its land constituted a small political entity, a state, like many others of its time and place. It was subordinate to a great empire, but was a distinct and autonomous unit, a part of the political structure of that empire. It had working institutions of self-government and politics. At the end of the

same period, by the seventh century, Israel in no way constituted a political entity. Such institutions of a political or juridical character that it had had, had lost the recognition and legitimacy formerly conferred upon them.

Moreover, when Israel looked outward, toward the world beyond its limits, the changes proved no less stunning. At the outset, Rome, and at the end, Rome, but what a different Rome! In the first three centuries, Rome was what it had always been, what its predecessors in the Middle East had always been: pagan, essentially benign toward Israel in its land. From the fourth century, Rome became something unprecedented: a kind of Israel and a kin to Israel, a knowledgable competitor, a powerful and canny enemy, a brother.

The modes by which the Jews, or, more to the point, the rabbis whose writings survive, proposed to symbolize the world had therefore to take up two contradictory worlds. On the one hand these "symbols of the stranger," of Israel's history and destiny, and of Israel's relationship to the outsider, dealt with a world in which Israel was like the outsider: a nation among nations, a political entity confronting another such entity, thus history among other histories. At the end, these symbols had to convey the reality of an Israel that was essentially different in genus from the outsider: no longer a nation in the sense in which other groups constituted a nation, no longer a political entity like others, no longer standing at the end of a history essentially consubstantial with the history of the nations.

What we shall see is the surprising fact that, so far as we are able to tell, the modes of political and social symbolization remained essentially stable in a world of change. More to the point, the outsider remained what he had always been, a (mere) pagan, part of a world demanding from Israel no effort whatsoever at differentiation. The "nations" were all alike, and Israel was still not essentially different from them all: consubstantial, thus judged by the same standards, but to be sure guiltless while the rest were guilty. What makes so puzzling the stability of the modes of symbolization of Israel and the nations, Israel's history and destiny, and the substance of Israel's doctrine, is a simple fact. In the interval, Christianity had not only come to full and diverse expression, it also had reached power.

But the modes of symbolization as revealed by the canonical writings read one by one show enormous and surprising change. Imagination, an act of extraordinary daring -- these characterize the later fourth and fifth century thinkers. They confronted an unprecedented challenge, and they responded in an unprecedented way, by determing the equivalence of the two great powers of the world, Israel and Rome. Of course there was nothing equivalent about the two, either in heaven (from sages' viewpoint on God's view) or on earth (from everyone else's viewpoint). But that is part of the amazing work at hand. Once more, therefore, we observe: the preceding statement is simply false. I missed the difference among the sources, therefore I saw everything as pretty much the same thing when it was not. And, to proceed:

In coming to power, Christianity drew upon essentially the same symbolic heritage to which Israel had long had access. To Christianity as much as to Judaism the pagan was a pagan, not differentiated; history began in Eden and led through Sinai to the end of time; the Messiah stood at the climax and goal of this world's history; revelation ("Torah") came from one God to unique Israel. True, for all forms of Christianity, the values assigned to the repertoire of symbols at hand hardly corresponded to those imputed by the Jews. But the symbols remained the same, and so Israel now resorted to what had become a shared symbolic system and structure to express its history and politics.

Under such circumstances, who would be surprised to learn that deep thought went into the revision of the available symbols, a restatement in such wise as to differentiate what had been treated as uniform, to redefine what had been grasped as settled? Surely the Christian, in the symbolic system of Judaism, should look like something other than the pagan, maybe worse but at least different. Certainly history as a mode of social symbolization should proceed on a somewhat different path from the one it had taken when the one God had not yet come to rule, when Israel's ancient Scriptures had not yet come to define the nature and destiny of humanity. Reckoning with the profound political changes at hand, we might imagine, should lead at least some profound thinkers to reconsider the symbolic system that had formerly prevailed or, at the very least, the nature and definition of symbols that had gone forward into the new age and remained vivid. After all, social change should generate symbol change, political change should make its mark upon the symbols of politics and society.

I now see that the thinkers at hand did reconsider the available symbolic system and effect considerable revisions of it -- at precisely the right points. And what follows also is simply wrong, for the reasons now amply spelled out:

> But if that is what reason dictates we should expect, it is not how things actually happened. ...it would take the rabbis of the canon of Judaism nearly a millenium to take seriously the specific character and claims of Christianity and to begin to counter in a systematic way the concrete assertions of that religious tradition. Before the High Middle Ages, Judaism would have nothing to say about, let alone to, Christianity. More probative, Jewish thinkers would maintain the fantastic pretense that nothing important happened in either the first or the fourth century, that is, in either the supernatural or the political world at hand. As we shall now see, one important indicator of that fact is the unwillingness of the rabbinic exegetes of the fourth and early fifth centuries to concede that Christians were different from pagans. On the contrary, the rabbinic sources treat all pagans as essentially faceless, and Christianity not at all, except as part of that same blank wall of hostility to God (and, by the way, to Israel).

When we consider the movement from the first two documents we examined to the third and the fourth, we realize that every word in the preceding discussion is wrong. In fact the documents brought to closure in the fourth century say something entirely different from those concluded earlier.

XI

Conclusion

The Methodological Upshot

What went wrong? The answer is simple. I began my research with perfect faith in a dogma of Judaism and therefore also of scholars of Judaism. It is that Christianity never made any difference to Judaism. So I took for granted, without knowing it, that I too would find that Christianity never made any difference. My original results then conformed to the premise with which I had commenced work. That is how I could earlier conclude, reflecting a consensus I myself simply took for granted instead of questioning:

> In fact it would be many centuries before Jews would take seriously, and in its own terms, the claim of Christianity to constitute a kind of Judaism, and not a kind of paganism. It would take a long time for Jews to distinguish the Christian from other outsiders. When that differentiation began to emerge, it would be in Christian Europe, on the part of Joseph Kimhi and Moses Nahmanides and others who had no choice. By that time, to be sure, "paganism" had long disappeared from the world of Israel's residency, on the one hand, and any expectation that Roman rule would give way to Israelite hegemony had lost all worldly credibility. Then, but only then, we find Jews confronting in a systematic way and with solid knowledge of the other side the facts of history that had emerged many centuries earlier.
>
> Whether a different symbolic system would have produced a more realistic and effective policy for the confrontation with triumphant Christianity we shall never know. For so long Israel had pretended nothing happened of any importance, not in the first century, not in the fourth. By the time people came around to concede that, after all, Christianity was here to stay and was essentially different from anything Israel had earlier encountered, it was an awareness too late to make such a difference in Israel's framing of its picture of the outsider and its policy toward the alien."

We now recognize that this statement is not only wrong, it is wrong-headed. The error is not niggling and it is not inconsequential. It is fundamental, because it is methodological. The methodological error is both general and specific. In general I erred by believing other people instead of asking how people knew the things they took for granted. I took over a prevailing attitude of mind -- and I did not even realize it. The specific error was that I failed to work along lines I myself had already discovered. I homogenized what should be analyzed and differentiated. I gave "the talmudic view of...," having spent many years trying to show that there is no such thing.

Let me in conclusion return to the questions with which we began and answer them:

[1] *If we find that each one of the documents says on its own essentially what all of the documents say together, so that the parts do turn out to be interchangeable, then imposing distinctions suggests differences where there is none....In that case, differentiation proves misleading.*

The outcome is that failing to differentiate among documents and to listen to the message of each on its own, I missed what in fact was a striking and fresh trait in one set of compilations. Not having heard the evidence of one canonical statement, I did not recognize the originality, the unprecedented nature, of another. So harmonization misled me. Now to turn to the opposite:

[2] *If, by contrast, when viewed one by one, our documents in fact do not say the same thing by themselves that all of them say when read together, our category, failing to recognize differences, suggests a unity and a cogency where there is none....In that case, not effecting a considerable labor of description of the documents one by one will obscure the very center and heart of matters: that the documents, components of the whole, are themselves autonomous, though connected (if that can be shown) and also continuous (if that can be shown).*

Clearly, the documents read one by one do yield insight that combining all their statements on a given topic does not bring to light. So, in sum, differentiating among documents shows us things that not differentiating among them obscures. Not seeing the books as individual statements obscured for me those shifts and turnings that now appear to respond to the movement of the wheel of history. And, it follows, the thinking at hand, concerning both the outsider in general and Rome in particular, the history of humanity but especially the history and destiny of Israel -- that thinking turns out, properly analyzed, to respond in a deep and systematic way to the single most considerable challenge the Jewish people in the Land of Israel was to face for the next fifteen hundred years: the rise of the Christian West as brother and enemy to Israel, the Jewish people. We who stand at the other side of the abyss mark the first generation to know that the siblings, Jacob and Esau, Israel and Rome, Judaism and Christianity, may learn to exchange the kiss of peace. And, as in the time of the meeting and reconciliation of the first Jacob and the first Esau, so today, it is at the very moment that Jacob, having labored in exile for so long, once more enters upon the land and the patrimony that is his.

Chapter Seven

Story, History, and Interpretation:
Moses In and Out of Context

i.   The Question at Hand

Does what Shakespeare ate for breakfast matter when I read Macbeth? And does Mozart's relationship with Salieri -- or with his father -- affect how I hear the Jupiter Symphony? These two questions make vivid a critical issue in interpretation, one which I shall spell out with specific regard to Moses. And Moses will be our example of a debate that concerns a much larger matter. At issue? The question concerns whether or not the context of a work of art dictates my appreciation of the contents of that thing. How much do I have to know about Robert Frost to appreciate *Stopping by woods on a winter eve*? Do I need to know how deep was the snow? And if I do not know that the English whipped the Spanish Armada, can I fully appreciate the spirit of Shakespeare's historical dramas? Having fired a barrage of questions, let me now move down from the shotgun to the rifle, for the issue is more precise than asking about breakfast and poppa.

The issue of interpreting the things people have made for our illumination presents subtleties and asks questions not readily answered. Obviously, we do not know what a poet ate for breakfast before that poet composed a masterpiece. But what if the poem deals with a belly ache, and what if we know that the poet got a belly ache from bad milk? Then we know something about the poem that we should not have known, if we did not know he drank sour milk. We know that the poem emerged from an immediate experience. Then we learn how the poet, through language, has turned a private anguish -- a belly-ache -- into something public, something with meaning and a message for others. Knowing (as we who saw Amadeus think we know) that Mozart's relationship with his father figured in Don Giovanni -- surmising that Mozart may have envied or identified with Don Giovanni -- imparts to that opera a depth, a terror, a psychological dimension, we should otherwise not grasp. And then we know the opera in a way in which otherwise we should not. Indeed, not knowing Mozart's psychological circumstances, we might not know the opera at all.

So it is easy to treat as trivial and unimportant the matter of history and circumstance: what was going on, what else was going on, when a story was told? To what setting did a writer speak when he or she told that story? And what problems did the work purport to solve? If we do not know that original context, if we cannot relate the work of art to its tradition, the work of fiction to its society, the work of poetry to the world of the poet, we also see the created thing as nothing other than a mere fact. It is something someone said, in our ignorance we think to whom it may concern. Then it is something about which, if we want, we can say anything we choose. We are not bound by time and circumstance (so we imagine) because the creative artist did not respond to context. The thing is there: we interpret it wholly in its own terms, therefore -- by definition -- wholly out of context.

ii.   The Importance of Knowing Context, Not Only Content

In my judgment treating as a matter of pure formality -- interpretation consisting of descriptive statements to which we impart portentous meaning -- "this is what it says, this is what it looks like" -- and ignoring the questions of where and when and why and in what tradition and in response to what issues allows for fraud. Specifically, the fraud is to make things up as you go along and turn your opinion of the moment into a judgment of a lasting work of creativity. Why fraud? Because, first, when we pay no attention to setting and tradition, we turn our opinion into judgment. Second, we never know whether or not we are right, so interpretation and criticism represent merely an exchange of personal opinions. Third, we permit no test of verification or falsification for our views, turning discourse into politics. And, finally, we remove from the realm of human experience the work that conveys to us a moment of humanity.

That is to say, we ignore the artist and pretend the art speaks on its own and by itself. So the art no longer captures a moment in a life. Literature read only in its social context yields sociology. But literature read wholly out of its social context speaks to us as we sit in the prison of our entire subjectivity. A work of art lives in more worlds than sociology or subjectivity. When I claim to tell you about those diverse dimensions of the life of art, one of the things I must be able responsibly to report is where the work began and what it meant to the people who first made it up and to the people who first received it: the context in history, in material life, in society. That is not all I must tell you, but it is where I have to begin. The alternative is to make things up as I go along and pretend to speak knowledgeably about what is in fact my own utterly private impressions: how I feel that morning, in place of how the artist felt that morning. So, to conclude this somewhat abstract discourse, knowing what Shakespeare had for breakfast may or may not matter, but knowing what I had for breakfast will surely tell you nothing worth knowing about Shakespeare.

iii.   From Policy to Personality: The Omniscient Know-Nothing

Now if that proposition strikes you as unspeakably obvious, I shall now show that it takes up a position on a seriously controverted and important issues. Specifically, the mode of interpretation consisting of treating a work of literature totally out of context -- and also not of literature at all -- has become quite stylish. People proud of their achievements in one field declare themselves experts in all sorts of other fields. In this regard, of course, the arrogance of the people in the most current and choices fields of learning -- nuclear physicists who make pronouncements on foreign policy, linguists who propose to settle issues of politics on the strength of their prestige in the narrow topic on which they know something, and, of course, God save us from the Noble Prize winners and the MacArthur Fellows! -- these people find particularly attractive the Bible in general, and the Old Testament in particular. The reason? Everyone knows the stories, more or less. Everyone cares. Enough people, indeed, revere the Scriptures so that you can always get attention. And, because so many people think they know the book, the responsibilities of serious learning (the amateurs maintain) impress nobody.

Now what, in fact, do the imperialists of the intellect propose to do? Quite simply, they open the Scriptures and free-associate, drawing heavily on what they do know to inform us yokels about the thing for which we care. I have heard Stephen J. Gould, for example, expatiate on the concept of time in the Bible in such a way as to suggest he had read a few bible-stories but not one sustained and responsible study of the concept of time in the Bible. In fact he conveyed superficial impressions and out-dated scholarship, knowing nothing of the hard and sustained work on the subject that a whole world of scholars have done. He announced his discovery of a mode of art that expresses that concept -- the layout of art in a cathedral he saw in Europe -- in utter ignorance of the fact that that mode of art forms a fixed convention in cathedral art from Trondheim (which I saw) to St. Chapelle, about which he spoke in excitement. But Gould is not to be blamed for believing his own press notices. What shall I tell you about distinguished scholars who, as part of the reversion to roots, discover in their prominent years that they would like to regain the religious condition of their youth. So they determine to open the Scriptures and read -- like Augustine -- but not to discover faith, or even to recover it. What they do is open, read, and, out of the resources of their own learning in their chosen field, free-associate. And, again, the free-association yields not some cocktail party chatter, or even a lecture for a Bible-study-group in a church or a synagogue, but a book. And then not a book deriving from a religious publisher, quite properly proposing to publish edifying documents of faith, but from a scholarly publisher.

Because I know one thing well, it does not mean I know something else at all. But that sort of humility, does not characterize intellectuals.

Since I am Jewish, I carry a special burden as a scholar of Judaism, because I have to take seriously the inanities that Jewish intellectuals pronounce on Judaism on the authority of their Jewish grandmother or some itinerant rabbi they fancy. "I'm Jewish, so I know the Bible" -- that is not an exaggeration of the prevailing attitude. Jews in general present their opinions on Jewish subjects not as primary data for the study of opinions Jews hold on Jewish subjects, but as Judaism: this is what it is.   And if ordinary Jews turn themselves from fish to ichthyologists, what shall we say of the intellectuals? No one has ever accused intellectuals of excessive humility. And in not a few instances scholars in the sciences and social sciences who just happen to be Jewish find irresistible the appeal of passing their opinion on Judaism, and that in every dimension. They will say -- as Michael Walzer does -- that they read a given portion of Scripture in the synagogue on the occasion of becoming a bar mitzvah, so they will write a book about that.   It is one thing for the inestimable Leonard Bernstein to write a Jeremiah Symphony, based on the modes of cantillation of the passage in the book of Jeremiah that he sang in the synagogue when he became a bar mitzvah. It is quite another for Michael Walzer, famous for whatever he is famous for, on the strength of whatever he claims to know about political history to tell us about Moses. He is not exempt from the rules of learning: mastering the text, but also mastering the scholarship on the text. Walzer typifies the childlike arrogance of people who, because they know one thing, assume they know everything.

iv.   Moses and Contemporary Scholarship in Political Science

Two political scientists, both of them Jewish, announce they know nothing about the sources or scholarship on Moses, an then proceed to prove it in rather pretentious books. I would have believed them had they merely said so. But both just now have published books on Moses, and, in both cases, claim to learn important laws of political science from Moses. One is Michael Walzer, *Exodus and Revolution* (N.Y., 1985: Basic Books), the other Aaron Wildavsky, *The Nursing Father. Moses as a Political Leader* (University, 1984: University of Alabama Press). So the figure of Moses proves remarkably contemporary, since prominent scholars claim to find in Moses fresh and important lessons for learning today. I too wish to learn from Walzer and Wildavsky, but not quite the lessons they propose to teach. For what I want to know is this: when today's scholars in acutely contemporary subjects, such as political science, turn to the Bible, what, in intellectual terms, do they propose to learn, and how do they wish to learn it? So we ask the figure of Moses to teach us yet another lesson about the intellectual history of the age. Let me frame the question I believe Moses answers today.

v.   The Question of Context and Meaning

The question is, do people tell us about Moses, or about themselves, when they tell us about Moses? That seems a critical issue. For if, as I believe, what people say through the centuries about Moses serves as a kind of barometer of intellect and culture of those centuries in which the figure of Moses persists, then we shall have to find out something about the climate of our own age from what contemporaries write about the age of Moses. And that is all that we shall learn. The question at hand -- Moses or us -- makes a difference. For when we answer that question, as I said in the beginning, we learn something exemplary about contemporary reading of ancient texts.

Specifically, we consider a most profound issue: when we read the texts of ancient times of our own civilization, and the texts of other civilizations altogether. The issue: may we take up and read, or must we travel a long road into the context and circumstance of those texts alien to our day and age? Wildavsky and Walzer think you can open ancient stories and learn modern lessons. Are they right? If they are right about Moses, then we can follow their example and read as if they were written this morning -- and with us in mind in particular -- Homer or Thucydides, the Gospel of Matthew or the history of Tabari, Machiavelli and Luther, not to mention Confucius, the Vedas, and Zoroaster. But if they are wrong, then the classics of ancient times and of other cultures than our own demand study only in context, only out of a process of learning and interpretation. If we cannot open and read and then say whatever we like and call it learning, then we have to undertake a process of mediation, a painful work of learning about the other in the terms and the setting of that other. We shall have to move from the world of ahistorical and asocial literary criticism of today, with its interest in formalities and its academicism, to the world of anthropology, broadly construed. That is to say, we shall have to treat the other as strange and unknown, something demanding from us humility and hard work, but as something we can know.

My view stated up front is this: we shall misunderstand the works of the other when we read them as if the authors wrote to whom it may concern, and not for someone in particular. That then is the choice: does context matter? or can we simply take up and read an ancient text, oblivious to its context and totally ignorant of what learned women and men have learned about that context -- that, and about the impact of context on interpretation, on meaning?

vi. Moses in Context: The Yahwist's Moses in the Imperial Age

To explain what I mean by the context of a story, and why I think that context makes a difference in our understanding of the content of a story, that setting affects the substance of a tale, I turn to Moses in particular. Again, using Moses as our example, we turn to stories told about Moses and ask how knowledge of the setting of that story dictates our understanding of the story. In fact, what conclusions should we draw from the knowledge of the world in which a story-teller told a story and in which an audience heard that story? My purpose is not to offend, but I have to tell you up front that the historical Moses, someone who really lived and led Israel and did the things the Bible says he did, does not define the issue. All we know is stories about "Moses," stories told long after the events they portray. Not only so, but these stories do not form a single tale. They constitute a pastiche, a collage, a mosaic. So when we ask about Moses in context, we do not mean the twelfth or thirteen century B.C., we mean some other century. Let me spell this out.

To understand the context, you have to know that the Five Books of Moses form a mosaic. The Five Books of Moses as we have them came together in the time of Ezra, around 450 B.C., that is to say, centuries after the historical Moses (if there was such a figure) actually lived. Diverse writers, flourishing at different times, contributed to that mosaic. The original context of a story about Moses, therefore, is not the final setting, in the Five Books of Moses as we have them. The original settings, that is, the circumstance in which stories about Moses were told, prove diverse. Each story-teller made his points in response to his age, to make points critical to the audience for which he told his story. Let me give three examples of how that fact affects the stories about Moses, one pertaining to Exodus's Moses, the other two to Deuteronomy's Moses.

In the time of king Solomon, people look backward to account for the great day at hand. This writer, who flourished around 950 B.C., is known by the name of God that he used in his stories, the Yahwist. He wanted to tell the story of the federation of the federated tribes, now a single kingdom under Solomon, with a focus on Zion and Jerusalem, the metropolis of the federation. What he did, then, is to tell the history (theology) of Israel from its origins, and he made the point that the hand of Yahweh directed events. What he wanted to know out of the past was the present and future of the empire and monarchy at hand.[1] This writer, the Yahwist, told the story of the creation of the world to the fulfillment of Israel in the conquest of the land. His purpose overall was to affirm that what happened to Israel -- its move from a federation of tribes to an empire under David and Solomon -- was the doing of God, whom he called Yahweh. Lee Humphrey's summarizes: "The Israel of the empire was Yahweh's creation for which Yahweh had a mission." The writer lays great emphasis on how God chose a particular person to carry out the mission: Abraham and Sarah, Isaac, Jacob, and onward -- all appeared unworthy and weak, but God chose them. The message, as Lee Humphrey paraphrases it, is this: "The Yahwist focused attention on just one man, then on twelve sons, then on a band of slaves in Egypt, then on fugitives in Sinai's wastes. Repeatedly endangered, seemingly about to vanish on many occasions, small, weak, and often unworthy, these ancestors of the Israelite empire of David and Solomon were sustained again and again, even in the land of the god-king pharaoh, because they were a chosen people, elected by a god who upheld and preserved them." That is the message.

The place of Moses in this picture? The Yahwist's picture reduces the covenant at Sinai to modest propositions; the legal stipulations are few (Humphrey, p. 76), focused in Exodus 34. The patriarchs take priority, the

---

[1] I follow the excellent and clear account of W. Lee Humphreys, *Crisis and Story: Introduction to the Old Testament* (Palo Alto, 1979: Mayfield Publishing Co.), pp. 65-78.

unconditional quality of the promises of God to Abraham -- and later to David -- dominates throughout. At issue then is the promises to the patriarchs and their children, not the contract between God and Israel. Israel is destined by divine grace for its present glory, in Solomon's time. So for the Yahwist, Moses is a minor figure relative to the patriarchs. And what is important about Moses is not the giving of law but the narratives of leadership, Exodus 1-24, 32, 34. And, it follows, *these we read as testimonies to the mentality of the Davidic monarchy*. So, the consensus concurs, when we tell the tale of the Golden Calf, the breaking of the tablets, and the forgiveness of God as an act of grace, we listen to sublime narratives told in the age of Solomon and to the world of Solomon: God's grace favoring Israel, in an age cognizant of grace, a powerful message to a self-confident empire -- in all, an American dream (to commit anachronism).

vii. Moses in Context: The Moses of Deuteronomy. A Moses for an Age of Crisis

Does the fact that the Yahwist's Moses speaks to the imperial age of Solomon make a difference? It surely did to the author of Deuteronomy, who gives us a different Moses. If we turn to the book of Deuteronomy, we find a very different picture from the picture we get in Exodus. Now there is a magnificent sermon, preached by Moses before his death, as a narrative of Israel's history. That sermon forms the setting for an enormous law code. At the heart of matters is this claim: here is God's law, which you will keep as your side of the contract that God made with you in bringing you out of Egypt and into the promised land. Moses now serves to validate the laws of the book at hand, that is, of Deuteronomy.

Does it matter? Why should we care about the point at which the Moses of the covenant of Deuteronomy made his appearance? To answer that question, we have to know why the covenant mattered, to whom it made a difference. We therefore ask, when did the book surface? It came to light toward the end of the seventh century, at about 620 B.C., forty years prior to the destruction of the first Temple of Jerusalem. What had happened in the period of the writing of Deuteronomy? Israel had spent a whole generation under Assyrian influence, and only now emerged from that sphere of cultural influence. It sought some other mode of defining itself and its life. It was part of a larger shaking of the foundations, as diverse people, finding in decay the political system that had long stood firm, began to ask about their own distinct and distinctive pasts. Some important segments of the book of Deuteronomy, particularly the legal ones, chapters 12-26, turned up at just this time. These chapters formed roots for the renewed, now independent Israel, of 620. A point of stress in these chapters is that in Jerusalem and only there Yahweh may be worshipped; only the priests of Jerusalem are valid. So the book of Deuteronomy in its earliest layer makes two points: first, one can worship only Yahweh, and, second, one can worship Yahweh only in Jerusalem. Moses then forms the authority for the story -- the authority, but not the leading actor. That is the first part of the story. But Deuteronomy answers a critical question, and, when the document reaches its final stage, forms part of a massive history of Israel, encompassing the books of Deuteronomy, Joshua, Judges, Samuel and Kings. That great work of historical narrative came into being, in its final composition, to answer a question of life and death: why have these things happened to us? The past must live again to explain the present and secure the future. Let me explain.

A second phase in the unfolding of the tale of the Deuteronomistic historians took place after the destruction of the Temple in 586. Then Moses would again serve, now to provide the authority for an explanation of the entire history of ancient Israel, culminating, as it had, in the tragedy at hand. Now Moses is law-giver, and the laws form the contract between Israel and God. Israel has violated that covenant or contract, and the result, the destruction, is at hand. Again Humphreys (p. 146): "In Judah and Jerusalem some would turn back to Moses, attempting to redeem the crisis of 587n B.C. [when the Temple was destroyed] by placing it in the theological framework of the old federation story of Israel's origins, for only in this way could Israel's tragic end be understood as the harsh but just action of its god Yahweh. In Moses, who had led Israel from Egyptian slavery, who had mediated the covenant on Mount Sinai, and whose death before the promise of land had been fulfilled had given an effective symbol to Israel's tragically unfulfilled promise, they found a mirror in which to view their own experience. This group found their charter in the book of Deuteronomy, which received its final form at their hands. From this base they reviewed Israel's history from the entrance into Canaan to the exile in Baby.lon after 587...They produced an extended theological survey of Israel's history that now comprises the books of Joshua through 2 Kings. Their book is called the deuteronomistic history because the basis for judgment is found in Deuteronomy." So the Moses of Deuteronomy is a great preacher and gives a sermon on the plains of Moab. The Moses at hand projects out of a secure past an account of the later issues and problems and doubts (Humphreys, p. 147). In Deuteronomy Moses says a great deal and does much less, in the Yahwist chapters of Exodus, Moses does much but gives few laws. So the contrast is clear.

What happens when we read the Moses of Deuteronomy in context? We can see each of the details of the picture -- the sermon, the laws -- as a statement to a particular group of people at a particular time. These statements -- admonitions, laws -- take on concreteness. We understand who speaks, we can describe the message, we know the purpose of the whole -- so we understand the matter at its depth.

What happens when we ignore context? We hear only the admonition and the laws and find ourselves able to say little about them in their original setting. The cost? We can do two things. We can paraphrase. And we can free-associate. We can paraphrase the story in our own words We can then supply a context of our own, out of our own minds, to give meaning and consequence to the admonition and the laws of Deuteronomy. We do not hear story-tellers telling people of their own age the meaning of what has happened to them -- an enormous message, encompassing the books of Deuteronomy, Joshua, Judges, Samuel, and Kings. Rather, we hear episodic sermons, made up for the occasion, which impose the conditions of a different age and a different world on the magnificent literature at hand.

When we take the Deuteronomistic picture out of its context, of course we join it to the Yahwist's portion of the book of Exodus as well. With what consequence? We join a number of quite diverse stories, each with its own tale to tell, and form them into a conglomerate, the Five Books of Moses as we have them all together, full of points of repetition, contradiction, and incongruity. So we mix pebbles and cookies and ignore the difference -- swallowing the whole thing all at once, choking on nothing. In other words, treating diverse stories as a single story, merely because they refer to a single person, requires us to ignore all manner of detail and contradiction. The Moses who leads the people, so paramount in the Yahwistic picture in Exodus, and the Moses who preaches a majestic sermon and provides a full code of laws, the Moses of Deuteronomy, form one and the same man only in the mind and imagination of people to whom the original stories, their context and meanings, made no difference.

And that brings us to the original exercise of harmonization, that is, to the work of the people who sewed the whole into a single cloak, or, to shift the metaphor, who took the pebbles of the Mosaic mosaic and erased the mortar of the margins. But they too had something in mind, and it has no bearing on the discoveries of the political scientists (to whom we shall ultimately return). The framers of the Pentateuch, for their part, had their message to deliver -- also an important one. Then the various Moseses of the antecedent writings formed into a single Moses, as diverse law codes became one, and varied and disharmonious messages from divinities with little in common became the one God who revealed the one unitary Torah to the one man, Moses, at Mount Sinai.

So much for the context of the original stories. What we learn is that Moses served the story-tellers of ancient Israel in whatever way they wanted him to. He was leader, he was law-giver, he stood by himself, he became the figure behind the later history of Israel from the Jordan to Jerusalem and thence Babylon. He was this, he was that, he was the other thing. In context, he emerges as a powerful and important figure, acutely relevant to the context which his diverse creators, the story tellers at hand, defined for him. So much for Moses in context: a set of stories, each formed in judgment of a sequence of circumstances, then all of them joined into a single harmonious message to a critical hour in Israel's history.

viii. Moses Out of Context: What Is at Stake?

From the formation of the Five Books of Moses into a single book the figure of Moses served, as I said at the outset, as a kind of barometer of the cultural climate. From what people said about Moses we learn a great deal about the time and place in which they spoke about Moses. And what we learn about Moses is how his name attracted the fantasies and hopes of the ages. If we wish to understand those fantasies, should we imagine we deal with one man, Moses, and with a single set of events? I think not. In fact we confront a whole set of stories, each with its own context and original point of importance and stress, each represented by its particular Moses. And if we do not ask about context as well as content, we do not grasp content. That is, we do not understand the stress and tension of a story, if we totally ignore the setting in which, to the story-teller, those points of stress and tension found resolution and imparted meaning. So we ask our opening question about knowing what the Deuteronomistic historians ate for breakfast, the gall and wormwood they had for lunch. Does it matter that they did their work to explain the crisis of 586? I think so.

Why does it matter, and what is at stake? The answer makes a difference because, as I have argued, the answer -- does literature relate to society, does the setting in which a story is told contribute to its meaning -- for us forms our approach to any document produced outside of our time and place. Do we understand, do we appreciate only within the limits of our context what has come to us from some other world entirely? Or do we have a task, in making our own and interpreting a classic, of placing into its formative context a poem or a work of music, a novel or a work of religious sentiment that we propose to naturalize into our world? This barrage of questions derives force from an explosive issue: what is at stake?

So what is at stake is the rule that will tell us how to appropriate for our own circumstance and use the heritage of humanity. What if we read Moses in context and what if we read Moses out of context?

If we read Moses in context, -- I claim -- we understand the story, its points of stress, its nuances, its generative tensions. Therefore, out of knowledge of context, we know what is at stake in the story, to whom the story matters, what its original meaning conveyed. And why do we want to know the answers to these questions? Because through those answers we can identify with the story. By this I mean that we can tell the story in address to an issue, a circumstance, which we, out of our experience, can understand.

We can identify with the story not when we turn the story into a tale of ourselves, but when we treat the story as a tale of something beyond ourselves -- but something to which we, too, can relate -- a very different thing. So we locate in our own circumstance those pertinent points of stress and tension that make the story relevant and interesting in its original setting, to its original story teller. So even the aesthetics of the story may speak to us in an authentic way.

And what if we read Moses out of context? Let me specify the costs. Then we bring to the story of Moses *only* the considerations of our own minds. We impose upon the stories at hand a unity that derives not from their setting -- in the Five Books of Moses, produced in the aftermath of the destruction of the state and of society in 586, -- but from ours. What difference does it make? To state matters quite simply, when we bring only ourselves, no information or insight beyond ourselves, we hear in the story only those messages that we did not need the story to convey to us -- that is, only what we knew before. For, without learning, without knowledge of the scholarly tradition on a story, of facts that help us understand the story, what do we have? What is that body of interpretation, the questions, the points of inquiry, that we bring to these stories? It is what we already know, what we already feel, what we already understand, about the world: our own circumstance, that alone. The story then repeats and recapitulates the reality we know, it does not convey a reality we need to learn. Can the stories about Moses enlarge our experience? Can they tell us something we do not already know? That seems to me the crux of the matter. And my view of the answer is simple. No, when all we bring is what we already feel and what we already know, then in those stories we shall discover only what we already are, but not what we are not yet -- and certainly not what we can become. We do not enlarge our vision, we do not broaden our range of experience, if we read the past only in the light of the present, and if we bring to the monuments of other ages or of alien worlds in our own time only what we already are.

So at stake in reading Moses out of context is whether we derive from those stories that broadening of vision, that lengthening of perspective, that access to things that did not happen to us but that can make a difference to us. And I think that when we come only with what we already know and feel, we fail to gain what the experience of to other times and places and person, recorded in the classics of alien and ancient ages. For we remain wholly within our own limits, the bounds of our imagination and our mind. Moses out of context tells us only the contents of our own minds, and Moses read in the imaginary and world of our minds -- a single story, not a set of stories, a story that takes place not in real time and among real people and in a real political setting, but only in our imagination -- that Moses teaches us nothing we do not already know.

ix. Moses in the Faith of the Synagogue and the Church

The rabbis and ministers and priests who read the Bible as God's word and preach the Bible in the context of the living faith of Judaism and Christianity bring to Moses a context of learning and discipline. They do not make things up as they go along and call it learning. Why not? Theirs is a context. That circumstance in which the stories are read brings to the Scriptures a rich and relevant body of interpretation. No one has an argument with those who believe and therefore ask their questions to the Moses who revealed God's will at Sinai, and whose life and words lie before us in the Torah, that is no longer "the Pentateuch" (let alone the conglomeration of J, E, P, JE, D, and the work of the Deuteronomistic historians!). Their Moses flourishes in the context of questions that derive not from this morning's newspaper or how I feel right now. They read Moses in the context of thousands of years of faith, their questions do not derive from their own experience alone, and, therefore, when the they come to Moses, they emerge from themselves. So the preachers amply meet the condition I defined a moment ago, the criterion of whether or not the encounter with Moses becomes more than a meeting with a mirror.

x. Wildavsky and Walzer: Moses in Invented Context

But what of the scholars of political science who wish to learn from Moses lessons important for political science? That is another matter. What we want to know is simple. What questions do they bring to the texts at hand? And, second, is their approach to the stories about Moses suitable to produce plausible answers to those questions. The answers to these questions derive from two places. First, what do they ask? Second, how do they find the answers. Walzer in his *Exodus and Revolution* treats the stories about Moses as a set of topics, thus "the house of bondage, slaves in Egypt, the murmurings, slaves in the wilderness, the covenant, a free people, the promised land, Exodus politics." His treatment of these topics begins with a biblical tale, and proceeds to broad free-associating on the topics at hand. Along the way, as he treats these topics, he tells us things he has found it in a rather superficial reading of a few of the scholarly books on the subject. He maintains, for one minor example, "Jewish messianic thought, and so all messianic thought, has its origins in this idea of a second Exodus." I cannot imagine a more extravagant, or a more ignorant, claim. But Walzer reads books that Harvard professors tell him to read, and, more to the point, he meticulously avoids reading books that Harvard professors tell him he does not have to bother to read. For there is a conventional list, a protocol that governs the books "our crowd" reads, and Walzer is certainly a member, in good standing, of one crowd, and not another. So Exodus and Revolution presents a picture in accord with the protocols of the scholars of Cambridge: we read Scholem, we read Urbach, but we do not read Mr. X and Miss Y; their books we ignore. Then, of course, we shall all praise one another and pretend there is no one else worthy not of praise but even of sustained interest. In this book Walzer is no scholar, nor even a theologian, he is nothing more than a ward politician among the party hacks of Cambridge. So much for what he has learned as a political scientist.

Wildavsky announces his interest very clearly in a chapter, "Why me? why Moses? Why leadership?":

I am attracted to the study of Moses for many reasons, three of which are related to leadership. The first is that the Mosaic experience is comprehensive, spanning the spectrum of regimes and the types of leadership associated with them. The second is that Moses, far from being beyond us, was full of human faults, from passivity to impatience to idolatry. ...The third is that Moses was a leader who taught his people to do without him by learning how to lead themselves."

Wildavsky further maintains:

"...understanding of the Mosaic Bible may be enhanced by treating it as a teaching on political leadership; second, that our understanding of leadership may be improved by considering it as an integral part of different political regimes. Moses' experience reveals the dilemmas of leadership under the major types of rule, from slavery in Egypt to anarchy before the golden Calf episode to equity...in the desert, until his final effort to institutionalize hierarchy."

From this program we conclude that the author reads the story as a unitary account of things that really happened. For otherwise he would have to tell us about *how* a given story, told at a given point, addresses problems of leadership under those circumstances in particular, at that time. For example, leadership in the time of the Solomonic empire evidently found useful a myth of grace. By contrast, leadership in the time of the breaking up of world empires (for Deuteronomy 12-26), found valuable a myth of totalitarianism: only here, only us. Again, leadership in the time of the destruction of the national polity (for the work of the Deuteronomic historians as a whole) demanded a myth of historical inevitability: the contract, its violation, but also, its potential for renewal. Moses serves all these myths, of course, and Wildavsky can have learned from biblical scholarship interesting lessons for sociology and politics (to name one splendid figure among many, Max Weber has shown how to study these matters for the interests of social science).

But seeing the diverse tales about "Moses" as a single unitary picture, Wildavsky can find in them that "spectrum of regimes and types of leadership" that he does. And why not, when, after all, what he sees as a "spectrum of regimes and types of leadership" is nothing other than a diverse set of stories, written by different people, at different times, for different purposes, and to make different points. All this Wildavsky rips out of context. Any other route would have demanded work -- serious learning -- and not the exercise of powers of free-association and undisciplined imagination, such that Wildavsky invests in this facile and ignorant book.

Now you must ask, Does it matter that Wildavsky treats as harmonious and unitary, in a context all its own, a set of tales that, in fact began in bits and pieces? The answer is yes and no. If he performs an act of mere literary criticism, for example, writing about Don Quixote as an example, in fiction, of such and such an ideal of life, then I think Wildavsky is right. For Moses as a single person, who lived out, in one lifetime, the pastiche of tales about the person named Moses, is a work of fiction. If Wildavsky were to turn, for example, with the same set of questions about the nature of leadership to Shakespeare's *Coriolanus* or *Macbeth*, he would provide an interesting account of Shakespeare's political theory. But he would not tell us much about the nature of leadership in Plutarch's Rome, or in Scotland in earlier times. Then what he would tell us is Shakespeare's theory of politics and leadership in Coriolanus, or even of women in politics (!), in Macbeth. But Wildavsky does not promise a picture of how a writer in the time of Solomon imagined political leadership -- and that we do know. Nor does he tell us how a write in the aftermath of the catastrophe of the destruction of the first Temple reflected on political leadership -- and that we do know. What we know he does not know, and what we do not know he wants to turn into knowledge and insight for political science.

So my problem with Wildavsky is that he brings to the text only what he finds in the text, reading the whole out of its context in real life, I mean, in diverse ages of material history and concrete society. One could in his defense claim that he proposes to read the stories as structuralists might, but Wildavsky claims no such sophistication. His is not the debate between marxist reading of literature in the social context and stucturalist reading of literature out of all material setting. He comes to the stories with a childlike faith in them and in himself. And he reads the stories out of his projection of himself onto them. That is why he treats as facts of real life what is nothing more than the invention of the people who pieced the whole together. To state matters simply: Wildavsky takes a document sewn together in the aftermath of an awful crisis at the end of a nation's life and reads it as the story of the *beginning* of that nation's life! You might as well treat Thomas More's *Utopia* as an account of the politics of a real place and a real time and write a book on political leadership in Utopia -- or in never-never-land in the time of Peter Pan. In fact we find ourselves, in this approach to Moses, among people who confuse fiction and history and turn the result into social science.

xi. Roots, Moses, Walzer and Wildavsky

Let me then compare our two Jewish social scientists, who propose to explore their "roots" . Walzer tells us, indeed, that for his bar mitzvah lection, we read Exodus 30:11-34:35: "At that time I took Hobbes's view...and argued with my teacher 'against the cruelty Moses for putting so many thousands to the sword'" (p. xi). With all due regard for Walzer's memories of his Jewish education, that education does not today suffice. The world has learned things about the passage Walzer read when he was thirteen years old. Walzer has learned things too. But not about his bar mitzvah lection. That remained preserved in amber, awaiting his mature years as a prestigious scholar. Then, in search of roots, he would return. Walzer is a heavy-weight, not an enthusiast. He announces program far less naive than Wildavsky's. He approaches:

> "an idea of great presence and power in Western political thought, the idea of a deliverance from suffering and oppression...I have sought to describe the origins of that idea in the story of Israel's deliverance from Egypt, and then to give a reading of Exodus, Numbers, and Deuteronomy designed to explain their importance for generation after generation of religious and political radicals. The escape from bondage, the wilderness journey, the Sinai covenant, the promised land: all these loom large in the literature of revolution."

I find this, on the face of it, plausible. For Walzer does not pretend to talk about the stories in their context; he brings his own context for the interpretation of the materials at hand. And what is that? It is, as he says, the effect of the stories about Moses among many later generations.

Would that Walzer had remembered, as he wrote the book, his original program. But, forgetful author like the rest of us, he moved from tracing the impact of stories on diverse generations backward to the events themselves. For Walzer wishes to do more than study how later generations received Moses. He confesses, "I want to pursue these imaginings, for they illuminate both the ancient books and the characteristically modern forms of political action...So I move back and forth between the biblical narrative...and the tracts and treatises, the slogans and songs, of radical politics..." I wish he had stayed among the slogans and songs. Then we should learn something about radical politics.

Again, Walzer says the right thing, but then -- forgetting his fine program -- does the wrong one. On the one hand, Walzer does not pretend to know what actually happened. He distinguishes the story from history: "The story is more important than the events." But the story constitutes an event, with a history of its own. At the same time, we have to ask at what point the story takes on a life of its own. Do we say "Moses did"? Then we use language that suggests we do know what really happened. Do we say, "The story says..."? Then we ask, which component of the story, and, more important, at the hands of which group of story tellers? Does Walzer grasp that fact? Alas, in no way. For he defines as his story not this bit and that piece -- nor even the picture of the whole deriving from the aftermath of 586. He tells the story in the setting of which it speaks, not in the context from which it emerged.

So, alas, Walzer takes up the story as a whole, with a beginning, a middle, and an end: problem, struggle, resolution, Egypt, wilderness, promised land (pp. 10-11). But we have a reasonably solid idea of who told that story as a whole, with is beginning, middle, and end, and where and when. As I said, scholarship in general concurs that the story reached its present condition in the aftermath of the destruction of the first Temple. then we are hearing a story about Egypt, wilderness, promised land, from people who are in the wilderness? or who are returning to the promised land. Do these facts not make an impact on how we shall read and understand the story? Or may we leap over the facts of the story as a whole (which, by his own word, Walzer has chosen to tell) and narrate merely the story *pretty much as it is told in Scripture* ?

In my view, if we bring nothing more to the story but the story itself, along with our own questions, we end up telling the story so as to say things we would want to say had the story never been told to begin with. We demean fundamentalism by calling this reading of Exodus fundamentalist. It is something else: it is making things up as you go along and calling the result scholarship. Wildavsky and Walzer would never dare to read a text of political science in so ignorant and impressionistic a manner. But, in search of roots, they leap directly into the holy books and speak with the authority they believe they bring from elsewhere.

xi. Making Things Up As You Go Along

Let me give a simple example of his "authoritative" address. What I mean to show is that he pays a heavy price, in understanding, for ignoring scholarship and leaping with perfect faith in his own knowledge directly into the text at hand. When he says, "A political history with a strong linearity, a strong forward movement, the Exodus gives permanent shape to Jewish conceptions of time," I wonder whatever he can mean, e.g, by "Jewish." Does he mean Jewish conceptions of time in the Judaism that flourished from antiquity to modern times? Then where does he find them? I have found that in the definitive Judaic literature of late antiquity, conceptions of time are not at all linear; they keep referring back to ideal time, specifically, in Genesis, at the creation and at the formation of the family of Israel, the Jewish people. In that sense they keep alluding to the cyclicality of time. How so? Israel now, in the fourth century (I refer to the conception of time and of history in Genesis Rabbah) lives out the lives of the patriarchs and matriarchs of Genesis. What happened to them happens now. The deeds of the one form paradigms for the other, not in a moral or ethical sense alone, but in a concrete historical sense. The framers of Genesis Rabbah and Leviticus Rabbah, at the end of the fourth century, interpreted the epochs of world history as recapitulations of the epochs of biblical history in the books of Genesis and Leviticus (but not Exodus, Numbers, and Deuteronomy, a fact that would have impressed Walzer had he done his homework). That theory of recapitulation is not "a linearity of time," and that is not a strong forward movement. It is just the opposite. Typology contradicts linearity, and Jews read Genesis typologically.

Walzer knows nothing of this. Why not? Because he has chosen to read the book of Exodus out of its context *and also out of the context of Judaism,* which, having become a bar mitzvah by reading these very tales, he claims to know in an expert way, and, of course, out of the context of learning. When Walzer speaks of "Jewish conceptions of time," he is pretending to know things that he does not know. A page later (pp. 13-14) he appeals to linearity in an appropriate way: "The appeal of Exodus history to generations of radicals lies in its linearity." Now that is a separate thing, I would assume even a valid statement. That statement stands on its own, as a fact, in the way in which the statement on the conception of time in Judaism is no fact at all.

Can I, should I, dismiss it all as mere homiletics? Why offend the great preachers of church and synagogue by equating free association with homiletics? So I think not, because I have too deep a regard for the holy calling of homiletics. The great preacher does not free associate, as Wildavsky and Walzer do.. The preacher does not make things up as he or she goes along, the preacher preaches the word of God, as these two reversioners to Judaism do not pretend to do (that far their reversion does not take them). The preacher does not make up messages of his own. His or hers is a different task altogether: to deliver God's word, in Scripture, to a living generation. I see nothing in common between the Moses of the homiletics of church and synagogue and the Moses of the political scientists. High-class free association you can do when you are a great professor in Berkeley or in the Institute for Advanced Study, centers of learning which give your voice resonance, and your opinions automatic audience. But that is something you cannot do when you are a professor at a mediocre ivy league college -- let alone a graduate student, all the more so a mere undergraduate. Then you come not merely with opinions and things you have picked up here and there. You come with a program of questions appropriate to the text and to the task, framed through learning, not through mere impressions, and aimed at producing insight into the text either as it came into being, or as it existed at some finite point in human history, or as it flourishes in some real circumstance in the world today. None of these tasks strikes Wildavsky and Walzer as urgent.

xii. At What Cost?

Walzer, the more prominent of the two, shows us. He says, "I want to focus instead on what happened in Egypt." I am puzzled on why he thinks he should. The book of Exodus does not tell us what happened *in Egypt*. Walzer will look in vain for a scholar of Exodus who thinks that the face of it, the details of the story require us to find out what was going that dark night in Egypt! What does the story tell us? It tells us what the Yahwist thought happened, and the Yahwist made up the stories in the time of Solomon. So if Walzer tells us what happened in Egypt,on the basis of what he reads in Exodus, then he might as well tell us on the basis of *A Man for All Seasons* what was going on in the state and church of England in the time of Henry. Or he might as well insist that we cannot read *A Man for All Seasons* unless we know what was going on in twelfth century England -- or unless we ask Richard Burton what he was thinking in those days (to close the matter at its absurd end).

So the cost proves considerable. We will not hear what the story does tell us, which is how people used their minds and imaginations to create a past commensurate with the present they perceived. But we do hear what the story does not tell us, which is what happened in Egypt. We will not take seriously the great work of imagination represented by Deuteronomy's centerpiece, the chapters that respond to the breaking up of the old empires. We will not bring sympathy and understanding to the enormous exercise of the Deuteronomic historians in bringing comfort to their people in the aftermath of catastrophe. None of this do we wish to hear. But it is what the Scriptures tell us.

Moses serves not as a fiction of the imagination of political scientists looking for proof-texts or for their own roots, though I hope they find them. "Moses" stands for the work of the creative minds of real people, facing real problems and showing us how they used their powers of imagination to solve those problems. That is why I argue in favor of reading Moses in his context, whether in Solomon's time, or in the age of the destruction of the first Temple in 586. That is when Moses really lived and led his people. That is when he counts. That is why he counts. That is not the only age in which he lived and the only reason that he mattered. But that is the point of entry into the stories. For where and when they were told, the context in which they were important -- these define, to begin with, the traits of the story that would exercise power afterward.

People who look to Exodus to tell us about Egyptian slavery or about important rules of political leadership also believe in Santa Claus and navigate by maps that show the world to be flat. But the world is round, and parents and not Santa Claus bring presents at Christmas. So, in all, let the political scientists look for their data in the world of political action, not in the realm of fiction read as fact. Or, if they prefer, let them read fiction for their facts. But then let them underscore that the facts are the figments of great minds: it is a fact that someone made up this story, and here is how that person imagines things to be. It is a fact that, through the ages, masses of men and women have responded to these stories. That is a fact worth studying, would that Walzer had remained true to his professed intent of studying it and telling us about it. But he studies Moses and Egypt and purports to know about Judaism and "the Jewish idea of time." If that is how political science will choose to enlighten us as to politics, however, I doubt that the practitioners of the field will enjoy the prestige that (in their minds at least) permit them to turn to the Bible, open things up, and read and comment as they go along -- without learning, without criticism, without discipline, without standards, without intellectual honesty.

xii. What Do I Learn from Moses in Context?   One Example

I find in the Moses of the Deuteronomic historians a powerful example of how people respond to precisely the situation in which we find ourselves. For, after all, the story from Deuteronomy through Kings tells us how to look back on a history now over but also how to look forward to we know not what. Moses served as the beginning, explaining what would happen in the end. He therefore delivered a message critical to a generation that lived through the end and faced the task of explaining it and thereby surviving. We who live today have witnessed many endings, and only a few beginnings. We in the West have seen the end of a stable and worthy system, with World War I. We have seen the outburst of barbarism, with World War II. We have lived through changes in the history of the West that lead us no one knows where. And we Jews have every day to take account of the destruction of one third of our people in death factories, including ourselves, had we been there. We look back on a world that is no more.

What if we had historians like the ones who compiled Deuteronomy, Joshua, Judges, Samuel, and Kings? What story would they tell us about the past, to lead us to a perception of a future we can endure? No one knows. We have no Deuteronomic historians to tell the history of the West from the beginning to the catastrophic century we now that now draws to a close. But we have the *example* of historians who, through the figure of Moses, performed a task of extraordinary power. They explained to their people why despite it all and against it all they should go forward. They told them that they retained the power to shape their own destiny, by living up to the terms of the contract they had with God. They brought them the hope contained in the lesson of disaster. This we learn when we listen to them where and when they spoke, cognizant of their audience and its problems, alert to the issues they had to sort out. I see this reading of Moses as a human achievement of extraordinary power. When we measure what they achieved against what none in our day has accomplished, we understand why Moses brought salvation -- if not in Egypt, then, at least, in Babylonia. So no, I do not think it matters that we do not know what Mozart ate for breakfast the morning he composed the final scene of Don Giovanni. And yes, I do think it matters, very much, to know that beneath the mask was the face of Leopold Mozart. For all of us have to sort out the relationships that chain us to parents with iron links of guilt, and all of us have to find our way out of this wretched century of ours. So we do well to listen to Don Giovanni in its context and to read the books of Deuteronomy through Kings that "Moses" wrote -- so to speak -- in 586. Then Don Giovanni makes us more than we were, by enlarging our imagination, and Moses too shows us how we can become greater than we ever dreamed. Knowing the context then draws us outward and upward from our context now.

Index